EXISTENTIAL PSYCHOTHERAPY
AND COUNSELLING

SAGE was founded in 1965 by Sara Miller McCune to support the dissemination of usable knowledge by publishing innovative and high-quality research and teaching content. Today, we publish more than 750 journals, including those of more than 300 learned societies, more than 800 new books per year, and a growing range of library products including archives, data, case studies, reports, conference highlights, and video. SAGE remains majority-owned by our founder, and after Sara's lifetime will become owned by a charitable trust that secures our continued independence.

Los Angeles | London | Washington DC | New Delhi | Singapore

EXISTENTIAL PSYCHOTHERAPY AND COUNSELLING

Contributions to a Pluralistic Practice

Mick Cooper

Los Angeles | London | New Delhi
Singapore | Washington DC

Los Angeles | London | New Delhi
Singapore | Washington DC

SAGE Publications Ltd
1 Oliver's Yard
55 City Road
London EC1Y 1SP

SAGE Publications Inc.
2455 Teller Road
Thousand Oaks, California 91320

SAGE Publications India Pvt Ltd
B 1/I 1 Mohan Cooperative Industrial Area
Mathura Road
New Delhi 110 044

SAGE Publications Asia-Pacific Pte Ltd
3 Church Street
#10-04 Samsung Hub
Singapore 049483

Editor: Susannah Trefgarne
Assistant editor: Laura Walmsley
Production editor: Rachel Burrows
Copyeditor: Christine Bitten
Proofreader: Kate Morris
Indexer: Martin Hargreaves
Marketing manager: Camille Richmond
Cover design: Shaun Mercier
Typeset by: C&M Digitals (P) Ltd, Chennai, India
Printed and bound by
CPI Group (UK) Ltd, Croydon, CR0 4YY

Library of Congress Control Number: 2014954255

British Library Cataloguing in Publication data

A catalogue record for this book is available from
the British Library

ISBN 978-1-4462-0130-5
ISBN 978-1-4462-0131-2 (pbk)

At SAGE we take sustainability seriously. Most of our products are printed in the UK using FSC papers and boards.
When we print overseas we ensure sustainable papers are used as measured by the Egmont grading system. We
undertake an annual audit to monitor our sustainability.

For Ruby – my beautiful, brilliant, precious jewel.

ilysm.

Contents

About the Author

Mick Cooper is a Professor of Counselling Psychology at the University of Roehampton, a chartered counselling psychologist and a UKCP-registered existential psychotherapist. Mick is author and editor of a range of texts on person-centred, existential, and relational approaches to therapy, including *Working at Relational Depth in Counselling and Psychotherapy* (Sage, 2005, with Dave Mearns), *The Handbook of Person-centred Psychotherapy and Counselling* (Palgrave, 2003, with Maureen O'Hara, Art Bohart and Peter Schmid), and *Pluralistic Counselling and Psychotherapy* (Sage, 2011, with John McLeod). Mick has led a range of research studies exploring the process and outcomes of humanistic counselling with young people, and is author of *Essential Research Findings in Counselling and Psychotherapy: The Facts are Friendly* (Sage, 2008). Mick lives in Brighton, UK with his partner and four children.

Acknowledgements

Over the past 15 years as a therapist, I have had the privilege of working with a number of remarkable individuals. For obvious reasons, I cannot name these clients here, but I have them in mind as I write this; and their courage to face their difficulties and to learn, relate and change has been a continuing source of inspiration to me.

I am very grateful to the many students, in the UK and internationally, that I have explored and developed the ideas and practices in this book with. Their warmth, insights and challenge have played an essential role in helping me shape and refine the ideas presented here.

I am enormously thankful to the many people who, over the years, have dialogued with me around existential ideas, and helped me deepen and develop my understanding of them. Thanks to Dan Burningham, who first introduced me to existential philosophy and literature; to my mum Kitty Cooper who, as an octogenarian, is still up for discussing Heideggerian ontology; to my partner Helen Cruthers, who has supported – and engaged with – my work for the past 20 years. Thanks also to Lucia Berdondini and Edgar Correia, who are always up for an argument about existential therapies over a glass or two of red wine; and to Katie McArthur, with whom I have had some great dialogues about dialogue.

In recent years, I have had the privilege of talking with two of the brightest young sparks in the existential therapies' field – Joël Vos and Daniel Sousa – and with two of the greatest sparks of them all. First is Ernesto Spinelli, who has been a continued source of support, inspiration and challenge; and to whom a debt of gratitude is owed for his willingness to stand by, and develop, his contribution to our field. Second is John McLeod, whose wisdom, insight and creativity have been a major influence on my thinking and practice in recent years.

Thanks to Graham Molyneux, my supervisor for many years; and to James Sanderson and Peter Baker, for their friendship.

As with many of us in the 'British school' of existential therapy, I am deeply indebted to Emmy van Deurzen, who instigated and inspired the existential approach in the UK, and who continues to be a source of learning, challenge and wisdom.

I am very grateful for the team at Sage, including Susannah Trefgarne, Laura Walmsley and Rachel Burrows, for their continued support, encouragement and efficiency. Thanks to the many reviewers and colleagues who took time to comment on the chapters or ideas in this book, including Martin Adams, Meg Barker, Rose Bedford, Windy Dryden, Pavlos Filippopoulos, Maria Gilbert, Darren Langdridge, Elena Manafi, Martin Milton and Diana Voller.

Several of the therapeutic methods outlined in this book, particularly in Chapter 3 on phenomenological practices, were taught to me during my four years' training in existential psychotherapy at Regent's College in London. Here, I am particularly indebted to Lucia Moja-Strasser, and to the many other trainers I had the privilege of working with over these years: Mike Harding, Ernesto Spinelli, Sarah Young, Simon du Plock, Hans Cohn and Freddie Strasser. Very special thanks are also due to my fellow trainees, Shari and Alan, for all their support, encouragement and resilience through some stormy seas.

Most of the text for this book has evolved from notes, slides and exercises developed for the existential workshops I have delivered since the publication of *Existential Therapies* in 2003. However, two sections of this book are fully updated and revised versions of previously published texts. The first part of Chapter 2, I and Thou, is based on 'I–I and I–Me: transposing Buber's interpersonal attitudes to the intrapersonal plane', published in the *Journal of Constructivist Psychology* (2003c, *16*(2), 131–153), reprinted by permission of Taylor & Francis LLC (www.tandfonline.com). Chapter 7, on interpersonal perceptions, is an extended and fully revised version of 'Interpersonal perceptions and metaperceptions: psychotherapeutic practice in the inter-experiential realm', published in the *Journal of Humanistic Psychology* (2009a, *49*(1), 85–99), reprinted by permission of Sage Publications Ltd (www.sagepub.com). In addition, I am very grateful to PCCS Books (www.pccs-books.co.uk), Sage Publications Ltd, the Society for Existential Analysis (www.existentialanalysis.org.uk), and Taylor and Francis LLC for kind permission to make available chapters and papers on the companion website. Thanks, also, to my co-authors who gave permission for these texts to be uploaded: Amy Chak, Flora Cornish, Meghan Craig, Helen Cruthers, Alex Gillespie, John McLeod and Joël Vos.

I would like to thank Michael Steger for kind permission to reproduce the Meaning in Life Questionnaire.

Finally, very special thanks, as ever, are due to Zac, Shula, Ruby (who also researched the fish pictures on page 173) and Maya – Helen and my four children. They provide all the love, acceptance and chaos that an existential therapist could ever wish for.

Companion Website

Existential Psychotherapy and Counselling: Contributions to a Pluralistic Practice is accompanied by a companion website hosting a wealth of downloadable materials and specially created video clips for trainees, lecturers and practitioners. The following pages offer a guide to these resources which can all be found at https://study.sagepub.com/cooper

Videos on the Companion Website

The following video tutorials are designed to introduce readers to key counselling skills, which can serve as the basis for existential counselling and psychotherapy practice. Each video explains a specific skill and incorporates relevant clips and discussions from two case studies, illustrating how these skills can be used in the counselling room. This icon indicates which parts of the text are accompanied by a video tutorial.

Active listening, Chapter 3, p. 75

This tutorial describes and demonstrates what active listening is, why it's important and how to tailor active listening to each individual client.

Minimal encouragers, Chapter 3, p. 76

This tutorial explains what minimal encouragers are, covering spoken and body language, how they can be an important part of the counselling conversation, and how to use them in your therapeutic work.

Reflecting, paraphrasing, summarising, Chapter 3, p. 76

This tutorial looks at reflecting, paraphrasing and summarising: what they mean in a counselling context, reasons why they're helpful and examples of how you might use them.

Asking open-ended questions, Chapter 3, p. 78

This tutorial explores what open-ended questions are, why they're helpful and explores the kind of questions you might ask to help people explore what they're experiencing. This is demonstrated further through case studies illustrating closed questions vs. open-ended questions.

Using symbols and metaphors, Chapter 3, p. 79

This tutorial considers how you might use symbols and metaphors to help clients talk about and reflect on their experiences. It also offers some examples of symbols and metaphors that might be useful.

Bringing things into the here-and-now, Chapter 3, p. 82

This tutorial explains why bringing things into the here and now can be valuable, offers advice on how you can make it as helpful as possible for clients, as well as some examples of how you can encourage your client to focus on what they are experiencing 'here and now' in the therapy room.

Dealing with ruptures, Chapter 3, p. 83

This tutorial looks at ruptures in the therapeutic relationship and how you might deal with them effectively, illustrated by examples.

Helping people re-decide, Chapter 4, p. 107

This tutorial looks at helping clients make decisions in their lives and chose to do things differently, the kind of questions you might ask to encourage this and some hints and tips about how to help clients make the best decisions for their future.

Using feedback measures, Chapter 7, p. 191

This tutorial explains the two main types of feedback measures: process and outcome measures. It considers the debates around these measures, how they can be helpful in therapeutic work and how you can make best use of them with your clients.

Downloadable Resources

The following resources are supplementary texts for the book. They are freely available for use, distribution and teaching without further permission, but please do not amend or revise in any way. This icon indicates where relevant downloadable resources are available on the companion website.

Chapter 1

- **An introduction to pluralism.** McLeod, J., & Cooper, M. (2012). Pluralistic counselling and psychotherapy. In C. Feltham & I. Horton (Eds.), *The Sage Handbook of Counselling and Psychotherapy* (pp. 368–371). London: Sage.
- **Existential therapy and research.** Cooper, M. (2004). Viagra for the brain: Psychotherapy research and the challenge of existential therapeutic practice. *Existential Analysis, 15*(1), 2–14.
- **Existential therapy and pluralism: notes.**
- **A personal perspective on social change.** Cooper, M. (2006). Socialist humanism: A progressive politics for the twenty-first century.

In G. Proctor, M. Cooper, P. Sanders, & B. Malcolm (Eds.), *Politicising the Person-Centred Approach: An Agenda for Social Change* (pp. 80–94). Ross-on-Wye: PCCS Books.

- **Protocols for a meta-analysis of existential therapies**. Reprint of: Cooper, M., Vos, J., & Craig, M. (2011). *Protocol for EXIST review*. Glasgow: University of Strathclyde.
- **Annotated existential therapies reading list.**

Chapter 2

- **Dialogue**. Cooper, M., Chak, A., Cornish, F., & Gillespie, A. (2012). Dialogue: Bridging personal, community and social transformation. *Journal of Humanistic Psychology, 53*(1), 70–93.
- **A moment of relational depth: notes.**
- **Strategies of Disconnection Inventory.**
- **Understanding client distress from a relational perspective: notes.**
- **The I–I and I–Me self-relational stances.** Cooper, M. (2003). 'I-I' And 'I-Me': Transposing Buber's interpersonal attitudes to the intrapersonal plane. *Journal of Constructivist Psychology, 16*(2), 131–153.

Chapter 3

- **Existential therapy and postmodernism.** Cooper, M. (1999). The discourse of existence: Existential-phenomenological psychotherapy in a postmodern world. *Journal of the Society for Existential Analysis, 10*(2), 93–101.
- **Self-plurality from an existential perspective.** Cooper, M. (1996). Modes of existence: Towards a phenomenological polypsychism. *Journal of the Society for Existential Analysis, 7*(2), 50–56.
- **Methods of personification.** Cooper, M., & Cruthers, H. (1999). Facilitating the expression of subpersonalities: A review and analysis of techniques. In J. Rowan & M. Cooper (Eds.), *The plural self: Multiplicity in everyday life* (pp. 198–212). London: Sage.
- **Existential black ice: notes.**
- **Evidence and examples critical of a phenomenological focus: notes.**

Chapter 4

- **The firm and gentle of existential practice: a group training exercise.**

Chapter 5

- **Existential therapy and genetics.** Cooper, M. (2001). The genetic given: Towards an existential understanding of inherited 'personality traits'. *Journal of the Society for Existential Analysis, 12*(1), 2–12.
- **Empathising with the anxiety of facing limitations: notes.**

Chapter 6

- **Existential perspectives on the past.** Cooper, M. (1998). 'The tools of being: An existential perspective on the past', *Counsellor and Psychotherapist Dialogue, 1*(3), 12–15.
- **Integrated psycho-social model of wants.** Cooper, M. (2012). *A hierarchy of wants: Towards an integrative framework for counselling, psychotherapy and social change.* Glasgow: University of Strathclyde.
- **Goals Form.**

Chapter 7

- **Exploring the inter-perceptual world.** Cooper, M. (2009). Interpersonal perceptions and metaperceptions: Psychotherapeutic practice in the inter-experiential realm. *Journal of Humanistic Psychology, 49*(1), 85–99.
- **Challenging clients' metaperceptions in the immediate here-and-now: notes.**
- **Metaperceptions: a group training exercise.**

Appendix

- Full results of survey of existential films, novels and songs.
- Weblinks.

1

Introduction

This chapter discusses:

- The background, rationale, aims, structure and intended audience for this book.
- Pluralism as a framework for conceptualising and practising existential therapy.
- The nature and scope of existential philosophy and therapeutic practice.

This book is born out of a passion and a love: for existentialism, for pluralism but, more than that, for the principles that underlie both these perspectives. For me, existential therapy is an attempt to engage with people in deeply respectful and valuing ways (Cooper, 2007), and pluralism is a framework that aims to deepen this engagement (Cooper & McLeod, 2011b). It is about striving to be truly open to the 'other-ness' of clients: not just *saying* that we are being open or theorising about it, but really, deeply, challenging ourselves to put our own assumptions and wants to one side to engage with our clients and their worlds. Yet neither existentialism nor pluralism suggests that we should negate our own knowledge or the expertise that we can bring to the therapeutic encounter. To 'be for' an other is also to be willing to draw on our own wisdom, insights and skills. This is where therapy becomes a genuine *dialogue*: an expert client, and an expert therapist, working together to help the client in the best way that they both can.

Existential therapy – like many other therapeutic approaches – is a diverse, vibrant, and wonderfully rich 'tapestry' of understandings and methods that has the potential to make a valuable contribution to the work of any counsellor, psychotherapist or psychologist (Cooper, 2003b; Milton, Charles, Judd, O'Brien, Tipney & Turner, 2003). The aim of this book is to lay out this tapestry in all its richness, so that readers of any orientation can incorporate these ideas and practices into their own therapeutic work.

A pluralistic framework for therapy

AN
INTRODUCTION
TO PLURALISM

The perspective within which these existential practices and understandings are framed is a *pluralistic* one. Pluralism is a way of thinking about therapy that has emerged in recent years (Cooper & McLeod, 2007, 2011b; McLeod & Cooper, 2012; McLeod, McLeod, Cooper & Dryden, 2014; Milton, 2010b). It is based on the philosophical assumption that 'any substantial question admits of a variety of plausible but mutually conflicting responses' (Rescher, 1993: 79). In other words, pluralism assumes that many different things can be 'right', and that it is often more constructive to allow multiple truths to flourish than to try and pin things down to a definitive single answer. This is particularly the case where questions are 'substantial', and nowhere is this more true than in questions of human being, functioning and therapeutic change. In relation to therapy, therefore, a pluralistic perspective suggests that there are lots of different ways of understanding why people get distressed, and lots of different ways of helping them. That is, no one therapeutic approach – existential or otherwise – has the monopoly on understanding the causes of distress or on the most helpful therapeutic responses. Such a stance challenges the *schoolism* that has been endemic in the therapy world (Cooper & McLeod, 2011b): that only *Therapy X* explains why people get distressed, or that only *Therapy Y* can help them. Instead, it argues that therapists should be open to respecting understandings and practices from across the counselling and psychotherapy field.

In this pluralistic approach, there is also an emphasis on acknowledging and appreciating diversity across clients, and recognising that different clients may benefit from different therapies at different points in time. As Boucher (2010: 159) writes, 'the basic tenet of pluralism is very simple – there are many people and they are all unique.' Hence, the approach is about trying to *tailor* the therapeutic approach to the individual client. It is about 'horses for courses' rather than 'one size fits all.'

Given this emphasis on valuing multiple perspectives and tailoring therapy to the clients' wants, a pluralistic therapeutic approach holds that *both* participants in the therapeutic dyad – the client as well as the therapist – have much to contribute to the process of deciding the most appropriate goals and methods for therapy. This means that a pluralistic approach emphasises *shared decision making* (Edwards & Elwyn, 2009) and *metatherapeutic communication* (Cooper & McLeod, 2011a): talking to clients about the process of therapy itself, including what they want from it and how they would like to try and get there.

These two basic principles of pluralism – that clients can be helped in many ways and that it is good to talk to them about what they want – can be held by therapists of any orientation. Therapists do not need to draw on practices from multiple orientations to do so. For instance, a therapist may choose to practise in a purely existential way, but at the same time appreciate the work that cognitive-behavioural and psychodynamic therapists do. However, this *pluralistic perspective* opens on to the possibility of *pluralistic practice*: drawing on multiple understandings and methods in the therapeutic work. A pluralistic approach also suggests that therapeutic effectiveness may be enhanced if practitioners draw on knowledge from multiple domains: personal experience, theory, practice and *research*. This last one has been particularly emphasised within the pluralistic approach (e.g., Cooper & McLeod, 2011b) because it has, traditionally, been neglected in the training of counsellors and psychotherapists (see, for instance, Morrow-Bradley & Elliott, 1986). In this respect, a pluralistic perspective advocates an *evidence-informed* approach to therapy: where evidence is treated as one – but just one – very valuable source of information on how best to help clients. (For a detailed discussion of the relationship between research and existential therapy, see Cooper, 2004c.)

EXISTENTIAL
THERAPY
AND
RESEARCH

Box 1.1   The pluralistic approach: FAQs

Does a pluralistic approach mean that you have to be able to offer every therapy going?

No, as indicated above, you can hold a pluralistic perspective without necessarily drawing on multiple therapeutic understandings and methods. Even if you do, no-one would ever be able to offer the 400+ therapies going, and it is an important ethical requirement that therapists have adequate training in whatever therapy they choose to offer. So pluralism is not about

(Continued)

(Continued)

trying to do a bit of everything. It is about being open to the value of multiple practices and understandings, and drawing on them as and when the therapist might have the appropriate expertise, and as and when that might be helpful to the client.

Isn't pluralistic therapy just the same as integrative/ eclectic therapy?

There is certainly a lot of overlap, and in many ways pluralistic practice – where a therapist is drawing on two or more approaches – can be considered synonymous with a 'collaborative integrative' way of working (van Rijn, personal communication, 2013). However, there are three important distinctions between a pluralistic approach and *integrative* practices (putting together different theories, Hollanders, 2014) or *eclectic* practices (selecting techniques from a number of different orientations irrespective of the underlying philosophies, Hollanders, 2014), *per se*. First, in many instances, integrative or eclectic models of therapy are *particular* combinations of therapeutic understandings and practices – such as Cognitive-Analytic Therapy (CAT, Ryle, 1990) – while a pluralistic approach refers to a more general openness to multiple therapeutic perspectives. Second, while many integrative and eclectic approaches *do* put considerable emphasis on shared decision making and a tailoring of the therapeutic work to the individual client (see, for instance, Lazarus, 1993), this is not inherent to either approach. Third, integrative and eclectic are descriptions of particular ways of practising therapy while, as we have seen, pluralism can also refer to a particular stance towards therapy as a whole.

Aren't we all pluralists anyway?

It is undoubtedly true that many counsellors, psychotherapists and psychologists do, already, think and practise in ways that we have come to describe as 'pluralistic'. Indeed, in a recent study of American psychotherapists, at least 98% identified with more than one therapeutic orientation (Cook, Biyanova, Elhai, Schnurr & Coyne, 2010). Pluralism, then, is less a 'shiny new' form of therapy, and more an articulation of what many therapists have thought and practised for years. Nevertheless, formally articulating it gives us the opportunity to research, develop and promote this way of working.

Most clients don't know what they want from therapy, or how to go about getting it, so why ask them?

Actually, in our experience, most clients are pretty able to say what they want from therapy, and offer some ideas about how they might get there

(Cooper, 2014; Cooper et al., submitted). Even if they cannot, inviting clients to do so at the start of therapy seems to help them feel more able to say what they want or prefer later on in the work.

If you just give clients what they want, aren't you in danger of 'colluding' with them?

Shared decision making is not about just doing whatever clients want. It is about involving them in the process of *dialogue*, and trusting that they – as well as the therapist – have something useful to contribute to this process. So if a therapist thinks that what a client wants is unhelpful or unreasonable, this is something they should bring into the dialogue. In this respect, a pluralistic approach does not imply an uncritical acceptance of the client's perspective, but neither does it allow for its uncritical negation (Borrell-Carrio, Suchman & Epstein, 2004).

So does that mean you can still work with the 'transference'?

Yes, but a pluralistic approach would aim to make this explicit and agreed at the start of therapy, so that there is consent from the client to do so.

Surely clients' goals and preferences for therapy change, so the ones that they first think of are not necessarily the ones that they will prioritise later on in therapy?

Exactly, so a pluralistic approach emphasises the need to continue dialoguing with clients about goals and methods as the therapy develops, not just as a one-off event.

Where can I find out more about the pluralistic approach?

An introduction to pluralism is available on the companion website. See also www.pluralistictherapy.com and Recommended reading at the end of this chapter.

AN
INTRODUCTION
TO PLURALISM

A *pluralistic* introduction to existential therapy

In recent years, a number of excellent introductions to existential therapeutic practice have been published (see Recommended reading, at the end of this chapter). However, the pluralistic principles underlying this book mean that it has a number of unique features:

- Therapeutic understandings are presented as *potential* means of helping clients make sense of their lives and problems – a 'narrative' that is useful for some clients some of the time – and not as universal truths.
- Therapeutic methods, likewise, are presented as ways of working with clients that may be very useful for some clients some of the time, but not as 'superior' or universally helpful practices.
- There is a discussion of who the existential methods might be most helpful for, and/or at what points in time.
- There is an attempt to try and detail specific pathways of change.
- A reflexive, critical standpoint is taken towards existential ideas and practices: emphasising their limitations as well as their potential contributions.
- Similarities and differences to other therapeutic orientations, in understandings and methods, are discussed – and in a way that values alternative perspectives.
- There is discussion, and illustrations, of how the methods might be practised alongside shared decision making.
- Clients' capacities for, and contribution towards, therapeutic change are acknowledged; and methods are discussed that can support this (e.g., self-help literature).
- Issues of social and cultural diversity are taken into account and discussed.
- Understandings and methods are explored, where possible, in relation to the available empirical research (both qualitative and quantitative).
- The existential approach, itself, is understood in a pluralistic way: as a complex diversity of understandings and methods, as opposed to a single, unified stance.

Given these features, this book is likely to be of particular interest to two groups of readers. First, for trainee and practising therapists from outside of the existential field who are interested in drawing on existential understandings and methods as part of their therapeutic work. This might be practitioners working in integrative, eclectic or pluralistic ways. It might also be single orientation practitioners – such as person-centred or cognitive-behavioural therapists – who are particularly interested in drawing on existential understandings and methods. Second, the book may be of particular interest to trainee and practising therapists from within the existential field, who are keen to work in more integrative, collaborative and pluralistic ways.

In addition, the book may be of interest to existential therapists – trainees or practitioners – who are hoping to develop their understanding of the approach and particularly the 'nuts and bolts' of what existential therapists actually *do*. For years, the nature of existential therapy has lain shrouded in mystery, with only 'inexact and complex' translations from theory to practice (Norcross, 1987: 54). More recently, however, existential authors have begun to detail their actual practice (e.g., Adams, 2013; Spinelli, 2007; van Deurzen & Adams, 2011) and this book hopes to continue this trend. In this respect, it aims to give readers a vivid, practical and down-to-earth guide to existential therapeutic methods, along with the theoretical understandings that guide these ways of working.

On the companion website, there is an extended discussion of the relationship between existentialism and pluralism, and the legitimacy (or otherwise) of practising existential therapy in this way. As discussed there, below, and in Cooper & Stumm (2015), the pluralistic approach can be seen as an extension of existential thought and practice, emphasising the collaborative relationship, the freedom for the client to choose, and an emphasis on the client's being-towards-the-future. It can also be seen as an existential perspective *on* existential therapy: a willingness to stand back from, and critique, any fixed 'truths'. On the other hand, however, a pluralistic approach could be seen as an adulteration of the core principles and practices of existential therapy. 'Have you ever mixed paints', asks 'Tristram Shandy' (2012: 8), 'and come up with brown?' Similarly, Spinelli (2014a: 9) argues that the principles of existential therapy are so radical and unique that they cannot be simply combined with more mainstream perspectives. Nor, he argues, can the existential approach be broken up into component parts and dispersed across different practices.

EXISTENTIAL THERAPY AND PLURALISM: NOTES

The present text is based on the former assumption: that existential therapy *can* be practised in a pluralistic way, and that the two philosophies are eminently compatible. However, a pluralistic approach needs to be pluralistic about pluralism. In this regard, the challenges of Spinelli (2014a) and others provide a welcome opportunity to reflect on, and refine, an understanding of effective therapeutic practice.

Personal foundations

This is a very personal book. Over the last 15 years, I have authored and co-authored a number of books, chapters and journal papers about existential therapy (Cooper, 2003a, 2003b, 2004b, 2008b, 2012b, 2012c; Cooper & Stumm, 2015; Craig, Vos, Cooper & Correia, in press; Vos, Craig & Cooper, 2014). However, this is the first text where I have detailed what *I* actually think – and, more pertinently, what I actually *do*.

This means, of course, that the understandings and practices described in this book are just *one* perspective on existential therapy (Cooper, 2003b); and different authors would – and do – describe the approach very differently. Where possible, I have tried to highlight this. In addition, the following paragraphs lay out my own background and interests, such that readers may be more able to see where my own biases are coming to the fore.

The foundations of my approach to existential thinking and practice lie in my four years' training as an existential counsellor and psychotherapist at Regent's College, London, in the late 1990s. This is one of two 'homes' for the British school of existential therapy (see below). Here, I was particularly drawn towards the relational, phenomenological approach of Ernesto Spinelli (1994, 1997, 2001, 2005, 2015), and of Lucia Moja-Strasser (e.g., Moja-Strasser, 1996). After this, I went on to teach on person-centred counselling courses, and became very immersed in the field of person-centred, experiential and humanistic counselling and psychotherapy (e.g., Cooper, Schmid, O'Hara & Bohart, 2013; Cooper, Watson & Hölldampf, 2010; Mearns & Cooper, 2005). This extended and deepened my interest in relational ways of working.

My passion for the existential approach, however, has always been tempered by a dislike of the more dogmatic, doctrinarian elements of this school (or, indeed, any school, Cooper & McLeod, 2011b). For me, the essence of this approach is a respect for otherness (see below), and a willingness to change, learn and grow. Hence, when I saw Heidegger's (1962) *Being and Time* treated like gospel, or when alternative therapeutic approaches like CBT were demonised, it felt to me that something very un-existential was going on. This led to the development, with John McLeod, of a *pluralistic* approach to therapy (Cooper & McLeod, 2007, 2011b, see above; McLeod & Cooper, 2012). For me, this was a way of articulating, and developing, what I found most precious in the existential and person-centred approaches (Cooper & McLeod, 2011a). Today, I would describe my practice as 'a pluralistic approach, primarily informed by person-centred and existential practices.'

As may be evident here, what is most fundamental to my thought and practice is a commitment to engaging with clients in a valuing, respectful and egalitarian way (Cooper, 2007; Cooper & McLeod, 2011a). For me, this stems back to a life-long commitment to a progressive political agenda (see Cooper, 2006).

A PERSONAL
PERSPECTIVE
ON SOCIAL
CHANGE

The approach outlined in this book has also been influenced by my own experiences as a client. I have struggled with periods of intense anxiety since a young child – and continue to do so – and have worked with a range of counsellors, psychotherapists and psychiatrists. One of the most important things I learnt from this is that many different things can be of help, and not necessarily the therapies I am most affiliated with. My most helpful therapists were a Kleinian psychoanalyst, a CBT nurse, and a CBT-ish psychiatrist; while my experiences of existential and person-centred therapy were very mixed. Indeed, over the years, the thing that I have probably found most helpful in addressing my anxiety has been regular intensive exercise; and I have also found anti-depressants extremely effective at a time of severe stress. Through my own experiences of anxiety, I have also come to feel that, sometimes, accepting the presence of a mental health problem is more helpful than battling to try and eradicate it.

Existential therapy: an introduction

Existential therapy may be considered one of the smaller therapeutic schools. A survey of American psychotherapists some years ago found that only around 4% identified with this orientation (Norcross, 1987). However, through the writings of such well-known advocates as Irvin Yalom and Victor Frankl, it has 'punched well above its weight': having a wide and pervasive impact on the psychological therapies field (Schneider, 2008).

There are many different ways of defining the existential approach to therapy (Cooper, 2003b), and what is or is not within this scope (see Box 1.2). Indeed, Norcross (1987: 42) writes that: 'Existential therapy means something to everyone yet what it means precisely varies with the exponent.' For van Deurzen (2012a), for instance, it is a therapeutic approach that draws on philosophy to help people think more broadly and address problems in living. For 'logotherapists' (e.g., Frankl, 1986), on the other hand, it aims to help people find meaning and purpose in their lives. And for some therapists associated with the existential approach (Yalom, 2001), it is not really a therapeutic orientation at all. Rather, consistent with the aims of this book, it is a sensibility and awareness that therapists of any orientation can adopt (Yalom, in Serlin, 1999).

Box 1.2 The scope of existential therapies: the EXIST study

The EXIST study was a recent research project that aimed to review the evidence for the effectiveness of existential therapies (Cooper, Vos & Craig, 2011; Vos et al., 2014). To do so, it needed to give a clear definition of what was, and what was not, considered an existential approach. To achieve this, a dialogue was initiated with leading figures in the existential therapeutic field. No consensus was achieved, but the definition taken forward by the researchers was as follows:

PROTOCOLS FOR
A META-ANALYSIS
OF EXISTENTIAL
THERAPIES

(Continued)

(Continued)

Existential therapies are therapeutic practices that: A) Explicitly uses the term 'existential' to describe either the therapeutic intervention or the focus of the therapeutic work; and B) Are based, primarily or wholly, on one or more of the following assumptions associated with the existential school of thought: i) that human beings are orientated to, and have a need for, meaning and purpose; ii) that human beings have a capacity for freedom and choice, and function most effectively when they actualize this potential and take responsibility for their choices; iii) that human beings will inevitably face limitations and challenges in their lives, and function most effectively when they face up to – rather than avoid or deny – them; iv) that the subjective, phenomenological flow of experiencing is a key aspect of human being, and therefore a central focus for psychotherapeutic work; v) that human experiencing is fundamentally embedded in relationships with others and with its world.

Therapies that were considered to fall within this scope included Daseinsanalysis (e.g., Boss, 1963), the British school of existential therapy (e.g., van Deurzen & Adams, 2011), logotherapy (e.g., Frankl, 1986), and the existential-humanistic approach (e.g., Schneider & Krug, 2010) (see below). Therapies that were considered outside of this scope – though known to be influenced by existential ideas – included gestalt therapy, contextual therapy, person-centred therapy and psychodrama.

Existential philosophers

At its most basic, an existential approach to therapy can be defined as a form of therapeutic practice that is based, primarily or wholly, on the assumptions associated with the existential school of thought (Cooper et al., 2011, see Criteria B, Box 1.2). A recent international online survey of over 1,000 existential therapists found that the following philosophers, in descending order, were considered most influential on practice (Correia, Cooper & Berdondini, 2014a):

1. **Martin Heidegger** (1889–1976): German philosopher who explored the nature of being. Earlier work emphasised resolution in the face of anxiety and mortality; later work emphasised an openness towards the world. *Key text: Being and Time (1926).*
2. **Jean-Paul Sartre** (1905–1980): French philosopher, novelist and social critic. Emphasised the freedom at the heart of human existence, and the angst, meaninglessness and nausea that it evokes. *Key text: Being and Nothingness (1943).*
3. **Søren Kierkegaard** (1813–1855): Danish philosopher, who criticised the passionlessness and conformity of nineteenth century

Christendom. Argued that human beings needed to turn towards their own subjective truths and make a personal leap of faith towards God. *Several key texts, including Concluding Unscientific Postscript to Philosophical Fragments (1846).*

4. **Martin Buber** (1878–1965): Jewish, Viennese philosopher and theologian. Emphasised the fundamentally relational nature of human being, and the importance of an 'I–Thou' humanising stance towards the other (see Chapter 2). *Key text: I and Thou (1923).*

5. **Friedrich Nietzsche** (1844–1900): German philosopher, who preached an atheistic gospel of aspiration towards the *bermensch*: the autonomous superman who creates his or her own values and morality. *Key text: Thus spake Zarathrusa* (1883).

(adapted from Cooper, 2003b)

There are many other philosophers associated with the existential school of thought (see Macquarrie, 1972). Simone de Beauvoir (1948a), for instance, developed an existential ethic of freedom, and wrote about the social and historical factors that could limit that freedom and choice (de Beauvoir, 1948b). Maurice Merleau-Ponty (1962) developed an embodied understanding of existence; and Albert Camus (1955: 11) explored issues of meaninglessness, writing that 'There is but one truly serious philosophical problem and that is suicide.'

Unfortunately, as this overview suggests, defining existential therapy in terms of existential philosophy does not make the approach that much clearer, as there are enormous variations in thinking across the field. For instance, while some are deeply religious (e.g., Buber, Kierkegaard, Tillich) others are committed atheist (e.g., Sartre).

The essence of existential philosophy

So what is it that draws all these diverse philosophies together under the same 'existential' banner? This question has been answered in many ways (e.g., Spinelli, 2015; Warnock, 1970), but perhaps the deepest unifying feature is a particular *ethic*. That is, a belief about how we should relate to, and conceptualise, human beings. More specifically, what each of the existential philosophers has done is to critique systems of thought that are seen as *de-humanising* individuals. That is, that reduce the complexity, uniqueness and inter-relatedness of human lived-existences to a set of impersonal statistics, laws, systems or absolutes (Cooper, 2003b). In other words, existential philosophers strive to call our attention back to the concrete realities of human lives, the 'man of flesh and bone' (de Unamuno, 1954), and to repudiate 'all idealisms, mysticisms, etcetera which prefer a Form to man himself' (de Beauvoir, 1948a: 145). These might be philosophical systems, such as Hegelianism (1949), which sees individuals as bit-players in some historical grand narrative; or technological (Guignon, 1993) perspectives, such as Freudianism (1923), which reduce the person down to mechanistic laws and drives. From an existential standpoint, when we see human beings in non-human terms, we do violence (Laing, 1967: 53) to people, and lose the very essence of who they are.

From this starting point, existential writers have then gone on to say something of what this actual human existence may be like (see Exercise 1.1). For instance, they have argued that we exist in-relation-to-others (Chapter 2), and that we have the capacity for freedom and choice (Chapter 4).

Exercise 1.1   Existential assumptions: What do you think?

Aim

To encourage you to reflect on some key existential assumptions.

The exercise

For each of the following quotes, consider how much you agree or disagree with them. You may also want to consider if there are ways in which you could modify the quotes to improve them. For instance, in the quote by van Deurzen, you may think 'challenge' is a better word than 'struggle'.

'All actual life is encounter' (Buber, 1970: 62).

'Human beings are nothing else but what they make of themselves' (Sartre, 1996: 259).

'The script of life is so unspeakably beautiful to read because death looks over our shoulder' (Buber, 1964: 91).

'He [or she] who has a why to live can bear with almost any how' (Nietzsche, quoted in Frankl, 1984: 97).

'[L]ife is an endless struggle, where moments of ease and happiness are the exception rather than the rule' (van Deurzen, 1998: 132).

Comment

Of course, there are no right or wrong answers here, but these quotes will give you a chance to think through some of the existential ideas that we will explore throughout this book.

Variations

If you are on a training course, this is a great exercise to do in small groups (say for 30 minutes), and you may find you only get through one or two of the quotes because there is so much to discuss. Make sure you spend some time getting clear on what the quote is saying. This exercise also works best if groups try as hard as possible to reach a consensus (rather than simply agreeing to disagree) so that the key issues can be really thrashed out.

The schools of existential therapy

In the first decades of the twentieth century, a number of psychiatrists across the European continent began to draw on existential and phenomenological (see Chapter 3) philosophy to develop ways of understanding – and engaging with – psychologically distressed individuals (see Ellenberger, 1958 for an excellent overview). This included Jaspers (1963), Binswanger (1958, 1963), Minkowski (1958) and Frankl (1984, 1986). Building on this work, a number of existential schools evolved in the twentieth century, each emphasising and drawing on different elements of existential thought. What each of these approaches had in common was the existential ethic of engaging with clients in deeply humanising ways. More than that, each of these existential therapies held that psychological difficulties arise when human beings become alienated from their own existences. Here, therapy was aimed at helping clients acknowledge, live 'in tune with' and make the most of the actuality of their lived-being.

Across the globe today, four main schools of existential therapy can be identified (Cooper, 2003b, 2012b). Research indicates that there is considerable overlap in the influences and practices associated with these schools, though the fourth – meaning-oriented approaches – stands somewhat distinct from the others (Correia, Cooper & Berdondini, in preparation-a).

Daseinsanalysis

This approach is based on the work of two Swiss psychiatrists, Ludwig Binswanger (1963) and Medard Boss (1979), and aims to radically revise the foundations of psychoanalytical practice. It conceptualises psychological distress in later-Heideggerian terms: as a 'closedness' to the being of the world. In practice, it retains many elements of classical psychoanalysis, such as dream analysis, but aims to cultivate a warm and permissive therapeutic relationship in which the client opens themselves up to the being of their world. It is currently practised in small pockets across the world, particularly Europe and southern America (Correia, Cooper & Berdondini, 2014b).

Existential-humanistic psychotherapy

Developed in the US in the 1950s by Rollo May and colleagues (May, 1969a; May, Angel & Ellenberger, 1958), this approach assumes that people experience psychological difficulties when they try to defend themselves against an awareness of such existential givens as death, freedom, meaninglessness and isolation (Yalom, 1980). Using a range of strategies from the highly interpretative to the warmly relational, existential-humanistic therapists try to help clients come to terms with the realities of their existences. Although just a small handful of existential-humanistic training institutes exist today (primarily in the US), it has been highly influential through the existentially informed writings of one of the best-loved psychotherapy authors, Irvin Yalom.

The British School of existential therapy

This builds on the work of the Scottish psychiatrist R. D. Laing (1965, 1969) in the 1960s, and emerged in London in the 1980s. It is still very active (Correia et al., 2014b) with a regular journal (*Existential Analysis*), training programmes and conferences. The principal driving force behind this school was Emmy van Deurzen (2009a, 2012a), whose approach draws extensively from philosophy, and encourages clients to live a vibrant and meaningful life in the face of inevitable challenges. Other authors within the British School, such as Ernesto Spinelli (1994, 2015), have adopted a more phenomenological and relational approach, emphasising the need to encounter clients from a stance of openness and 'un-knowing'. Recent years have seen the dissemination of this approach across several European countries, including Denmark, Greece and Portugal; as well as Australia.

Meaning-oriented therapy

'Logotherapy' was developed by Victor Frankl in the 1920s and 1930s. This is a form of existential therapy that specifically aims to help clients discover meaning and purpose in their lives. It uses a range of relatively directive techniques, including Socratic dialogue, which challenge clients to discover what is genuinely meaningful in their lives. In recent years, the Austrian psychiatrist Alfried Längle has developed a logotherapeutic approach called Existential Analysis, which combines traditional logotherapeutic concerns with a broader range of existential understandings and practices. This is one of the most prevalent forms of existential practice today (Correia et al., 2014b). Recent years have also seen the development of a number of other meaning-oriented therapies, such as Wong's (1998) meaning-centred counselling and Breitbart et al.'s (2010) meaning-centred group psychotherapy for patients with advanced cancer.

Dimensions of existential therapies

Across these schools of existential therapy, there are a number of differences in the way that therapists work. Some approaches, for instance, use a lot of techniques (e.g., meaning-oriented therapies), while others adopt a more relational stance (e.g., daseinsanalysis). Similarly, some tend to focus at the level of psychological, individual processes (e.g., the existential-humanistic approach), while others tend to bring in a more philosophical perspective (e.g., van Deurzen). In general, however, there is a 'hard'–'soft' dimension underlying these different practices (Cooper, 2008b) – or what Meg Barker refers to as a 'firm'–'gentle' dimension (personal communication, 2014) – with some existential therapists adopting a relatively challenging and directive approach, and others working in a more exploratory and client-led way.

To a great extent, where existential therapists stand on this firm–gentle dimension will be dependent on how much they believe human beings are – and can be – honest with themselves. If they believe that human beings suppress into their unconscious an awareness of their true existential condition, then a relatively challenging, interpretative approach may be adopted (e.g., Yalom, 1980). If, on the other hand, they believe that human beings can be relatively conscious of what they are experiencing and why (Spinelli, 1994, 2015), then a gentler, more exploratory approach may be seen as sufficient.

The outcomes of existential therapies

So does existential therapy actually make a positive difference to clients' lives? Of course, existential therapists would love to think so, but how do they actually know? No doubt, clients often tell them that the therapy has been helpful, but perhaps they are just trying to please them (Rennie, 1994), or justify to themselves the time and expense of therapy. And although existential therapists may see positive changes in their clients, perhaps this is the therapists trying to justify to themselves the work they do, or something that would have happened anyway over time.

For these kinds of reasons, in the world of counselling and psychotherapy today, there is a growing expectation that psychological practices are supported by 'objective' evidence that they bring about positive change. Typically, this means data from empirical study such as randomised controlled trials (RCTs), which test whether people who participate in therapy 'improve' significantly more than those who do not. This raises, however, a whole host of challenges for existential therapists. As we have seen, 'existential thinking emerged precisely as a reaction to the kinds of assumptions implicitly held within such empirical research' (Cooper, 2004c: 5): for instance, that 'objective truths' are more important than subjective experiences, that human change can be conceptualised in mechanistic terms, or that statistical averages can tell us something about individual human experiences. Indeed, even the concept of 'improvement' raises challenges for an existential perspective: improvement according to whom? (For further discussion of the relationship between existential therapy and research see the companion website, also Finlay, 2012).

EXISTENTIAL
THERAPY
AND
RESEARCH

Consequently, 'systematic, corroborative evidence for existential therapy is relatively limited' (Schneider & Krug, 2010: 93). Indeed, in a review of the evidence for the existential therapies in 2002, Walsh and McElwain (2002) did not cite a single experimental study in support of an existential approach. More recently, however, existential writers have begun to engage more fully with the outcome research (e.g., Cooper, 2004c; Craig et al., in press; Langdridge, 2012; LeMay & Wilson, 2008). Sometimes, this is out of pragmatism: a concern for the future of existential therapies; sometimes out of methodological pluralism: a belief that outcome research is one, albeit just one, legitimate form of inquiry; and sometimes out of a belief that outcome research can challenge our pre-existing assumptions and biases (Cooper, 2004c, 2010). In addition, since the 1980s (e.g., Greenberg, Koole & Pyszczynski, 2004; Spiegel, Bloom & Yalom, 1981), there has been a strand of psychology and psychotherapy researchers with an interest in existential themes such as death and meaning, but with no particular affiliation to the more philosophical and epistemological elements of existential thought.

In our EXIST review (Box 1.2, Vos et al., 2014), we identified 15 RCTs which evaluated the outcomes of existential therapies, involving a total of 1,792 participants. Most of these studies focused on the effectiveness of time-limited, group-based and often highly structured existential programmes for people with chronic and terminal physical illnesses, particularly cancer (e.g. Breitbart et al., 2010; Kissane et al., 2003; Spiegel et al., 1981). This means that it is difficult to generalise from the results of these studies to other forms of existential therapy, or other populations. Nevertheless, we did find that existential therapies – particularly the meaning-oriented approaches (see above and Chapter 6) – had the potential to bring about significant positive changes, particularly in increasing a sense of meaning and in reducing depression and anxiety. In a more recent study, an existentially informed therapy also did well against psychodynamic therapy for particular kinds of clients with 'treatment-resistant' depression (Stålsett, Gude, Rønnestad & Monsen, 2012).

In addition to these RCTs, the EXIST review found another 20 or so studies that looked at how a range of clients (e.g., people with alcohol problems, in prison, or attending a general psychotherapeutic practice, see Crumbaugh & Carr, 1979; Längle et al., 2005; Whiddon, 1983) had fared in existential therapy from beginning to end. Generally, what these studies showed is that clients in existential therapies improved on a range of indices, at levels that are fairly commensurate with other therapeutic approaches. In one of the most recent studies of this type, Rayner and Vitali (in press) looked at the outcomes of a short-term, structured programme of existential therapy in a London primary care setting. They found that around half of the participants showed significant clinical improvement – similar to the proportions improving in CBT and other therapeutic practices (Gyani, Shafran, Layard & Clark, 2013) – with low drop-out and relapse rates. As Schneider and Krug (2010: 94) recently put it, then, the outcome evidence for existential therapies is at a 'nascent but promising stage'.

About this book

Finally, by way of introduction, a few words about the structure and content of this book.

Each of the main chapters in this book focuses on a key facet of how existential therapists have described human being. Hence, following this introduction, Chapter 2 looks at human being-in-relation-to others, and Chapter 3 focuses on the experiential principles underlying existential work. In Chapter 4, freedom and choice are examined, followed by an exploration of the limitations of existence in Chapter 5. Another core existential theme, meaning and purpose, is addressed in Chapter 6. The focus of Chapter 7 is somewhat more idiosyncratic, but closely linked to existential ideas: interpersonal perceptions and 'metaperceptions'. Finally, in Chapter 8, there is a discussion and summary to draw the book together.

Chapters 3 to 7 are divided into two main parts. The first, 'understandings', presents a range of concepts and ideas – philosophical, psychological and psychotherapeutic – that can inform therapeutic reflections, formulation and practices. The second, 'practices', then looks at how these ideas can be applied in therapeutic work. Here, a range of client examples and dialogues are given to try and make the application of these ideas as concrete as possible. Each of these chapters concludes with critical reflections, in which the limitations as well as the strengths of these understandings and practices are discussed. This is followed by questions for reflections and suggestions for how these ideas might be followed up if you are interested: for instance, books, websites and articles. There are also various exercises, boxes and recommendations for reading throughout the chapters. (Please note that the exercises invite you to reflect on personal material. It is important, therefore, to only undertake those that you feel comfortable with; and do make sure there is someone available for you to debrief with, should the need arise.) Finally, a number of resources have been made available on the companion website: https://study.sagepub.com/cooper. These are a range of published papers of relevance to the current text, group exercises and some further notes (essentially, writings for this book that did not make it into the final edit!). Videos are also available which discuss further, and illustrate, a number of the basic counselling practices.

As indicated above, many client examples and dialogues are presented in this book. In all instances, details of the clients have been disguised to preserve their anonymity. In some cases, clients' narratives have been combined to further enhance anonymity and/or to emphasise teaching points. As much of the practice detailed in this book took place in a research clinic, I have had the opportunity to draw on actual recordings of sessions, or written feedback from clients, as well as data from psychotherapy outcome tools such as the Patient Health Questionnaire measure of depression (PHQ-9, see Kroenke, Spitzer & Williams, 2001). Consequently, some of the examples given of therapeutic work or feedback are verbatim, and it is indicated where this is the case. In other instances, client–therapist dialogues have been reconstructed after the session; and in some instances are entirely hypothetical.

Like many existential therapists, my practice has primarily been with adults, and on a one-to-one basis. As a consequence, this book does not directly address existential practice with children (see Quinn, 2010; Scalzo, 2010), couples (see van Deurzen & Iacovou, 2013), groups (see Breitbart et al., 2010; Cohn, 1997), or communities (see Mosher & Hendrix, 2004). I have also not focused explicitly on existential *coaching* (see van Deurzen & Hanaway, 2012) though the focus of coaching on 'self-development rather than pathology' (van Deurzen & Hanaway, 2012: xvii) suggests that it does fit very well with an existential stance.

Summary

This book aims to describe existential ideas and practices, as embedded within a pluralistic approach to therapy. It is primarily written for counsellors and psychotherapists outside of the existential field who are interested in drawing on this approach, as well as integratively minded existential therapists. Existential therapies are a range of practices, based on existential philosophy, that try to help clients acknowledge – and make the most of – the realities of their lived existences. The evidence for this approach is limited but promising.

Recommended reading

The ten most influential existential texts

A recent online survey of over 1,000 existential therapists, from across the globe, identified the texts that were most frequently considered to have influenced practice (Correia et al., 2014a). Each of these provides an ideal starting point for recommended reading in the existential field (though you will need to know German to read #10!). The top ten texts, in descending order (and referencing the most recent editions), are:

1. Frankl, V.E. (1984) *Man's Search for Meaning*. New York: Washington Square. Bestselling account of Frankl's experiences in the Nazi death camps, arguing that meaning, freedom and dignity can still be found in the midst of the most horrendous suffering. Includes a concise introduction to logotherapeutic principles and practice.
2. Yalom, I.D. (1980) *Existential Psychotherapy*. New York: Basic Books. Yalom's *magnum opus*, detailing the manifestations of, resistances to, research about, and therapeutic work with four 'ultimate concerns' of existence: death, freedom, isolation and meaninglessness.
3. Spinelli, E. (2015) *Practising Existential Therapy*, 2nd edn. London: Sage. Practical introduction to existential therapy based around a relational, three-phase model of practice.
4. Frankl, V.E. (1986) *The Doctor and the Soul: From Psychotherapy to Logotherapy*. New York: Vintage Books. Clearest, most comprehensive, and most detailed presentation of logotherapeutic principles and practice.
5. van Deurzen, E. (2009) *Everyday Mysteries,* 2nd edn. London: Sage. In-depth presentation of the theory and practice of a philosophically focused existential practice.
6. van Deurzen, E. (2012) *Existential Counselling and Psychotherapy in Practice*, 3rd edn. London: Sage. Accessible and practical introduction to van Deurzen's existential approach.
7. Spinelli, E. (2005) *The Interpreted World: An Introduction to Phenomenological Psychology*, 2nd edn. London: Sage. Introduction to phenomenology and its implications for psychology and psychological practices.
8. Yalom, I.D. (2001) *The Gift of Therapy: Reflections on Being a Therapist*. London: Piatkus. Tips from the master, with a particular emphasis on

(Continued)

(Continued)

the importance of being real with clients and working with the here-and-now relationship.

9. Yalom, I.D. (1989) *Love's Executioner and Other Tales of Psychotherapy*. London: Penguin. Classic, compelling and vivid compilation of existentially informed client studies.
10. Längle, A. (1988) *Sinnvoll leben: Eine praktische anleitung der logotherapy*. NP-Verlag: St Pölten. A practical guide to a contemporary logotherapeutic practice (German language).

Existential therapy: introductions

Of the ten most influential existential texts (above), Spinelli's *Practising Existential Therapy* (#3) and van Deurzen's *Existential Counselling and Psychotherapy in Practice* (#6) give the most practical introductions to contemporary existential theory and practice. Other introductory texts to consider are:

May, R. (1983) *The Discovery of Being*. New York: W.W. Norton and Co. Classic introduction to the existential approach.
Cooper, M. (2012) *Existential Counselling Primer*. Ross-on-Wye: PCCS Books. Concise overview of existential understandings and methods.
Langdridge, D. (2012) *Existential Counselling and Psychotherapy*. London: Sage. Existential therapy from a contemporary British school perspective.
Cooper, M. (2003) *Existential Therapies*. London: Sage. Critical review of the principal schools of existential therapy.

Chapters introducing the core principles and practices of existential therapy can also be found in most of the handbooks of counselling and psychotherapy, such as Dryden and Reeves' *The Handbook of Individual Therapy* (Sage, 2014, 6th edn), Feltham and Horton's *The Sage Handbook of Counselling and Psychotherapy* (Sage, 2012, 3rd edn), and Messer and Gurman's *Essential Psychotherapies* (Guilford, 2013, 3rd edn).

There are a range of YouTube videos introducing, discussing and demonstrating existential therapy. A good place to start is the playlist 'Popular existential therapy & existentialism videos', which includes my own introduction 'UA: Existentialism'.

Existential therapy: case studies

Yalom's *Love's Executioner* (#9) gives a brilliantly written account of an existentially informed practice, though it leans heavily to a psychodynamic approach. For an equally engaging read, which is, perhaps, more representative of contemporary existential practice, try:

Spinelli, E. (1997) *Tales of Un-Knowing: Therapeutic Encounters from an Existential Perspective*. Ross: PCCS Books.

Existential therapy: in-depth analysis

Yalom's *Existential Psychotherapy* (#2) gives one of the most comprehensive, detailed accounts of existential themes; while van Deurzen's *Everyday Mysteries* (#5) gives an in-depth analysis of the philosophical foundations of existential practice. If you loved Yalom's text, and are looking for something even more comprehensive, detailed and practical, try:

Bugental, J.F.T. (1981) *The Search for Authenticity: An Existential-Analytic Approach to Psychotherapy* (exp. edn). New York: Irvington.

This book is strongly influenced by humanistic and psychodynamic assumptions, and is not easy to get hold of (current online price is £304.01!), but it's a forgotten classic of the existential therapy literature and well worth borrowing from a library if you can.

For another very rich and critical exploration of key existential principles, with a particular focus on their relationship to psychodynamic ideas and practices, try:

Boss, M. (1963) *Psychoanalysis and Daseinsanalysis*. New York: Basic Books.

For a range of contemporary writings on existential therapy and the philosophy underlying this practice, see *Existential Analysis*, the journal of the UK Society for Existential Analysis (existentialanalysis.org.uk). See also The New Existentialists, at www.saybrook.edu/newexistentialists.

For a comprehensive review of the evidence base for existential therapeutic practice, see:

Craig, M., Vos, J., Cooper, M. & Correia, E. (in press) Existential psychotherapies. In D. Cain, K. Keenan & S. Rubin (eds), *Humanistic Psychotherapies*. Washington: APA.

Existential philosophy: introductory texts

Cox, G. (2009) *How to be an Existentialist: Or how to Get Real, Get a Grip and Stop Making Excuses*. London: Bloomsbury. Hugely witty, irreverent and accessible: a brilliant introduction to Sartrean-based existentialism. See also Cox (2012) which extends these reflections.

(Continued)

(Continued)

Wartenberg, T.E. (2008) *Existentialism: A Beginner's Guide*. London: Oneworld. Succinct, informed and very readable: one of the best contemporary introductions to existential philosophy.

Warnock, M. (1970) *Existentialism* (rev. edn). Oxford: Oxford University Press. Classic introduction to key existential thinkers.

Cooper, D.E. (1999) *Existentialism*. Oxford: Blackwell Publishers Ltd. Useful introduction to the principal concepts of existentialism.

Guignon, C.B. (2002) Existentialism. Available from http://www.rep.routledge.com. Very brief, but enormously lucid, accessible and incisive summary of existential thought.

Pluralistic therapy

Cooper, M. & McLeod, J. (2011) *Pluralistic Counselling and Psychotherapy*. London: Sage. Definitive guide to pluralistic thinking and practice.

Cooper, M. & Dryden, W. (2016) *The Handbook of Pluralistic Counselling and Psychotherapy*. London: Sage. Comprehensive tome on all aspects of pluralistic practice.

AN
INTRODUCTION
TO PLURALISM

McLeod, J. & Cooper, M. (2012) Pluralistic counselling and psychotherapy. In C. Feltham & I. Horton (eds), *The Sage Handbook of Counselling and Psychotherapy* (pp. 368–371). London: Sage. A very brief and concise introduction to the pluralistic approach. Available on the companion website.

McLeod, J., McLeod, J., Cooper, M. & Dryden, W. (2014) Pluralistic therapy. In W. Dryden & A. Reeves (eds), *Handbook of Individual Therapy*, 6th edn (pp. 547–573). London: Sage. A more detailed summary of a pluralistic perspective.

Manafi, E. (2010) Amor Fati*: existential contributions to pluralistic practice. In M. Milton (ed.), *Therapy and Beyond: Counselling Psychology Contributions to Therapeutic and Social Issues* (pp. 171–187). London: Wiley-Blackwell. Succinct summary of existential therapy within a pluralistic worldview, with an excellent client study.

2

Relational Foundations

This chapter discusses:

- The centrality of the therapeutic relationship to existential thought and practice.
- Buber's concept of the *I–Thou* attitude and its application to therapy.
- *Dialogue*, *relational depth* and *co-presence* as articulations, from an existential perspective, of the optimal therapeutic encounter.
- The reasons why an I–Thou therapist stance may be helpful for clients, and the particular clients it may be most helpful for.

From Daseinsanalysis (e.g., Boss, 1963) to existential–humanistic therapy (e.g., Bugental, 1978), a common feature of nearly all existential therapies is an emphasis on the quality of the client–therapist relationship. Yalom (1989: 91) puts this most succinctly when he states: 'It's the relationship that heals, the relationship that heals, the relationship that heals'. He also writes, 'In my work with clients, I strive for connectedness above all else' (2008: 206).

Consistent with this, when existential therapists are asked what they do with clients, they are most likely to describe their practice in relational terms: for instance, being caring, empathic and working in the here-and-now (Correia, Cooper & Berdondini, in preparation-b; Norcross, 1987; Wilkes & Milton, 2006). Similarly, independent observers are most likely to rate existential practice in terms of relational activities (Sousa & Alegria, in preparation), for instance 'Therapist is sensitive to the patient's feelings, attuned to the patient; empathic.' Most importantly, perhaps, when clients are asked what is most significant in their sessions of existential therapy, they again cite the relational dimension (Olivereira, Sousa & Pires, 2012).

This emphasis on the therapeutic relationship is not exclusive to the existential therapies: person-centred therapists (e.g., Schmid, 2006), gestalt therapists (e.g., Hycner, 1991), psychodynamic therapists (e.g., Stern, 2004), feminist therapists (e.g., Jordan, Kaplan, Miller, Stiver & Surrey, 1991) and integrative therapies (e.g., Clarkson, 2003), for example, all give the quality of the therapeutic relationship similar prominence. Indeed, research suggests that relational practices are the most common feature of all psychotherapeutic work (Cook et al., 2010). Nevertheless, the philosophical and ethical grounding of existential therapies gives it a particularly rich understanding of what it means to relate to clients in a deeply therapeutic way.

I–Thou and I–It

Martin Buber's (1958) writings on the *I–Thou* attitude has informed much existential work (e.g., Friedman, 1999; Spinelli, 2007), and provides an essential articulation of the existential ethic and therapeutic stance. Buber (see Chapter 1) developed his ideas from a fertile stream of nineteenth and twentieth century religious existentialism (Bergman, 1991). Here, he transposed notions of receptivity and dialogue towards God into notions of receptivity and dialogue towards one's fellow human beings (Cooper, Chak, Cornish & Gillespie, 2012). Buber remained deeply religious throughout his life; but argued that the path towards a 'higher spiritual presence' was through in-depth encounters with other human beings. For him (1958: 99), God was the 'Centre' where the 'extended lines of relation' meet.

Buber's (1958: 15) concept of the I–Thou and I–It stances are articulated in his 1923 text, *I and Thou*, which remains one of the most influential writings in the existential psychotherapy field (Correia et al., 2014a, see Chapter 1). The book opens with the following lines, and it is worth spending a little time focusing on them to get a flavour of Buber's writings and ideas:

> To human beings the world is twofold, in accordance with their twofold attitude.

> The attitude of human beings is twofold, in accordance with the two-fold nature of the primary words which they speak.

As can be seen, Buber's (1958: 15) style of writing is poetic and somewhat quixotic, so what does he actually mean? Here, Buber is suggesting that there are two fundamentally different ways in which we can encounter our world; indeed, the very world that we encounter depends on the stance that we take towards it.

> The primary words are not isolated words, but combined words.
>
> The one primary word is the combination I–Thou.
>
> The other primary word is the combination I–It; wherein, without a change in the primary word, one of the words He or She can replace It.

Here, Buber (1958: 15) is making three key points. First, that our primary being is not as isolated entities – like 'me', 'you', 'she' or 'it' – but as *beings-with-others*. In other words, as with the many *intersubjective* philosophers (see, for instance, Crossley, 1996), Buber is suggesting that we are fundamentally and inextricably linked with the people around us. That is, our sense of separation and individuality is, to some extent, an illusion. 'If you consider the individual by himself,' writes Buber (1947: 247) 'then you see of man just as much as you see of the moon; only man with man provides a full image.'

Second, Buber is suggesting that this being-with-others can take two forms: an *I–Thou* stance, and an *I–It* stance. The I–Thou stance is when we relate to the other as a human being; whereas the I–It stance is when we relate to the other as an object-like, dehumanised 'thing'. We will explore this in much more detail below. This leads on to the third key point that Buber is making in this passage: that, in the I–It stance, we can just as well be relating to a person or an inanimate object, like a chair; it does not matter. It is the same, de-humanising stance.

Buber (1958: 15) concludes this passage by stating:

> Hence the I of humans is also twofold.
>
> For the I of the primary word I–Thou is a different I from that of the primary word I–It.

In other words, our very being is dependent on the stance that we take towards others and our world. It is not, for Buber (1958), that we exist, and our world exists, and then we take an attitude towards it. Rather, for Buber, it is a stance towards the world – a relationship – that comes first, which then defines both the world and who we are in relation to it.

So what are these two different modes of relating? In *I and Thou*, Buber (1958) maps out a range of differences between them, and these will be described in the sections below, with specific reference to the therapeutic relationship. However, it is important to bear in mind that these differences are not isolated, independent dimensions; but inter-related parts of two very integrated ways of being (Cooper, 2003c). 'Buber's texts are fractal in structure' write Goldenberg and Isaacson (1996: 118); 'Whenever one draws out a piece and magnifies it, it turns out to be a microcosm of the whole'.

'Standing alongside' the client

One of the first distinctions that Buber (1958) makes between the I–It and I–Thou attitudes is that, in the former, the other is *experienced*; whilst in the latter, the other is *related to*. What he means by this is that, in the I–It attitude, we distance ourselves from another: they become something apart from us, something to which we *direct* our attention. So, for instance, we might survey, study or measure them; in the same way that we might study or measure a chemical molecule. This is illustrated in the top image in Figure 2.1, with the 'self' looking directly at the 'other'. By contrast, writes Buber (1958: 22), 'I do not experience the man to whom I say *Thou*, But I take my stand in relation to him'.

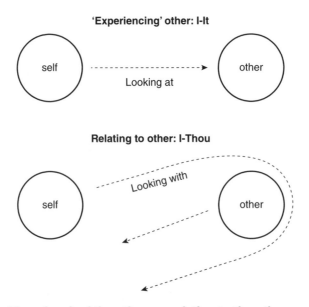

'Experiencing' other: I-It

self - - - - - - - - - - - - - -> other

Looking at

Relating to other: I-Thou

self   Looking with   other

Figure 2.1   'Experiencing' the other vs. relating to the other

Here, the other is not an object that we inspect, but a fellow human being that we stand alongside as they engage with their world. We do not look *at* them, but *with* them: a being to be understood, not analysed (May, 1983). This, for Spinelli (2015: 13), is the original meaning of the term *therapeia*: 'the enterprise of "attending to" another via the attempt to stand beside, or with, that other as he or she is being and acts in or upon the world'.

In relation to therapeutic practice, this aspect of the I–Thou stance has many parallels with the person-centred concept of *empathy*. This can be defined as 'entering the private perceptual world of the other and becoming thoroughly at home in it' (Rogers, 1980: 142). Here therapists are akin to 'fellow travellers', 'a term that abolishes distinctions between "them" (the afflicted) and "us" (the healers)' (Yalom, 2001: 8). We journey with our clients as they explore and experience their world: listening to what they see and feel, reflecting it back, asking questions, and providing companionship and support. Like fellow travellers, we do not focus 'in' on our clients: observing them, analysing them, and trying to explain why they do what they do. Indeed, it would be a very irritating travelling companion who spent all their time observing and analysing us! Rather our focus is outwards, alongside the other: seeing their world as they see it. For instance:

Therapist/fellow traveller:	What does it look like over there?
Client/traveller:	I'm not sure. I think it's a bit like _____.
Therapist/fellow traveller:	Oh yeah, I think I can see that too. Are you saying it's _____?
Client/traveller:	Well, sort of, but I meant more that I can see _____.
Therapist/fellow traveller:	Oh, ok, I get that. It's like _____. And can you tell me a bit more about what that's like...

Given this focus on being alongside clients, existential therapies tend to differ from more *interpretative* approaches – such as psychodynamic therapies – which focus *in* on trying to explain to clients why they act and feel in the ways that they do. Existential therapies also tend to eschew the process of 'formulation' or 'assessment' (Norcross, 1987), in which a psychological account is developed of how clients' problems have emerged. This focus on *being with* the other also differs from more psycho-educational approaches – such as cognitive-behavioural therapy – where the therapist encourages the client to see and do things in new ways.

For Buber (1958), standing alongside the other in an I–Thou stance also means that we are not trying to *do* something to them. That is, the other should not be a medium for our own desires. Therapeutically, this suggests that we need to develop an awareness – through supervision, personal therapy, or other forms of self-development – of our own wants in the therapeutic work, such that we are able to put them to one side (i.e., *bracket* them, see Chapter 3).

Relating to the client as subject, not object

A closely associated facet of Buber's (1958) I–Thou attitude is that, here, the other is related to as a *subject*: as a source of agency and experiencing. By contrast, in the I–It attitude, the other is experienced as an *object*: an entity, a thing, an 'it'. In terms of therapeutic practice, this might mean that a client diagnosed with depression is seen, first and foremost, as a person who is striving to cope with their sadness and hopelessness; and not as 'a depressive'. For Buber (1958: 21), 'If I face my human being as my *Thou*, and say the primary word *I–Thou* to him, he is not a thing among things' (p. 21). Rather, she or he remains a vibrant, dynamic humanity: a 'psychic stream' (Buber, 1988: 70).

In this respect, existential approaches to therapy tend to avoid the use of diagnostic categories (for instance, Laing, 1965): that is, labelling clients according to some pre-defined taxonomy. Indeed, Buber (1947: 29) states that real human encounter begins 'when the dictionary is put down'. Instead, existential therapists tend to use terms like 'problems in living' (DuPlock, 1997) to describe the kinds of difficulties that clients might be facing. This is an attempt to take a *de-pathologising* stance: viewing clients as functioning human subjectivities (albeit ones facing difficulties in their lives), rather than malfunction machines in need of repair (Frankl, 1988).

Acknowledging the client's freedom

Relating to an other as a subjectivity also means acknowledging their capacity for freedom and choice (Chapter 4). This contrasts with the I–It stance, in which the other is construed in determined, mechanistic terms. Here, again, we see the ethical core of the existential approach. Frankl (1986: xxvii), for instance, writes: 'When we present man as an automaton of reflexes, as a mind-machine, as a bundle of instincts, as a pawn of drives and reactions, as a mere product of instinct, heredity and environment, we feed the nihilism to which modern man is, in any case, prone.'

This existential emphasis on engaging with clients as freely choosing beings is partly why some existential therapists have rejected the use of techniques (May, 1958; Mullan, 1999). This is seen as doing something *to* the client, rather than as fostering the clients' own agency and choice.

Listening holistically

For Buber (1958), another facet of the I–Thou stance is that the other is related to *as* a wholeness: beheld and engaged with in her or his totality. Indeed, for existential therapists such as Binswanger (1963) and Spinelli (2015), the essence of an existential approach is to undercut such dualities as mind/body, cognitions/emotions, and even self/other, to reach the integrated experiencing that precedes such divisions. This contrasts with the I–It stance, in which the other is viewed as a 'compound' that can be broken down into its constituent atoms (Heidegger, 2001). An example of this is Freud's (1923) 'id', 'ego' and 'superego'.

Buber (1958: 19–20) gives a vivid description of what it means to relate to an other in this holistic way when he describes two very different modes of encountering a tree. He writes:

> I consider a tree....
>
> I can classify it in a species and study it as a type in its structure and mode of life.
>
> I can subdue its actual presence and form so sternly that I recognise it only as an expression of law....
>
> I can dissipate it and perpetuate it in number, in pure numerical relation.
>
> In all this, the tree remains my object, occupies space and time, and has its nature and constitution.

Here, Buber is describing what it means to relate to the tree in an I–It way. He then goes on to write:

> It can, however, also come about, if I have both will and grace, that in considering the tree I become bound up in relation to it. The tree is now no longer It. I have seized by the power of exclusiveness.
>
> To effect this it is not necessary for me to give up any of the ways in which I consider the tree. There is nothing from which I would have to turn my eyes away in order to see, and no knowledge that I would have to forget. Rather, is everything, picture and movement, species and type, law and number, indivisibly united in the event.
>
> Everything belonging to the tree is in this: its form and structure, its colours, a chemical composition, its intercourse with the elements and with the stars, are all present in a single whole.

This is the I–Thou stance, in which everything is experienced as a unified whole.

In therapeutic terms, what Buber (1958) is describing here can be called *holistic listening* (Mearns & Cooper, 2005). It is a 'breathing in' of the other in their totality, rather than a focusing down on one particular element. This is similar to Freud's 'evenly hovering attention' (quoted in Safran & Muran, 2000: 55): a relaxed openness to everything the client brings. Note, here, how Buber says that this stance does not require us to 'turn our eyes' from any aspect of the thing we are encountering. So it is not to ignore that a client has been diagnosed with depression, or that they come from a particular culture, or that they have had a traumatic past; but to see all these elements as part of an integrated whole.

Being open to the otherness of the client

When Buber (1958) describes relating to the tree in an I–It way, he writes about 'subduing' its actual presence 'so sternly that he recognises it only as an expression of law.' What he means by this is that the actual tree in front of him is forced to fit into his preconceived notions of what a tree is. In fact, from this stance, he does not really encounter the tree at all – what he encounters is a 'mirror' of his own assumptions and schemata (Wood, 1969). To give an analogy, it is as if he is looking through the lens of a telescope, but all he is really seeing is something pasted on to the end of it. The actual object he thinks he is looking at is obscured and beyond his gaze.

In relation to therapeutic practice, then, if I meet my client first and foremost as a label – for instance, as a 'borderline personality' – then I am not really meeting my client at all. Rather, I am simply meeting my assumptions and expectations about what he or she is like. So I see in my client the 'attachment difficulties' that I presumed he would have, or 'his' manipulative behaviour. But, in each of these cases, the actual, complex, multifaceted, unique individual in front of me is obscured: his presence has become subdued so sternly that, now, he is only an expression of psychological 'laws'. In the I–Thou stance, by contrast, I allow myself to recognise that this particular 'depressive' experienced a loving relationship with his parents, or that he is a profoundly creative and able person. It means, in the words of the post-existential French philosopher Emmanuel Levinas (1982), that I am open to the *otherness* of the other, that I have a 'non-allergic reaction with alterity' (Levinas, 1969: 47). Here, the self does not attempt to 'neutralise' the other; but recognises and acknowledges his or her fundamental unknowability (Cooper, 2009b).

This openness to the otherness of clients means meeting them from a place of *indefiniteness* (McArthur in Cooper & Ikemi, 2012) or *un-knowing* (Spinelli, 1997). It can also be described as bringing to the encounter *genuinely unfinished opennesses* (Cooper & Spinelli, 2012): where we engage with the other opened up to learning and discovering more. From a Buberian standpoint, it is only through this unfinished-ness and un-knowing that we can genuinely receive into ourselves others and encounter them in an I–Thou way. In other words, if we meet them from a stance of definiteness, completeness and certainty, what more could we – or would we want to – take in?

An openness to the otherness of the other also means a willingness to respond in different ways to different clients: adjusting and altering our behaviour depending on that client's unique, individual needs and modes of engagement. As Yalom (1999, 2001) puts it, we must create a new therapy for each individual client. We may find, for instance, that one client wants us to challenge her ways of thinking, while another wants us to focus principally on providing him with space to talk. Adopting an I–Thou stance, then, means personalising our therapy, as developed within the pluralistic approach (see Chapter 1). This contrasts with an I–It stance in which we come to treat each client as essentially the same.

Confirming the client

Affirming the otherness of the other relates closely to Buber's (1958) concept of *confirmation*, another key facet of the I–Thou stance. Friedman (1985) defined this as 'an act of love through which one acknowledges the other as one who exists in his own peculiar form and has the right to do so' (p. 134). There are clear parallels here with Rogers' (1957) concepts of 'unconditional positive regard' and non-judgmental acceptance – particularly the emphasis on the acceptance of others in their wholeness – and research suggests that clients do experience this as a significant part of existential therapy (Olivereira et al., 2012). However, in emphasising the confirmation of others in their 'own peculiar form', a Buberian perspective particularly emphasises the acceptance of others in their *difference* from the I. In other words, it is an affirmation of others across a 'bridge' of difference: that they and we are fundamentally unique, and that those differences – at both ends – are to be welcomed, prized and affirmed. Indeed, as Buber (1958) points out, to merge with another is not to encounter them: we cannot encounter something that we are.

This emphasis on confirming-the-other-across-difference has important implications for existential therapeutic practice, particularly when contrasted with a classical client-centred approach (Merry, 2004). The classical client-centred therapist strives to 'stand in the shoes' of clients and experience their world as they experience it. For much of the time, the existential therapist strives to do the same (see above). Yet, from an existential standpoint, there are also times when therapists may choose to encounter clients from a standpoint of otherness: to present them with ideas, understandings or perspectives which lie outside of clients' own frames of reference. In this respect, as Friedman (1985: 199–200) writes, the existential therapist 'does not lose his centre, his personal core, in an amorphous meeting with the other. If he sees through the eyes of the other and experiences the other's side, he does not cease to experience the relationship from his own side.'

Suppose, for instance, that a client is talking about a fear that others experience here as incoherent. Here, an empathic person-centred or existential response might be to confirm that experiencing, for example, 'It sounds like you are really scared of sounding unclear.' An existential therapist, however, might also then go on to engage with that experiencing from a more 'external' standpoint. For instance, 'I know you are afraid of sounding incoherent, but my experience of you is that you are actually very clear'. Of course, many person-centred therapists would do something similar – construed in terms of *congruence* (Rogers, 1957) – but the existential emphasis on confirmation across *difference* means that existential therapists may be more willing to introduce, transparently, their own frame of reference into the dialogue. In Spinelli's (2015) terms, this is a willingness to *be-for* the client, as well as to *be-with* them.

In this respect, a useful skill for therapists to develop may be the capacity for *affirming dissensus* (Cooper & Ikemi, 2012). This means the ability to communicate warmth and positive regard to clients, while at the same time a fundamentally different view on how their world might be. For instance:

Client:	I feel like everyone really hates me.
Empathic response:	I really get a strong sense of how much you think people hate you.
Affirming dissensus:	I really get a strong sense of how much you think people hate you, and I know that's how you feel; but when you describe your relationships with others I get a sense that lots of people really like you. And that's my experience of you too – as a really likeable person.

Such a response aims to respect the phenomenological reality of the client (see Chapter 3), but to also bring in other possibilities and perspectives: the otherness of the therapist. In doing so, it moves further away from a classical, non-directive person-centred standpoint, and towards a more cognitive therapeutic approach. Here, the therapist may actively (but respectfully) challenge the client's perception of their world. An example of how this can be helpful to clients comes from 'Angela', an existential therapy client interviewed in Edwards and Milton (2014: 49). She states:

> I was banging on about something. It was one of those situations where 'I knew I was right,' and suddenly she [the therapist] kind of stepped forward, almost took her therapist hat off, and said, 'actually I don't agree,' and she told me how she felt in the same situation. It was brilliant, it was the most wonderful way of 'vooom', and, of course, I thought how ridiculous, these are my hang-ups. She only did it that once, and it was so powerful... it's still with me, it helped me to be honest with myself in a way.

Buber's (1958) confirmation can also differ from a Rogerian (1957) unconditional positive regard in that it is an *active prizing* of a client's being, as opposed to a more neutral non-judgemental acceptance. In other words, therapists might go beyond communicating to clients that they are 'ok' however they are; to expressing a positive perception of their being: as 'courageous', or 'talented' or 'amazingly resourceful' individuals. Obviously, such a perception cannot be forced, but if a therapist perceives a client in this way, then from an existential perspective, there is no reason to hold it back. Indeed, to the extent this may not be how a client sees himself or herself, it is an example of affirming dissensus: gently and positively challenging a client with an alternative, and hopefully more *salutogenic* (i.e., wellbeing promoting) worldview.

Throughout my 20 sessions with Rima, for instance, I had a sense that I was with a remarkable young woman. Despite constant life challenges and disappointments, she put everything in to therapy: always trying to see what she could learn from it and how she might move forward in her life. And there was something about her that seemed to really reach out to people – to me – in a very caring and compassionate way; some deep capacity to accept and to be with others. In our last session together, she talked about her experiences of therapy; and I, then, shared those perceptions that I had had of her: that I thought she was remarkable, and courageous, and able to touch others in a very deep way. Rima sat quietly and expressed surprise: 'those are just normal qualities', she said. But later in her feedback on the session she rated this exchange as 'greatly helpful', writing 'It was challenging for me to hear how Mick perceived me, but I hope that one day I might be able to really take it in'.

In these respects, Friedman (1985: 138) writes that 'Real confirmation cares enough about the other person to wrestle with him, for him – confirming him even while opposing him'. This is consistent with empirical research which suggests that clients often want their therapists to challenge them (Aylindar, 2014), and find feedback of positive benefit (Claiborn, Goodyear & Horner, 2002). Recent research also suggests that one of the things that clients may find most helpful in therapy is not unconditional acceptance, *per se*, but a sense that their therapist genuinely *cares* about them (see Bedi, Davis & Williams, 2005; Knox & Cooper, 2010; McMillan & McLeod, 2006). This is a feeling of really mattering to their therapists: that their therapists are interested in them and willing to 'go the extra mile'. One client, for instance, described how helpful it had been when their therapist said, 'Call anytime, or just come in anytime, and there will be someone here, even if I'm not here' (Bedi et al., 2005: 318).

Relating to the client *as* a wholeness

As we have seen, Buber (1958) states that an *I–Thou* attitude is one in which we relate to the other as a whole. For Buber, however, such an *I–Thou* attitude also requires *us* to bring *our* own totality into the encounter. '[T]he primary word [I–Thou] can only be spoken with the whole being' writes Buber, 'He who gives himself to it may withhold nothing of himself' (p. 23). In therapeutic terms, this means that therapists need to be aware of, and able to draw on, all aspects of themselves – their vulnerabilities and strengths, their cognitions and emotions, their wisdom and their humour – right down to their very 'wordless depths' (Buber, 1947: 42). It means, as with person-centred *congruence* (Rogers, 1957), that the therapist is more than just a professional role; but a fully fleshed out, four-dimensional human being: a 'Mick' or 'Joanna' or 'Deena'; albeit a Mick- or Joanna- or Deena-who-is-focused-on-their-clients.

Box 2.1 Are you *you* in the therapeutic encounter?

An interesting test of how genuine you are in your therapeutic work is to ask yourself whether you 'change' as a person when you go from everyday life to working with your clients. Does it feel, for instance, that you seem to move through an 'invisible curtain' and start to talk differently (e.g., hushed tones), sit differently, or say things that you never normally would (e.g., 'I really hear that', 'I'm wondering if you feel safe here?', 'Let's just stay with your experiences'). Obviously, as counsellors and psychotherapists, there are some things we need to *do* differently to everyday life – in particular, staying focused on the other – but if we are different as a person, it may be interesting to reflect on how and why this happens. From an existential standpoint, we should just be 'ourselves' in the therapeutic relationship; albeit ourselves in a focused and 'disciplined' way, attending to the psychological needs and experiences of the other.

This emphasis on being real, authentic and 'just yourself' in the therapeutic relationship is one of the hallmarks of an existential approach to therapy (Bugental, 1978; Mullan, 1999; Yalom, 2001), and has been identified by clients as a significant part of the existential therapeutic process (Edwards & Milton, 2014; Olivereira et al., 2012). One aspect of this authenticity is a willingness to engage with clients in relatively relaxed and informal ways (see Box 2.1): for instance, making cups of tea for clients or even going out for walks with them (Mullan, 1995; Spinelli, 2001). This flexibility of therapeutic boundaries is something that clients in existential therapy have described as helpful (Edwards & Milton, 2014), and may also be found in humanistic and CBT practices. However, it contrasts with more psychodynamic approaches, where there is a stronger emphasis on boundaries, consistency and engaging with clients in a more 'neutral' way. Laing (1985: 143) illustrates these differences:

> In a recent seminar that I gave to a group of psychoanalysts, my audience became progressively aghast when I said that I might accept a cigarette from a patient without making an interpretation. I might even offer a patient a cigarette. I might even give him or her a light.
>
> 'And what if a patient asked you for a glass of water?' one of them asked, almost breathlessly.
>
> 'I would give him or her a glass of water and sit down in my chair again.'
>
> 'Would you make an interpretation?'
>
> 'Very probably not.'
>
> A lady exclaimed, 'I'm totally lost.'

A second aspect of being real with clients is *self-disclosure*: 'Therapist statements that reveal something personal about the therapist' (Cooper, 2008a: 187). In general, existential therapists have encouraged a relatively disclosing approach. Yalom (2001: 92), for instance, writes:

If patients want to know whether I am married, have children, like a certain movie, read a certain book, of felt awkward at our meeting at some social event, I always answer them directly. Why not? What's the big deal? How can one have genuine encounter with another person while remaining so opaque.

Consistent with the broader psychotherapy research (Hill & Knox, 2002), self-disclosures tend to be experienced by clients as a helpful element in existential therapy, revealing the therapist as 'a real/similar human being' (Olivereira et al., 2012: 297). Indeed, research suggests that clients can even experience the disclosure of therapists' vulnerabilities and insecurities as helpful (Edwards & Milton, 2014; Olivereira et al., 2012). First, it may help them feel more trusting of the therapist (Olivereira et al., 2012). Second, it may help them see that the therapist, as a vulnerable human being, cannot 'make' them change. Rather, it is something that they will need to make happen themselves (Farber, 1967). Third, it may help them feel more empowered, because the relationship is more equal. One client in existential therapy, for instance, reported:

[The therapist] said, 'I've got a really bad cold, fluey sort of cold it makes me feel so depressed I almost feel like committing suicide'. I gave him a big hug and I said I hope you feel better soon. I felt wonderful about that... that he'd shared that with me. Vulnerability is important for someone's humanity, that person-to-person relationship. (Edwards & Milton, 2014)

What is also evident from the research (Hill & Knox, 2002; Olivereira et al., 2012), however, is that self-disclosure should be used sparingly, judiciously and cautiously. Indeed, even Buber (1947) warns against a 'universal un-reserve'. As with all therapists' responses, the question, here, is whether or not the self-disclosure is 'relevant for the mentioned issue' (Olivereira et al., 2012: 296). From a pluralistic standpoint, this is particularly whether or not the self-disclosure is relevant to the client's therapeutic goals. For instance, if a client's goal is to understand why her relationships break down, it might be helpful for a therapist to share that, at times, she can feel rejected and dismissed by the client. However, if the client has come to therapy to work through a bereavement, such a disclosure may be quite irrelevant and inappropriate. In this respect, it is also important for therapists to ask themselves whether their desire to self-disclose comes from their own particular wants and interests – 'countertransference' – rather than being a genuine response to their clients.

For therapists to be able to draw on different aspects of their experiencing – and also to know whether their experiencing is more about them than their clients – it is probably essential that they have developed an *accepting embrace* of these different aspects of them-selves (Spinelli in Cooper & Spinelli, 2012). If a therapist, for instance, feels ashamed of her feelings of vulnerability, it is unlikely that she will draw on these to help inform her therapeutic work. Buber (1947: 39) writes: 'in order to be able to go out to the other you must have the starting place, you must have been, you must be, with yourself.' This, again, highlights the importance of the personal developmental agenda for therapists.

This capacity to express all of our being extends right to the very 'edges' of our awareness (Cooper & Ikemi, 2012). This is the ability to access and articulate thoughts, feelings and *felt senses* (Gendlin, 1996) that are just emerging into our consciousness. Like unfinished open-nesses, these are responses to the client that are indefinite, uncertain and half-formed: question marks rather than answers. For instance, 'I just get this sense of relief as you say that, do you feel that too?' or 'I'm just feeling that you might be annoyed with me, is that right?' Of course, as tentatively felt experiences, such responses need to be shared in very tentative ways – they may be entirely tangential to what clients are experiencing. But if therapists are empathically attuned to their clients, from the whole of their being to the whole of the clients', then what is emerging at the edges of the therapist's experiences may reflect something of the client's too.

One of the edges of their experiencing that it may be useful for ther-apists to draw on is their bodily responses. This can be described as an *embodied empathy* (Cooper, 2001a), complementing the more cognitive and affective forms of responding that therapists may be more familiar with. For instance, a therapist might share with a client: 'When you talk about your relationship with your mother, I get a real sense of pressure on my shoulders', or 'I can feel those butterflies in my stom-ach as you talk about that'. Used sparingly and tentatively, such responses may help clients to connect more fully with their own bodily felt responses, and go deeper into their experiencing (see Cooper, 2013b).

A willingness to take risks

To open ourselves up to the otherness of the client, and to be fully pres-ent in the face of that, is to take a risk. It means allowing an encounter to evolve in ways that we cannot predict or control (Leontiev, 2013). It is a 'perilous' and 'unreliable' meeting, in which 'the well-tried context' is 'loosened' and the potential for having our 'security shattered' (Buber, 1958). It means to take the risk of *trusting* our clients (Boszormenyi-Nagy & Krasner, 1986). Yalom (2001: 26) writes 'I urge you to let your patients matter to you, to let them enter your mind, influence you, change you – and not to conceal this from them.'

Not surprisingly, then, when therapists are asked what facilitates a moment of in-depth meeting, their most common response is that it is this act of taking a risk with their clients (Cooper, 2005, unpublished). In particular, it is the times when they realise that they have fallen into a routinised, incongruent way of relating to clients; and take the risk of sharing what is really going on. In the first 20 minutes of a session with Sonya, a long-term client, for instance, I listened as she shared with me things that she frequently shared: her feelings of frustration with her partner, her sense that the world was unjust, her incredulity at how brutal other people could be. I reflected and summarised her percep-tions; but 'underneath' I felt distanced and a bit confused: why was she telling me this again? At first, it did not even occur to me to share this with Sonya. I did not want to hurt her feelings; and, indeed, research shows that providing clients with negative feedback can be quite harmful at times (Cooper, 2008a). As my feelings persisted, however, I took the risk of sharing this with her, in a way that I hoped would not be experienced as critical. 'Sonya', I said, 'I'm aware that you often talk about how unfair and brutal the world seems, and I just don't quite understand why it's so important for you to tell me this. Can you tell me?'

Sonya went quiet for a bit. 'I think', she said gently, 'it's something about feeling like you don't really understand what it is like for me outside in the world, how hard the world can be. It's like you live in this world of being a professor and an academic and don't realise that things out there are really *tough*'.

Sonya smiled at me apologetically and I smiled back: 'It's like even here', I said, 'you feel that I just don't get how tough things feel, that must be so isolating'.

Sonya went on to talk about her deep sense of isolation in the world; her feeling of being cut off from everyone around her – even from me, the person who was supposed to understand her most. And, as she talked, slowly and with emotion, it felt like the distance between us began to reduce. Through taking the risk of sharing something of my genuine experiencing with Sonya, it felt like an invitation had been extended to her to share something of her own.

Dialogue and meeting at relational depth

In his 1929 essay *Dialogue* (in Buber, 1947), Buber moves on from talking about the particular stances that individuals can take towards each other towards an exploration of the kinds of relationships that can exist *between* persons. Here, Buber describes a form of relating that he terms *genuine dialogue* (or sometimes just *dialogue*). This is essentially equivalent to two people encountering the other in an I–Thou way. From an existential standpoint – as well as a pluralistic one – it can be considered an optimal form of therapeutic relating. (For an in-depth discussion of dialogue at the intrapersonal, interpersonal and social level, see Cooper et al., 2012).

DIALOGUE

Buber (1947) contrasts genuine dialogue with monologue (where both parties relate to the other as an It), and also to 'monologue disguised as dialogue'. Buber considers the latter most prevalent in the world of his day (and that was before text messaging and online chat ☺). By this, Buber means a form of communication that has a semblance of interpersonal openness and receptivity, but is essentially a turning towards, and concern with, oneself: a 'reflexivity' rather than a genuine reaching out to an other. Here, he writes, 'two or more men, meeting in space, speak each with himself in strangely torturous and circuitous ways and yet imagine they have escaped the torment of being thrown back on their own resources' (p. 37). In this 'duologue' (van Deurzen & Adams, 2011), each individual's concerns are not with learning from the other, but with self-presentation and self-enhancement. Spontaneity and transparency are replaced with artifice, phoniness and manipulation. Buber (1947: 38) vividly describes a number of forms of communication that make up this 'underworld of faceless spectres of dialogue'. In *debate*, for instance, he writes that points are not made as they exist in the protagonist's mind, but are designed to strike home as sharply as possible – a 'word duel' that is far more about self-aggrandisement than any genuine learning. And in *speechifying*, he writes, 'people do not really speak to one another, but each, although turned to the other, really speaks to a fictitious court of appeal whose life consists of nothing but listening to him' (1988: 68–69).

Relational depth is a concept closely related to dialogue. It was introduced by the person-centred therapist Dave Mearns (1997, 2003) – and developed by Dave, myself and other colleagues (Knox, Murphy, Wiggins & Cooper, 2013; Mearns & Cooper, 2005: xii) – to describe, 'A state of profound contact and engagement between two people, in which each person is fully real with the Other, and able to understand and value the Other's experiences at a high level'. As moments in therapy, it can be considered synonymous with times of genuine therapeutic dialogue, with therapists and clients experiencing a powerful sense of intimacy, reciprocity and 'co-flow' (Cooper, 2013a). Research indicates that nearly all therapists, and around 80% of clients, have experienced such moments of in-depth relating in therapy (Leung, 2008). Research also suggests that feelings of connectedness tend to be experienced *synchronously*: that is, experienced by therapist and client at about the same time (Cooper, 2012a).

A MOMENT OF
RELATIONAL
DEPTH: NOTES

(An extended example of a moment of relational depth is given on the companion website.)

At these times of relational depth, there is a strong element of *mutuality*: the therapist affects the client, but the client also affects the therapist. This is a common thread across Buber's concepts of the I–Thou stance and dialogue (Wood, 1969), relational depth (Murphy, 2013) and much existential therapeutic work (Yalom, 1999). That is, the existential therapist strives to create a relationship that is bi-directional and relatively 'egalitarian': where the client is not only 'done to', but also a 'do-er'. Consistent with this, research suggests that clients in existential therapy do feel empowered and validated by being invited to relate to their therapists in a cooperative way (Olivereira et al., 2012). More broadly, research suggests that clients do better in therapy when there are higher levels of mutuality (Murphy & Cramer, 2014; Orlinsky, Rønnestad & Willutzki, 2004). That is, when they feel empathic or accepting towards their therapists as well as vice versa.

Although existential therapists may hope to engage their clients in a genuinely dialogic and mutual way, there is an important difference between the I–Thou stance and dialogue/relational depth. Therapists can choose to engage their clients from an I–Thou stance, but they 'cannot will relation' (Farber, 2000b: 84). Dialogue and relational depth are *two*-person phenomena: it is the client, as much as the therapist, that brings this about. Therapists, then, cannot create relational depth on their own. Moreover, to try and make genuine dialogue or relational depth happen would be a contradiction in terms. As we have seen, dialogue requires an engagement with the other that respects their freedom, and does not treat them as a means to an end.

Presence and co-presence

Given that therapists cannot evoke dialogue or relational depth, these phenomena can only be understood as *descriptions* of what might take place in therapy. By contrast, the I–Thou stance gives more guidance on how therapists may choose to relate to their clients. And, in this sense, the concept of the I–Thou attitude may be more directly relevant to therapist training and practice. Nevertheless, an understanding of the optimal therapeutic encounter in terms of dialogue and relational depth raises some important considerations and possibilities regarding therapeutic practice.

A useful way of articulating this, and drawing together this exploration of the existential relational stance, is through the concepts of *presence* and *co-presence*. Presence is a concept that is widely used in the existential and humanistic fields (e.g., Geller, 2013), and can be defined as being 'totally in the situation' (Bugental, 1976: 36). In other words, when we are present to other people, we are responding to them as they are, in the here-and-now. Presence, then, is synonymous with the I–Thou stance: it is about meeting others in their present and particular being. It is an engagement with others as we are and as they are, without preconceptions, distortions or disguises.

James Bugental (1976), one of the founders of existential-humanistic psychotherapy, goes on to suggest that presence has two wholly inter-related, aspects: a willingness to be impacted upon by a situation (*receptivity*), and a willingness to share oneself in a situation (*expressivity*, see Figure 2.2). This can be a useful framework for thinking about what it means to encounter the other from an I–Thou stance. Here, we *receive* into the 'core' of ourselves (Leontiev, 2013) the client as a freely choosing, holistic subjectivity; and take the risk of *expressing* our core essence in an integrated, honest way.

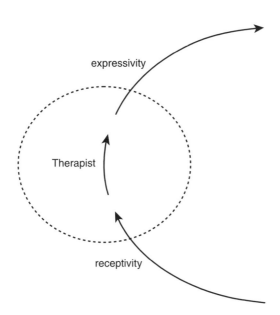

Figure 2.2 Presence

Framed in this manner, dialogue and relational depth can be conceptualised as manifestations of *co-presence*: where both clients and therapists are able to receive the other and express their genuine being in response. This is illustrated in Figure 2.3, where the 'wordless depths' of both therapist and client are connected in an on-going, dialogical cycle. My client, for instance, tells me about her sense of shame;

and, as I listen to this, I feel an uncomfortableness throughout my body. I share this with her and she says that she feels it too – like a gawky, pathetic teenager. She tells me about her first date and how her father laughed at her when he found out. The shame feels more visceral and I reflect this back....

This model of co-presence suggests four points of 'therapeutic leverage' when we think about ways in which we might deepen the level of relating in our counselling and psychotherapy work.

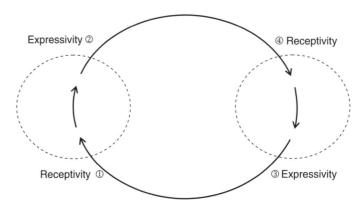

Figure 2.3   Co-presence and four points of 'therapeutic leverage'

First, we can work on enhancing our receptivity towards our clients. As one facet of the I–Thou stance, we have already looked at different ways in which this might be achieved. This includes listening holistically, and in embodied ways, to our clients; receiving their humanity and subjectivity rather than it-ifying them; and bracketing assumptions and prejudices to take in the full totality of their otherness. It also means looking at what our own blocks to presence and connectedness might be (see also the Strategies of Disconnection Inventory in Cooper, 2013b, also available on the companion website).

STRATEGIES OF DISCONNECTION INVENTORY

Second, we can focus on enhancing our expressivity towards our clients. This is the other facet of the I–Thou stance that we have explored in this chapter, and involves taking the risk of recognising and expressing – where appropriate – our authentic, felt response to the client.

The third point of leverage that this framework points to involves helping clients enhance their levels of expressivity. This is a more challenging focus because it is outside of our control. It is the 'grace' that Buber (1958) refers to in his description of encountering the tree. We can 'will' to encounter the other, but this is insufficient in itself: the other must open up to us. Moreover, clients that we work with may have 'withdrawn from world into inner citadel of self' (Laing, 1965: 80) as a means of self-protection. However, many of the methods discussed in the next chapter on phenomenological practice may help in this process (Chapter 3). Creating a 'safe', consistent and appropriately boundaried space may also be important here, so that clients feel that they can share whatever they want without undesired or unpredictable consequences. In addition, there may be a wide range of more active methods, exercises and forms of questioning – as particularly developed in the experiential therapies, such as focusing and two chair work (e.g., Gendlin, 1996; Greenberg, Rice & Elliott, 1993) – that can help clients express their experiencing in deeper and more authentic ways. Indeed, research suggests that therapists can play a key role in either deepening or flattening clients' levels of experiential engagement (Sachse & Elliott, 2002).

Finally, there is the question of how therapists might help their clients develop greater levels of receptivity towards them. This is, perhaps, the most challenging point of leverage to consider: how do you help another be more open to you? As Buber (1947) suggests, in many instances, we will be encountering clients who are unable or unwilling to enter into genuine dialogue (see the companion website). These are clients who are speechifying, trying to debate with us, or otherwise closed to our otherness, and may not be aware that they are doing so. So how do we help clients create 'chinks' in their own armour (Schneider, 2000)? Creating a safe, caring and well-boundaried space may, again, be important here, in helping clients feel that they can trust their therapists to open up to them, and meet them from a place of genuinely unfinished opennesses. Knowing their therapists will not violate or exploit any opennesses may also be important; and this means therapists expressing themselves in sensitive, non-threatening and affirming ways – even when in dissensus (see above). In addition, if a client's lack of receptivity seems to be a real barrier to therapeutic progress, despite the levels of care and affirmation offered, it may be appropriate for therapists to raise this with their client, and explore the process in more detail. This may range from a relatively gentle prompt: for instance, 'I get a sense that what I said didn't seem helpful to you' to a more direct challenge 'I sometimes feel that it's really hard for you to take in what I say, is that right?'

UNDERSTANDING CLIENT DISTRESS FROM A RELATIONAL PERSPECTIVE: NOTES

The therapeutic value of in-depth relating

The existential emphasis on the establishment of an in-depth, dialogical relationship is well supported by empirical research in the field.

Analyses of data from hundreds of studies indicates that the therapeutic relationship is probably *the* most important predictor of therapeutic outcomes – aside from what the clients, themselves, bring to therapy – accounting for around 12% of the total variance in client outcomes (Crits-Christoph, Connolly Gibbons & Mukherjee, 2013; Norcross, 2011; Norcross & Lambert, 2011). Drawing on an extensive body of data, the second American Psychological Association Task Force on Evidence-Based Therapy Relationships concluded that 'the therapy relationship makes substantial and consistent contributions to psychotherapy outcome independent of the specific type of treatment' (Norcross & Wampold, 2011: 423); and that 'The therapy relationship accounts for why clients improve (or fail to improve) at least as much as the particular treatment or method' (Norcross & Wampold, 2011: 423).

More specifically, the particular qualities of the therapeutic relationship that have been shown to be associated with positive outcomes are closely related to those advocated by Buber and the existential therapists. Empathy – the therapist's capacity to stand alongside the client – has been identified by the APA Task Force as one of four 'demonstrably effective' elements of the therapeutic relationship (Elliott, Bohart, Watson & Greenberg, 2011). Evidence for the quality of the *therapeutic alliance* (Horvath, Del Re, Fluckinger & Symonds, 2011) is at a similar level. This refers both to the bond and the level of collaboration between therapist and client. Positive regard – the therapist's confirmation of the client – has a somewhat lower level of empirical support, but this is primarily because less research has been conducted. However, it is still identified by the APA Task Force as a 'probably effective' element of the therapeutic relationship (Farber & Doolin, 2011). Congruence/genuineness is identified as an element that is 'promising but insufficient research' (Kolden, Klein, Wang & Austin, 2011). In addition, recent research suggests that relational depth may be an important predictor of outcomes (Wiggins, 2011); with clients who reported greater depth of relating at significant moments in therapy showing greater reductions in psychological distress. Clients in existential therapy have also reported the value of being able to relate to their therapists on a deep personal level (Edwards & Milton, 2014).

What this research does not address so fully, however, is *why* the therapeutic relationship might be a key contributor to positive therapeutic outcomes. Four potential reasons are outlined below.

A crucible for facilitative therapeutic work

At its most basic, a therapist's adoption of an I–Thou relational stance may provide a conducive context for clients to carry out a wide range of self-exploratory – and developmental – activities. Through feeling listened to, empathised and affirmed – and through experiencing the therapist as a caring and genuine human being – clients may experience a sense of safety that allows them to disclose 'aspects of their self that are, for them, the most profound aspects that they can rarely face themselves and would *never* share with another' (Mearns & Cooper, 2005: 50). Through the articulation and exploration of such experiences, clients may then be able to develop greater insights into themselves and their behaviours; and find new, and potentially more constructive, ways forward in their lives.

Helping clients connect deeply with themselves

When clients are asked why an experience at relational depth is helpful to them, the most common response is that it facilitates their connection *with themselves* (Knox, 2013). This is consistent with the ideas of the influential developmental psychologist Lev Semonich Vygostky (1962): that the way we relate to others becomes the way we relate to ourselves. Indeed, many therapists will have heard their clients say that they carry a 'little voice' of the therapist 'inside their head': offering supportive or reassuring words, or asking them questions about what they are doing and feeling.

In previous writings (Cooper, 2003c (available on the companion website); 2004a, 2005a), I have suggested that we might refer to an internalised I–Thou relation as an *I–I* self-relational stance. This contrasts with an *I–Me* self-relational stance, which is an intrapersonal version of the I–It attitude. In the I–I stance, people relate to themselves, or different aspects of their experiencing, in an empathic and affirming way; open to – and owning of – their own *self-otherness* (Cooper & Hermans, 2007). For instance, a client might acknowledge that he can experience intense feelings of vulnerability, and that this is a meaningful and legitimate – albeit painful – means of experiencing his world. By contrast, in the I–Me self-relational stance, people objectify, criticise and disown some aspects of their being; or explain their behaviour in mechanistic ways (Boss, 1963). So here, for instance, the client might feel very ashamed of the fact that he feels vulnerable; or he may see this as something that takes him over and needs to be removed (Spinelli, 1994). In this I–Me self-relational stance, the vulnerability is not construed as a living, meaningful part of his being; but as a 'thing' (de Beauvoir, 1948a; Sartre, 1958) which lies outside of the self-construct.

Relating to ourselves in an I–I way may be psychologically beneficial for several reasons (Cooper, 2003c, 2004a). First, it is synonymous with

THE I–I AND I–ME SELF-RELATIONAL STANCES

feeling good about who we are – *all* of who we are – rather than ashamed or critical of different aspects of our being. Second, it means lower levels of 'internal conflict', which is known to be a key predictor of psychological distress (e.g., Michalak, Heidenreich & Hoyer, 2004). Third, it means that we can draw on all of our qualities and abilities all of the time, rather than having certain aspects of our being suppressed or denied (see Chapter 3).

Experiencing connection with the therapist

A third reason why the experience of in-depth connection with a therapist may be helpful to a client is because of the *salutogenic* potential of in-depth relating, *per se*. That is, a regular hour of close, personal connection each week with another human being may provide clients with the 'deep soul nourishment' (Hycner, 1991: 61) that they need to help them feel less isolated, better about themselves, and more able to function in their world. This is consistent with a range of theories – existential (e.g., Trüb, 1964) and otherwise (e.g., Baumeister & Leary, 1995; Bowlby, 1969; Ryan & Deci, 2000) – that suggest that people have a fundamental need for close connection with others (see Mearns & Cooper, 2005).

Such a viewpoint is supported by a wide body of research, which shows that feeling connected to others is one of the best predictors of subjectively reported mental wellbeing (e.g., Aked, Marks, Cordon & Thompson, 2008). For instance, spending time with friends and family 'are among the most valued and enjoyed pursuits in which people are engaged' (Salmela-Aro & Little, 2007: 207), and establishing close relationships are amongst the most important goals in people's lives (Salmela-Aro & Little, 2007). People who are happier also tend to feel that they have friends to count on and trust (Helliwell & Wang, 2010); and spend more time with family, friends or romantic partners (Diener & Seligman, 2002). Conversely, poor or absent interpersonal connections are associated with the existence of mental health problems (e.g., Aked et al., 2008). People with depression, for instance, tend to have less intimate, less confiding and less responsive relationships; and, in many cases, lack close relationships altogether (e.g., Segrin, 2001). A lack of perceived connection to others is also strongly implicated in suicidal desire, with research indicating that a thwarted sense of belongingness and social isolation are amongst the strongest and most reliable predictors of suicidal ideation (You, Van Orden & Conner, 2011). Indeed, the quality and quantity of interpersonal relationships is also one of the strongest predictors of mortality and physical health, with research showing that individuals with adequate social relationships have a 50% greater likelihood of survival compared to those with poor or insufficient relationships (Holt-Lunstad, Smith & Layton, 2010).

Developing the capacity to relate deeply with others in their lives

This experiencing of in-depth connection with a therapist may also help clients develop the capacity to relate more deeply to *others* in their lives – such as friends, partners and colleagues – and thereby accrue all the benefits, identified above, more of the time. Indeed, around half of the clients interviewed by Knox (2013) identified 'improved relationships with others' as one of the key outcomes of relating at depth. This might happen through a variety of inter-related processes. First, the experience of relating deeply with the therapist may help clients feel more confident about doing this in other relationships. Second, in therapy, clients may develop skills in in-depth relating – for instance, learning to disclose feelings of vulnerability, or learning to 'take in' the other (see above) – which can then be transferred to other relationships. Third, as clients talk about their deepest feelings and thoughts, they are likely to become more aware of these, and therefore more able to share them with others in their lives: hence establishing deeper levels of closeness, connection and assertive communication.

This re-connection may not just be with specific others, but with one's *community* (Friedman, 1985; Trüb, 1964). From this perspective, psychological distress can emerge when people become isolated from the social world around them: the groups, the networks, the public spaces in which they can meet and interact. Here, the value of a therapist is not just as a specific individual, but as a representative of the wider community. If clients can take the first steps towards engaging with their therapists, it may pave the way towards a broader re-engagement with the whole social world around them.

Critical reflections

Is it true that it's the relationship that heals?

As we have seen, research findings in the psychotherapy and counselling field tend to support the claim that an empathic, affirming and genuine relationship are associated with positive therapeutic outcomes. However, it would be erroneous to conclude from this that 'It's the relationship that heals' (Yalom, 1989: 91). This is for several reasons. First, although the quality of the therapeutic relationship is one of the strongest predictors of therapeutic outcomes, it is not the only one and not, actually, *the* strongest (that is client factors, Orlinsky et al., 2004). Second, the fact that a *correlation* exists between the quality of the therapeutic relationship and client outcomes does not *prove* that the former causes the latter. It may be, for instance, that clients who do well in therapy (perhaps because of the techniques used), start liking their therapists more. Third, research shows that clients can do well in therapeutic interventions that have only a limited amount of relational contact, such as guided self-help programmes (Barak, Hen, Boniel-Nissim & Shapira, 2008). This suggests that, while the therapeutic relationship may have the *propensity* to be healing, it would be wrong to conclude that *all* healings happen in relationship. Indeed, as many of us will know, watching a film, listening to a song, or reading a novel can also all have a deeply therapeutic effect (see Appendices).

What kind of relationship is most therapeutic?

There is also the question of the *kind* of relationship that is most therapeutic. Dialogical philosophy (Buber, 1947, 1958), as we have seen, points towards a therapeutic relationship that is relatively warm, personable and open. However, from some more psychoanalytic and interpersonal perspectives (e.g., Wolitzky, 2003), such a relationship may be seen as undermining the potential for real therapeutic change to occur. From these standpoints, clients experience psychological difficulties because they relate to others in dysfunctional ways, often as a consequence of projecting powerful unconscious expectations and feelings onto the other. Here, if a therapist can allow these feelings to emerge in the therapeutic relationship – the *transference* – he or she can help the client gain more insight into them, and respond to them in a different way. The problem from this perspective, then, is that if the therapist is too warm, friendly and personable, clients may never really experience these powerful feelings towards their therapist. That is, they never connect with that rage: or other powerful feelings like desire, loss or fear of abandonment. Or, if they do, they may feel too ashamed and protective towards their therapists to share it with them. Hence, from this perspective, an I–Thou relationship – by being overly warm and caring – may never allow the client to work through their core interpersonal patterns.

Indeed, this critique of a Buberian position might even be made from an existential perspective. Philosophers such as Sartre (1958) have argued that the nature of human being is to be in conflict. If, as Sartre (1989: 45) writes 'Hell is – other people!' then learning to deal with the realities of human aggression, tension, objectification and existential isolation (Yalom, 1980) may be more therapeutic than bathing in the temporary 'allure' of an I–Thou connectedness.

Personalising practice

Each of these criticisms raises important challenges to a Buberian therapeutic stance. However, when a Buberian approach is situated within a pluralistic framework, they are much less problematic. Rather, these challenges are an opportunity to refine, develop and tailor practice. Here, a dialogical, I–Thou stance towards clients is not claimed to be *the* most effective way of helping others. Rather, it is seen as a particular therapeutic stance that may be particularly helpful for particular clients at particular points in time through particular pathways of change. Virtually nothing is known, at this point, about when, where, and with whom an I–Thou stance may be most helpful. However, based on the analysis presented in this chapter, it seems reasonable to suggest that it may be most appropriate for clients who:

- Want a supportive, non-judgemental 'space' in which to explore their experiences and issues;
- Want to develop – or would benefit from developing – a more positive, supportive and understanding attitude towards themselves: less self-critical, judgemental and ashamed;
- Experience a lot of internal conflict and want to overcome it;
- Want to understand and accept all the different facets of their being;
- Are isolated from others or from their community, and want to be more connected and in relation to others.

Summary

From the standpoint of most existential therapies, the therapeutic relationship is a principal facilitator of positive therapeutic change. Buber's concept of the I–Thou stance articulates what many existential therapists would consider to be the optimal therapeutic stance: a holistic, affirming openness to the client as a freely choosing subjectivity. This can be considered one side of a dialogical, in-depth relationship, whereby the client also enters into the relationship in an open and expressive way. This relational stance may be indirectly helpful to clients by providing a supportive environment for which to talk about the key issues in their lives. More directly, it may also help them connect with themselves, their therapist, and with others in their lives. From a pluralistic standpoint, we need to be wary of claiming that 'it's all about the relationship' – it may be more or less helpful to different clients at different points in time – but there is very good evidence to suggest that, in many cases, it is a key element of positive therapeutic change.

Questions for reflection and discussion

- Think of a time when you have experienced relational depth (in or out of therapy). What was that like for you, what impact did it have on you?
- How easy do you find it to relate to others in an I–Thou way? What, for you, can get in the way of adopting that stance?
- What kinds of clients do you think benefit most from an in-depth therapeutic encounter?

Recommended reading

Philosophy

Buber, M. (1958) *I and Thou* (R.G. Smith, Trans.) 2nd edn. Edinburgh: T & T Clark Ltd. Essential reading for therapists wishing to adopt an existential relational stance. Not the easiest of texts, but worth sticking with.

Buber, M. (1947) Dialogue, in *Between Man and Man* (R.G. Smith, Trans.) (pp. 17–59). London: Fontana.

Anderson, R. & Cissna, K.N. (1997) *The Martin Buber – Carl Rogers Dialogue: A New Transcript with Commentary*. Albany, NY: State University of New York Press. New transcription of the infamous dialogue between Rogers and Buber, exploring such issues as mutuality, inner dialogue, and acceptance/confirmation.

Research

Cooper, M. (2008) *Essential Research Findings in Counselling and Psychotherapy: The Facts are Friendly*. London: Sage. Chapter 6 summarises the research on the therapeutic relationship.

Norcross, J.C. (ed.) (2011) *Psychotherapy Relationships that Work: Evidence-based responsiveness* (2nd edn). New York: Oxford University Press. Definitive summary of the research on the therapeutic relationship.

Practice

Friedman, M. (1985) *The Healing Dialogue in Psychotherapy*. New York: Jason Aronson, Inc. Reviews and develops the various dialogic approaches to therapy, deeply rooted in a Buberian perspective.

Spinelli, E. (1997) *Tales of Un-Knowing: Therapeutic Encounters from an Existential Perspective*. Ross-on-Wye: PCCS Books. A series of vivid and evocative client studies that beautifully exemplifies the existential relational stance.

Yalom, I.D. (2001) *The Gift of Therapy: Reflections on Being a Therapist*. London: Piatkus. Guidance on existentially informed relational practice (#8 of top ten, see Recommended reading, Chapter 1).

Mearns, D. & Cooper, M. (2005) *Working at Relational Depth in Counselling and Psychotherapy*. London: Sage. Describes and illustrates the nature of a relationally deep encounter, with guidance on practice and personal development. For a more contemporary and research-informed text, see: Knox, R., Murphy, D., Wiggins, S. & Cooper, M. (eds) (2013) *Relational Depth: New Perspectives and Developments*. Basingstoke: Palgrave.

3

Working Phenomenologically

This chapter discusses the existential understandings that:

- Existence is the essence of human being, and experiencing is a core component of that existing.
- Experiencing can be defined as all that goes on for us that we can be aware of.
- Our experiencing can be primary or secondary, pre-reflective or reflective.
- Greater acceptance, and awareness, of our experiencing can lead to greater wellbeing.

It then goes on to describe the practices of:

- Bracketing, staying descriptive, horizontalisation and verification.
- Inviting clients to explore their experiencing.
- Listening, minimal encouragers, reflections and paraphrasing.
- Highlighting contradictions in clients' narratives.
- Asking experiential questions.
- Using symbols and metaphors.
- Unpacking experiences in the here-and-now.
- Personifying different modes of experiencing.

Research suggests that phenomenological methods are amongst the most characteristic practices of contemporary existential therapists (Correia et al., in preparation-b). They are also rated by clients as amongst the most significant (Olivereira et al., 2012), and are key competencies for existential therapeutic work (Farber, 2010). This puts them on a par with the relational stance discussed in Chapter 2. Indeed, much of the work that existential therapists do can be described as a relational–phenomenological practice. As will be seen, the phenomenological principles and practices described in this chapter also share a great deal of overlap with the relational ones, albeit emerging from a very different philosophical lineage.

Understandings

The primacy of experiencing

For existential philosophers like Kierkegaard (1992) and Schopenhauer (1969) – as well as Buber (1958) – human being cannot be truly understood from an external, *objective* perspective. To do so, writes Schopenhauer (1969: 100), is like going round a castle and 'looking in vain for an entrance'. Rather, from an existential standpoint, we can only understand human life from 'within' (Jacobsen, 2007: 20): in terms of the *subjective*, concrete experiencing of existence.

This was also the starting point of Edmund Husserl, a German philosopher who lived from 1859 to 1938. Like the French philosopher Descartes, Husserl (1960: 1) wanted to achieve a 'complete reforming of philosophy into a science grounded on absolute foundation'. He asked, therefore, what can we know with absolute certainty, and concluded that the most fundamental source of all knowledge is our *experiencing*. This is the 'inner evidence' that is given to us intuitively in our conscious awareness of things. In other words, before there is any objective 'reality', any scientific knowledge, even any 'self', there is our experiencing of the world: the moment-by-moment 'I am perceiving this', 'I am feeling that' (see Exercise 3.1). Through this inquiry, Husserl founded phenomenology – 'the study of the essence of conscious experience' (Smith & Woodruff Smith, 1995: 9) – which remains an important philosophical movement to this day (Moran, 2000).

Phenomenology was adopted and adapted by many of the twentieth century existential philosophers (e.g., Heidegger, 1962; Merleau-Ponty, 1962; Sartre, 1958), and hence became integral to much existential therapeutic practice. Indeed, the existential therapeutic approach is sometimes referred to as the *existential–phenomenological* approach (e.g., Barren, 2005). However, other therapeutic approaches have also drawn extensively from phenomenology, such as person-centred (Cooper & Bohart, 2013) and gestalt (e.g., Hycner & Jacobs, 1995) therapies, and there are also many links with more mindfulness-orientated, 'third wave' CBTs (Nanda, 2012). This accounts for many of the similarities across these schools of practice. A phenomenological approach to therapy can also be considered consistent with a contemporary, 'postmodern' worldview, and this is discussed in more detail in Cooper, 1999a.

EXISTENTIAL
THERAPY
AND
POSTMODERNISM

Exercise 3.1   Developing an awareness of your experiencing

Aim

To help you explore, and develop an awareness of, the nature of experiencing.

The exercise

For five minutes, say to yourself everything you are experiencing *as* you experience it. Begin each statement with, 'Right now I am experiencing…'; for instance, 'Right now I am experiencing a tightness in my back', 'Right now I am experiencing a sense of tension', 'Right now I am experiencing the sound of the cars outside'.

Comment

This is a common exercise on counselling or psychotherapy programmes – across orientations – and is an excellent means of developing self-awareness. It can be quite tricky to carry on for five minutes, but remember that you can always articulate any uncertainty or discomfort you have, for instance 'Right now, I am experiencing a sense of confusion and of not knowing what to say!'

Variations

- Think of a particular point in your life, perhaps one that feels of significance to you, and take five minutes to describe what you were experiencing *then*, using the stem, 'At that point, I *was* experiencing…' Again, try and stay with just describing what you were experiencing (so, for instance, don't give an 'external' account of what happened, *per se*).

- Try doing these exercises with a partner (five minutes each) either describing what you are experiencing now, or what you experienced at a particular point in the past. As a first stage, the partner's role can be just to listen. As a second stage, the partner's role can be to respond in ways that help the person describe their experiencing (for instance, listening, prompts or asking questions). This latter exercise can be a very good way of developing counselling skills, as essentially its focus is on learning to help clients 'unpack' (see below) their experiencing.
- Based on what you were describing about your experiencing, spend a few minutes (either alone or with a partner) on the following questions:
  - How would you define 'experiencing'?
  - What would you consider the essential features of experiencing? (For instance, 'It has a dreamlike quality', 'I always feel it in my body'.)
  - What kind of things *are* experienced (e.g., feelings) and what kind of things are not (e.g., unconscious processes)?
- The next time you are watching a film or TV programme, choose a character, and try to imagine what they are experiencing as the story develops. For instance, are they feeling afraid, or anxious, or wondering what they should do next? To facilitate this process, you might want to look at Box 3.1, and consider the different elements of experiencing. For instance, what might they be feeling? Thinking? Sensing in their body? Desiring? Perceiving? Thinking about others in this way – rather than in terms of how they appear from the outside – may help you develop the ability to empathically tune in to others.

The nature of experiencing

Experiencing can be defined as all that is going on for the person at any given moment which is potentially available to awareness (Rogers, 1959). It has a number of essential, invariant qualities (Cooper & Bohart, 2013).

Flowing

First, as Buddhist scholars have argued for many millennia, experiencing is not an object-like entity. Rather, it is a dynamic flow, continually changing over time. 'It is a process, an activity, a functioning, not a bag of static things' (Gendlin, 1962: 30). For this reason, existential therapists are often wary of using noun-like terms to describe human existence, such as 'the self' or 'the psyche' (Spinelli, 1994). Indeed, for Merleau-Ponty (1962: 434), human being is an 'anonymous flux', which only later comes to be associated with a specific sense of self.

In-the-moment

Second, experiencing has an in-the-moment quality to it: it is what is immediately present to us. As Rogers (1959) states, this might include elements of the past or future, but our experiencing is not the past or future, *per se*, only their resonances in the present.

Personal

Third, closely related to this, experiencing has a personal, subjective quality to it: it flows from and to us. So an actual, external event is not what we experience; what we experience is how that event is *to us*.

Available to awareness

Fourth, for something to be experienced it must be *potentially* available to awareness. This means that something can be part of our experiential field if we are not consciously focused on it: for instance, the sound of someone talking behind me. However, something which is entirely beyond the grasp of our conscious awareness (like the metabolism of fats in my body) cannot.

Holistic

Fifth, our experiencing is 'primordially and constantly *whole*' (Heidegger, 1962: 225). That is, at any one time, my experiencing is a unified phenomenon rather than a set of independent occurrences. Right now, for instance, I can feel the touch of the keyboard under my fingers, the slight aching in my shoulders, and the sound of a dog barking outside, but it is not three separate experiences. Rather, it is a single, coherent gestalt.

Bodily

Sixth, 'experience has a bodily dimension to it. It is sensory, visceral and affective, a "psycho-physiological" flow' (Cooper & Bohart, 2013: 108). Merleau-Ponty (1962: 138–139), who particularly developed this aspect of experiencing, wrote that 'Consciousness is being-towards-the-thing through the intermediary of the body'. For him the body was like the 'canvas underlying the picture' (Merleau-Ponty, 1962: 293). That is, not something that can be separated from the mind, but something that always infuses our experiencing.

Towards something

For Husserl (1960: 33), perhaps the most fundamental characteristic of experiencing is that it is *intentional*: directed towards something outside of itself. 'Consciousness' writes Husserl, 'is to be consciousness *of* something'. So, for instance, the dog bark, the shoulder ache, and the computer are all things outside of my 'self', without which I could not have that experiencing. In this respect, as Laing (1967: 18) writes, 'My experience is not inside my head. My experience of this room is out there in the room'.

This concept of intentionality has important implications if we understand human beings *as* their experiencing. It means that 'As human beings, our primary dwelling is "outside" in the space of action constituted by relations to things, plants, animals, other human beings, ourselves...' (Boss, 1963: 33). In other words, as suggested by Buber (1958, see also Chapter 2), human beings are not self-enclosed entities, but 'openings' to the world and to others. Heidegger (1962) refers to this as *being-in-the-world*, and illustrates it with a diagram (Figure 3.1). Here, being is portrayed as an arc, which receives into itself the being of the world (the arrows, Heidegger, 2001).

Interestingly, Rogers (1959: 197) does not describe experiencing in these terms. In fact, for him, experiencing takes place 'within the envelope of the organism'. This has important implications for the way in which therapy is understood and practised. Within Rogers' person-centred approach, the emphasis tends to be on helping individuals change how they relate to themselves, such that they can become more embracing of the whole of their internal experiencing (Rogers, 1951, 1959). By contrast, within an existential approach, because individuals are seen as embedded within their world, there may be more focus on helping clients to address challenges and difficulties in their relationship to the world 'outside'. This will be evident throughout this book. The existential focus on being as in-the-world also contrasts with a cognitive approach, where the source of difficulties is again located within the person. Cognitive therapists are fond of quoting the Greek philosopher Epictetus: 'Men are disturbed not by things but by the views which they take of them' (in Beck, John, Shaw & Emery, 1979: 8). By contrast, from an existential perspective, the things-in-themselves are seen as having much more potential to be disturbing.

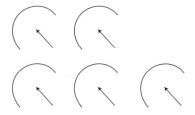

Figure 3.1   Heidegger's (2001) depiction of being as in-the-world

Intelligible

Finally, from an existential perspective, our experiencing towards the world has a quality of *intelligibility* (Laing, 1965). It is always a meaningful and comprehensible response towards the world: there 'for a reason', and not something that is simply irrational, ad hoc or meaningless. In *The Divided Self* (1965) and *Sanity, Madness and the Family* (Laing & Esterson, 1964), Laing argues that even psychosis can be understood in this way: as a sane response to an insane environment.

The phenomena of experiencing

Table 3.1 gives a summary of the kind of phenomena that would typically form part of our experiential field, and those that would not, *per se* (that is, we may have an experience *of* them, but they are not forms of experiencing, in themselves). This table may be of practical utility because it gives an indication of the kinds of phenomena that would typically be the subject of a phenomenologically oriented therapeutic inquiry (such as feelings and thoughts), and those that would not (such as non-conscious psychological mechanisms).

Table 3.1 Phenomena that are experienced and are not experienced

Phenomena that are experienced	Phenomena that are not experienced, *per se*
Feelings	Behaviours
Emotions	External events
Thoughts	Truths
Bodily sensations	Other people's experiences/behaviours
Desires, intentions, wants	Non-conscious biological processes
Perceptions, narratives, meanings,	Psychological mechanisms
self- and other-constructs	Unconscious processes
Consciousness	An object like 'self', 'parts' of a self

Primary and secondary experiencing

We experience our world, but we also experience our experiences. For instance, right now I am experiencing the tree outside my window. But I could also notice that I am looking at that tree, or I could feel guilty that I am looking at the tree instead of writing this chapter. Within the phenomenological field, various terms have been used to describe these two forms of experiencing. Most commonly, they are referred to as 'straightforward' (or 'pre-reflective') and 'reflective' experiencing (Husserl, 1960; Langdridge, 2012; Spinelli, 2005), respectively, and

Spinelli (2015) has recently proposed equivalent terms of 'worlding' and 'worldview'. For the purposes of this book, the terms *primary* and *secondary* experiencing are used (Dewey, 1958). The term 'reflective' experiencing is also used, but in a slightly different sense (see below).

Primary experiencing refers to our immediate feelings, thought and desires towards-the-world. I sip a glass of white wine, for instance, and experience a sharpness at the back of my throat, or I talk in front of a large group of people and feel scared. By contrast, our secondary experiencing is our feelings, thought and desires *about* our experiencing. I wonder, for instance, why I do not like the taste of the wine; or I feel anxious that I will start to tremble when talking in public.

The intelligibility of primary experiencing

This distinction between primary and secondary experiencing is central to several phenomenological and existential theories of the aetiology (i.e., development) of psychological distress, particularly those that are closer to a humanistic perspective (e.g., Bugental, 1981; Laing, 1965; May, 1969b).

The fundamental assumption underlying these theories, as discussed above, is that our primary experiencing is an intelligible and meaningful response to our world. It is an intuitive 'grasping' of that which we encounter and its values (Scheler, 1967). So, for instance, I experience sharpness in response to the acidity of the wine; or I feel love towards my child in response to their beauty, preciousness and 'radiance' (von Hildenbrand, 2009). Here, I am not simply *constructing* my experience. Rather, my experiencing emerges through encounter with the actual world around me. This means that my primary experiencing has a certain givenness: it is not easily modifiable. I could not taste the wine and choose to experience it as delicious: I may tell myself, at the secondary level, that it is; but my underlying primary experience remains. Furthermore, from a more humanistic–existential standpoint, there is a certain 'rightness' to my primary experiencing (e.g., Bugental, 1981; Rogers, 1959). That is, as organisms, we know what is most maintaining and enhancing to our being, and our primary experiencing is an expression of this 'actualising tendency' (Bugental, 1981).

'Positive' and 'negative' secondary experiencing

Given these assumptions, from this existential-humanistic perspective, psychological wellbeing is associated with acknowledging, affirming and attuning to this primary experiencing. Concomitantly, psychological distress is associated with relating to our primary experiencing in 'negative' ways (e.g., Bugental, 1981; Laing, 1965; May, 1969b; Rogers, 1959).

This negative secondary experiencing may take the form of the I–Me self-objectifying stance discussed in Chapter 2. Other examples of negative secondary experiencing might be:

- Feeling that we are abnormal for having the primary experiences we have (for instance, 'There must be something wrong with me to feel so tearful all the time').
- Feeling isolated and alone for how we are experiencing (for instance, 'No one can understand how unhappy I am').
- Feeling burdened by our experiences (for instance, 'I feel so weighed down by all this guilt').
- Feeling overwhelmed by our experiences (for instance, 'I feel that I just can't cope any more with all this anger').
- Feeling confused by our feelings (for instance, 'I just don't know what's going on with me any more').
- Worrying that we will not be able to get over our feelings (for instance, 'I am so scared I will always feel like this').
- Becoming obsessed with, and ruminate on, our feelings (for instance, 'I can't stop thinking about how anxious I feel').

Denial and distortion

Phenomenological therapists have also suggested that we may go on to deny or distort what we experience at the primary level (e.g., Rogers, 1959; Spinelli, 1994). So, for instance, instead of acknowledging that the wine tastes like vinegar, I may recall it as a 'delightfully tart bouquet of fruit notes with an under-hint of lightly glistening diesel'. Or, if I feel ashamed of getting anxious when talking in public, I may try to push this experiencing to the back of my mind. This can be described as *self-deception* (Sartre, 1958), or what Bugental (1981) refers to as being *inauthentic*. Essentially, it means that my secondary experiencing of my primary experiencing does not accurately match that primary experiencing (Bugental, 1981).

The 'they'

Primary experiencing is a direct, immediate relationship to our world, but the way in which we think and feel about this experiencing – our secondary experiencing – is likely to be strongly mediated by the social world around us. For many existential and humanistic thinkers (e.g., Bugental, 1981; May et al., 1958; Rogers, 1959), it is through this social influence that we come to be inauthentic and alienated from our primary experiencing. For instance, as suggested in Chapter 2, we can internalise others' objectifying views towards us, such that we come to experience ourselves in an I–Me way. Or we can 'introject' the social judgements that others make about our primary experiencing. Here, existential philosophers have spoken of 'the jostling crowd, the mass, the mob' (Kierkegaard, 1992: 67), 'the rabble' (Nietzsche, 1967: 148), 'the they' (Heidegger, 1962) who come to define how we act and relate to our being.

Existential and humanistic therapists (e.g., Laing & Esterson, 1964; Rogers, 1959) have also described how those closest to us, particularly our parents, can act in ways that lead us to distort or deny our own primary experiencing. Laing and Esterson (1964: 94), for instance, give a number of examples where the experiences of young people diagnosed with schizophrenia are clearly invalidated by their parents.

Mother: I think we've got on very well together. I don't think we've had any real disturbances over the years.

Daughter: The only thing is that you are a domineering character.

Mother: Well being a business-woman, Claire, that comes with it you see, I've always been –

Daughter: I like to submit rather than argue against your decision.

Mother: Yes I suppose so at times.... But we seem to have got on very well throughout the years.

Daughter: Oh yes, but as I say with you a domineering character.

Mother: We've always worked in with one another.... we've been able to overcome these things.

Here, the daughter's attempts to voice the difficulties she experiences in relation to her mother are constantly discounted by the mother. Through such interactions at an early age, suggests Laing (1965), we can become so alienated from our own primary experiencing that we no longer know what is real and what is phantasy.

Sedimentation

Our primary experiencing, as we have seen, is an ever-changing flow. But our secondary experiences can become *sedimented* (Ihde, 1986; Spinelli, 2001). This means that it can become fixed and calcified: laid down in a rigid and inflexible way that obscures the changing flux of primary experiencing. I come to believe, for instance, that I *always* like expensive Pinot Noirs, and never reflect back on my actual experiencing to check if this is true or not.

The self-concept

In both Spinelli's (1994) and Rogers' (1961) phenomenological theories of the aetiology (i.e., development) of distress, particular difficulties emerge when we develop a sedimented *self-concept* (or *self-construct*). This self-concept can be understood as the constellation of beliefs that we have about ourselves, which acts as the 'central structure and first structure through which all information flows' (Markus & Sentis, 1982: 65). So I look at myself, for instance, and see a man who appreciates fine wines; who is brave and invulnerable. But what gets concealed here is all the primary experiencing: the vulnerability, the sense of failure, the actuality of what I do and do not enjoy. We can think of this as like wearing a mask. There is a wealth of movement, fluidity and nuance going on at the primary level: the face. But this is hidden behind a static and unmoving visage. And because this self-concept is the central structure through which I make sense of the world, it affects all my behaviours. So I become a person who joins wine clubs, goes sky diving: I act *as* my mask. But my face, my real face, remains unseen and un-responded to: ignored, isolated and alone.

As suggested in Box 3.1, it may also be that we have multiple self-constructs: different masks that we wear at different times in our lives (Cooper, 1996).

Box 3.1 Modes of existence

Numerous psychologists and psychotherapists have hypothesised (e.g., Rowan, 2010), and evidenced (Lester, 1992; Rosenberg & Gara, 1985), that we may have multiple constructs of who we are. These can come online and offline at different times. There may be times in my life, for instance, when I see myself as courageous and strong; but there may be other times when I 'flip' into a sense of myself as vulnerable and weak; and there may be other times when I see myself as a loving parent, or as a romantic Valentino, or as a pathetic depressive. And, as each of these self-concepts come online, certain sets of experiences may come to be denied, while others may become more available to reflective awareness. So, for instance, at the times when I see myself as a pathetic depressive, I may be very aware of all the times I have felt sad in my life; and virtually unable to recall the times that I have felt happy or contented. Yet if I move into a sense of myself as a loving parent, those same periods of sadness may seem very remote, and I am now much more 'in touch' with the times I have felt loving and caring to others.

An implication of this understanding is that some – or, perhaps, all – of us do not experience the world in a smoothly consistent way; and neither do we experience it as a gradual movement from one way of experiencing to another. Rather, it suggests that we may go through quite sudden changes in how we experience the world: for instance, from courageous and bold one moment to vulnerable and scared the next. From an existential–phenomenological standpoint, these can be described as 'modes of experiencing' (Cooper, 1999b, see also Cooper, 1996, available on the companion website), ways of encountering the world that constellate around a particular sense of self. For instance, Rima, introduced in Chapter 2, would sometimes come to sessions feeling buoyant and positive about life. But there were other sessions in which she would turn up and it was immediately apparent she was in a very different mode: her shoulders hunched, looking at the ground, avoiding eye contact. When we unpacked this mode of experiencing further, Rima described it as feeling like she was a vulnerable, tiny little girl, huddled up at the bottom of a deep dark well. And, as with being at the bottom of a well, Rima felt at these times no hope that she could ever climb back to a more 'positive' state of being. Inevitably, however, she did, and finding how she moved from one mode of being to the other became a key part of the therapeutic work.

SELF-PLURALITY FROM AN EXISTENTIAL PERSPECTIVE

As well as being fully constellated modes of encountering the world, these different modes of being may take the form of 'voices': ways of talking to ourselves that seem to have distinctive characteristics and qualities. Across the psychotherapeutic literature, probably the most commonly discussed voice is the 'inner critic' (e.g., Elliott, Watson, Goldman & Greenberg, 2004), and we will explore an example of therapeutic work with this voice later on in the chapter.

If you are interested in reflecting on your own self-constructs/modes of experiencing, there are many different exercises you can try. For instance, find yourself a calm, quiet place, and close your eyes. Then imagine a bus is coming along, and all your different 'selves' are on it. Imagine the first 'self' coming off the bus. What does it look like? What does it do? What does it want? When you have a good sense of it, imagine the next 'self' coming off, and keep on going until you feel that you have met all your principal modes of being. Now spend a little time noticing how the different characters interact with each other. Who gets on with who, which 'selves' do not like each other? Finally, imagine the selves getting back on the bus and say 'goodbye' to them for now. For more examples of how you can explore these different modes of being, see Cooper and Cruthers (1999).

METHODS OF PERSONIFICATION

Secondary experiencing and psychological distress

From a phenomenological–humanistic standpoint, relating to our primary experiencing in negative ways is likely to lead to a range of psychological difficulties. This hypothesis is well-supported by the empirical evidence, which indicates that people who score higher on tests of authenticity – that is, more in tune with, and accepting of, their primary experiencing – are 'more satisfied with life, higher in self-esteem, less depressed and anxious and more alert and awake. They also have less physical symptoms such as headaches, aches and pains' (Cooper & Joseph, in press). So why might this be the case?

First, as we saw in Chapter 2, if we do not acknowledge and accept our primary experiencing, it means that we are likely to feel bad about ourselves as, by definition, we are rejecting certain elements of who we exist in the world. And, even if we deny those aspects of our experiencing, they do not go away, because they emerge from our genuine encountering with our world. So the fact that I do not acknowledge, for instance, that I feel afraid of talking in public does not stop it happening. Rather, it just means that it takes me by surprise whenever it happens, and I am thrust back into secondary feelings such as shame and self-hatred.

This leads on to a second reason why such a negative stance towards our primary experiencing can be problematic: the anxiety that our primary experiencing will 'return'. I can try to say to myself, for instance, that I do not really get anxious talking in public, but at some level I also know how anxious I can get. So when I think that I may have to do a presentation at college, or talk to my line manager, I end up lying awake at night in a state of fear. My denial of my anxiety has done nothing to make it go away: I remain haunted by its possibility.

This leads on to a third reason why relating negatively to our primary experiencing is so problematic and, for Bugental (1981), is the primary source of all neurosis. Because our primary experiencing does not go away, we must build up ever more sophisticated defences to try and 'keep it at bay': defences that, themselves, will inevitability falter. To try to avoid the anxiety of speaking in public, for instance, I might decline invitations to do presentations, or even stay at a lower grade at work so that I do not have to do them. I create a fixed, defensive, limited structure for my self. This can bring some temporary relief but is ultimately doomed to fail. I *have* to talk to people, engage in a public way, and so my only option is to shore my defences up further and further: for instance, by withdrawing entirely from the workplace. 'Each of us', writes Bugental (1981: 43), 'is like a person who pays blackmail to keep a feared reality from becoming manifest'. And, as with most blackmailing, the price to pay keeps getting higher and higher. In this way, *existential anxiety* becomes *neurotic* or *pathological anxiety* (Tillich, 2000): a frantic running away from reality that has the potential to spiral down into severe and chronic mental distress.

Closely related to this, if our secondary experiencing negates our primary experiencing, it can set up a whole range of *vicious circles* which can be the source of intensely distressing psychological experiences. This has been very well-documented in the cognitive and behavioural field (e.g., Williams & Garland, 2002). Take the example, for instance, of feeling anxious and ashamed about feeling scared when talking in public. I stand up, notice a slight tremor in my voice, worry that I am going to look ridiculous, and as a consequence feel even more anxiety. That, then, worsens my fear that I am going to look ridiculous, and leads me to spiral further and further down into a full blown panic attack. By contrast, if I had just acknowledged and accepted my anxiety, it is very likely that it would have eventually subsided on its own (Marks, 1978). These vicious circles may be the reason why, in certain areas of our lives, we can sometimes feel like we are on 'existential black ice' (see the companion website).

EXISTENTIAL
BLACK ICE:
NOTES

Fifth, if we ignore or discount our primary experiencing – an intuitive, intelligible perceiving of the world – we are likely to spend more of our lives doing things we do not like, and less doing things that we do. If I deceive myself into thinking, for instance, that I really like the vinegary taste of the £14 Pinot Grigio, I could end up choosing to drink a lot more of it, and foregoing the cheaper wine that I may, actually, experience more pleasure in drinking. In this respect, by discounting our primary experiencing, we can fail to actualise our possibilities and potentialities, realising 'only a fraction of what is latent in our lives' (Bugental, 1981: 47).

Finally, if we have a 'difficult' relationship to our own primary experiencing, this may lead to a more difficult relationship with others (which, as we saw in Chapter 2, can then have a negative effect on our own wellbeing). This is because, if we do not acknowledge or accept our own experiencing, it is unlikely that we will be able to communicate this to others in clear and assertive ways (see Chapter 7). Consequently, others may be less aware of what we are wanting, and therefore less able to respond to us in ways that feel rewarding and satisfying. It can also leave others feeling confused, as we may be giving very mixed messages to others about what we want. Someone may pick up from my primary experiencing, for instance, that I need comfort and nurturing; but on the basis of my secondary experiencing I may be telling them that I need independence and space.

Reflective experiencing

One particular form of secondary experiencing, however, that can be seen as having a critical place in establishing good psychological health is *reflective experiencing*. This is where we consciously reflect on what we are experiencing, or have experienced, and acknowledge it in an accurate way: for instance, 'Right now I am feeling cold', or 'When my mother spoke to me like that I felt very afraid'. Schopenhauer (1969: 84) likens such reflective awareness to an actor 'who has played his part in one scene, and takes his place in the audience until he must appear again'. *Reflective* experiencing can be contrasted with *pre-reflective* experiencing: things that go on for us that we do not consciously attend to (see Box 3.2). 'Reflective experiencing' is often used as synonymous with secondary experiencing, but it may be useful to distinguish the two. This is because our secondary experiencing may be taking place at a pre-reflective level. For instance, I may be telling myself I am pathetic for feeling scared of public speaking, but not really conscious that I am doing so. Also, secondary experiencing may give us a very inaccurate representation of what we are thinking or feeling at a primary level.

Box 3.2   Pre-reflective experiencing and the unconscious

Pre-reflected experiencing, as discussed in this chapter, has many similarities with the psychodynamic concept of the 'unconscious'. However, there are also some important differences (Spinelli, 2001), and some existential therapists have been fiercely critical of the concept of the unconscious (Boss, 1963; Sartre, 1958; Spinelli, 1994). In the phenomenological model, pre-reflected experiencing, as experiencing, is always *potentially* available to awareness. By contrast, in a psychodynamic model, the term 'unconscious' refers to processes and dynamics that lie *outside* of the grasp of consciousness (hence the inclusion of 'unconscious' processes as a non-experiential phenomenon in Table 3.1).

   This distinction has important implications for clinical practice. If experiencing cannot be consciously accessed, as per the psychodynamic model, then there is a need for therapists' interpretations as means of helping clients to understand their psychological processes. However, if all experiencing has the potential to be consciously accessed, then interpretation plays less of a significant role. Rather, the key therapeutic strategy is to help clients broaden out *their own* reflective awareness of their experiences. Boss (1963) argues, on the principle of Occam's razor (we should use the simplest theory possible), that we should not invoke the unconscious as conscious explanations tend to do. However, from a pluralistic stance, there may be times when clients cannot access the reasons for their behaviour, and here interpretation may play a valuable role.

The therapeutic value of reflective experiencing

As with many therapies (Cooper, 2008a), helping clients to develop a reflective knowledge and awareness of their experiencing is an essential component of the existential–phenomenological therapeutic process (Olivereira et al., 2012). And, indeed, there is reliable evidence that the 'deeper' clients go into their experiencing in therapy – focusing on 'inner' feelings and sensations, as opposed to impersonal, externally oriented content (Klein, Mathieu-Coughlan & Kiesler, 1986) – the better they tend to do (Hendricks, 2002; Orlinsky et al., 2004). But why might this be the case?

Insight

At the most basic level, if clients are reflecting on their experiencing – both primary and secondary – they are likely to develop a greater understanding of how they are in the world. They may recognise, for instance, that they experience a deep love for their child, or that they are very critical towards their own feelings of vulnerability. Research indicates that, for many clients, this enhanced insight – in itself – is identified as one of the most helpful aspects of therapy (Timulak, 2007). This may be because it helps clients feel more in control of their lives, less overwhelmed by their feelings, or less confused about why they do the things that they do.

From the humanistic–phenomenological position discussed above ('primary and secondary experiencing'), what is particularly important is that clients develop a greater insight into their primary experiencing, as well as the negative secondary experiencing that may suppress and distort it. Through therapeutic reflection, for instance, a client may come to recognise that she *really* feels more attracted to women than men, and that this is something she has always felt too ashamed to admit. Such a process then paves the way for clients to find more authentic ways of being in the world (see below).

Doing things differently

By developing greater reflective awareness, we may then be more enabled to change the way we *act* towards the world: to reconfigure our lives in ways that are more satisfying, fulfilling and authentic. Frankl (1986) refers to this as *self-transcendence*: the capacity to stand back from a situation and work out what is best. This might be at the behavioural level. For instance, through phenomenological exploration, I may come to realise that I often feel very vulnerable around my partner, and that this is because I experience her as critical and judgemental. Knowing this, I can then decide to behave in a different way: for instance, I might decide to challenge her, or to leave the relationship. Alternatively, it might be that I can change the way that I relate to myself or how I choose to think. For instance, if I recognise that the reason I have panic attacks is because I worry about worrying, then I can choose to think about my anxiety in a different way: for instance, that it is something that is unpleasant but survivable. Reflective awareness, then, gives me some distance from my pre-reflective experiencing to do things differently. Rather than being up against a cliff face, desperately trying to scramble up in whichever way looks best, I am standing back from the mountain, and am able to consider carefully the best way to ascend.

Box 3.3   The three Rs of therapy: reflecting, re-evaluating and re-deciding

We can think about the phenomenological therapeutic process – perhaps all therapeutic processes – in terms of three Rs: *reflecting*, *re-evaluating* and *re-deciding*. Clients are encouraged to reflect on their experiencing, and this may lead to a re-evaluation of the ways in which they are doing things. As a consequence of this, then may then 're-decide' their choices, and find ways of doing things that are potentially more satisfying. There is then the potential to reflect on how this impacts on their life, re-evaluate it again, and continue on the cycle of finding more satisfying and fulfilling ways of being. In this chapter, we mainly focus on the reflection stage, but the stages of re-evaluating and re-deciding are particularly central to Chapters 4 and 5.

Being more authentic

In terms of changing how we think, from the humanistic–phenomenological position described above, one of the most helpful things we can do is to find more positive ways of relating to our primary experiencing. I may not be able to change how the wine tastes to me (my primary experiencing), but I can change whether I berate myself for this experiencing or simply accept it (my secondary experiencing). Hence, through reflective experiencing, we can come to accept, acknowledge and actualise our primary experiencing more fully. We can become more authentic (Lander & Nahon, 2005). This, then, may negate the distressing effects of relating negatively to our primary experiencing (see above). We can feel better about ourselves. We can be less afraid of unwanted primary experiences returning. We avoid the neurotic activity of building up complex psychological defences that are doomed to fail, and can steer clear of vicious psychological circles. By being more authentic, we can also do more of what we like and less of what we do not like, and we can also form clearer and more rewarding relationship with others.

Internalising a more positive self-relational stance

From a humanistic–phenomenological position, the salutogenic potential of phenomenological reflection in therapy also comes from the fact that it is carried out *in the presence of* an affirming, 'thou-ifying' other (see Chapter 2). Its clients can talk about their primary experiencing to another who is validating and confirming of it, then it becomes possible that the client can internalise a more positive relational stance to their own primary experiencing (see the companion website).

THE I–I AND I–ME SELF-RELATIONAL STANCES

This process may be reflective and conscious. It may be, for instance, that a client thinks, 'If this experienced professional sitting opposite me doesn't think I am so crazy, then maybe I am not'. There is also the potential, however, that it could take place at a more pre-reflective level: the kind of 'relational healing' discussed in Chapter 2. Here, for instance, a client lays out all those aspects of his primary experiencing that he most despises: his feelings of rage, jealousy, vulnerability and fear. And, by seeing that his therapist still likes and values him *despite* this, his negative associations to those primary experiences may lessen.

Methods

Chapter 2 introduced the idea that the existential therapeutic relationship is like journeying alongside clients and helping them to reflect on what they are experiencing. This, in many respects, is also the essence of the phenomenological therapeutic process, with clients invited to *unpack* (see Box 3.4), or 'clarify', their experiencing. This process might also be described as 'putting a magnifying glass' (Yalom & Elkin, 1974) over specific incidents and events in our clients' lives, so that they can etch out all the experiencing and emotions.

Box 3.4 Unpacking

A term that is sometimes used to describe this process of phenomenological exploration is *unpacking* (e.g., Cooper, 2012b). Here, one might imagine that the client has many boxes stored away in their attic (that is, pre-reflected experiences), and the process of phenomenological exploration is to unpack these boxes and to find out more about what the client actually thinks and feels. In this process, it may be particularly important to unpack boxes that have been hidden away for many years; or those that are in the corners of the attic that the client has almost entirely lost sight of; or those that are

(Continued)

(Continued)

particularly frightening for the client to look in to. More generally, therapy can be seen as an opportunity to unpack experiencing that the client may find difficult to unpack with other people in their lives. In the context of an affirming, skilled, dialogic relationship, the client may feel safe – and motivated – enough to start unpacking even the most terrifying of boxes; and begin to realise that what they find there is not monsters and demons, but an experiencing that is always intelligible.

Basic principles

In relation to psychology and therapeutic practice, four basic principles, or steps, of the phenomenological process are frequently described (e.g., Adams, 2013).

Bracketing

Bracketing is a process of setting aside 'our initial biases and prejudices of things'. It involves suspending our expectations and assumptions, so that we can focus on the actual data of our clients' experiencing (Spinelli, 2005: 20). Bracketing means listening to our clients from a place of 'naivety' (Ihde, 1986; Moja-Strasser, 1996) and 'un-knowing' (Spinelli, 1997); as if we are hearing their experiencing for the first time (Ihde, 1986). Bracketing is synonymous with the process of being open to the otherness of the client (Chapter 2), and of meeting them from a place of indefiniteness and genuinely unfinished opennesses. It also has many similarities with the person-centred concept of 'unconditional positive regard' (Bozarth & Wilkins, 2001); and of managing our 'countertransference'. This means trying to ensure that we do not impose our own wants or expectations on to clients.

Bracketing is of particular importance if we want to help clients access their primary experiencing. This is for two reasons. First, as we have seen, primary experiencing often becomes obscured by the views, demands or expectations of others. Hence, to help clients develop insight into how *they*, uniquely, experience their world, it is important that we do not impose *our* own views and biases onto them. Second, as we have seen, the nature of primary experiencing is to be changing, ambiguous, unstable and temporary (Cayne & Loewenthal, 2011). Hence, if we impose a set of assumptions onto this, we may be doing little more than contributing to the build-up of further sedimentation.

Bracketing our own agenda in the therapeutic work can be particularly challenging. In fact, given the existential assumption that we always act towards the world in purpose-oriented ways (see Chapter 6), we cannot *not* want certain things in our work with clients. This agenda may be very well-intentioned, and potentially pre-reflective. For instance, we may want to make our clients feel better, educate them, or simply help them improve their lives (Moja-Strasser, 1996). This is not something we can rid ourselves of, and it is also of little use to feel bad about it. Rather, what is important is to be reflectively aware of our agenda, such that we are more enabled to put it to one side. Here, Adams (2001: 73) proposes some useful questions we can ask ourselves:

- What do I want for my client?
- If I was to give my client some advice right now, what would it be?
- Do I feel a different way towards this client rather than towards that client? And what is this about?

Bracketing can be very challenging because it may require us, as therapists, to bear some difficult emotions. Take the following example. As a therapist, part of my pre-reflective agenda is to feel good about myself and the work that I do: that I am a competent practitioner. So, suppose I am working with a long-term client who starts to take anti-depressant medication, and suppose they start to say that the drugs are really helpful: more helpful, in fact, than anything we have done together. How will I feel? Possibly quite hurt. As a consequence, I might start nudging the client towards seeing their medication in a more negative light: 'Have you thought about the side-effects?' Or I might interpret the client's behaviour in a more self-enhancing light: 'Perhaps you are telling me how good the drugs are because you are actually angry with me?' (and not because the drugs are actually more helpful than the therapy!). Do not underestimate, therefore, the challenge of bracketing. If it feels easy to do, it may be because your core beliefs have not been challenged to a sufficient degree.

Staying descriptive

The second step in the phenomenological method is the 'rule of description', the essence of which is *'Describe, don't explain'* (Ihde, 1986: 34). Here, we are urged to refrain from producing interpretations, hypotheses or theories as to what clients are experiencing, and instead to keep strictly to the phenomena as 'directly visible' (Boss, 1979). So, for instance, if a client dreams of eating a hot dog, what is explored is that dreamt-experiencing of eating a hot dog (Boss, 1977: 79): 'How did it taste?' 'What was it like?' 'What were you feeling as you ate away at it?' There is no attempt, here, to interpret some 'deeper', unconscious meaning.

Below are some examples of descriptive, and non-descriptive, responses:

Client:	It just seems like whenever I feel stressed, my partner is *more* mean to me. There's no support there. Every time I get hurt she just pulls away.
Descriptive response (reflection):	So it feels like, when things are difficult for you, your partner gets more distant rather than closer.
Descriptive response (asking question):	So tell me what that's like? What is it like for you when you're feeling hurt and she pulls away?
Non-descriptive response (interpretation):	It sounds like you experience your partner in the same way that you experience your father.
Non-descriptive response (other-focused):	I can't believe she acts like that – she's got more problems than you!

Horizontalisation

Third, there is the 'rule of horizontalisation', which 'further urges us to avoid placing any initial hierarchies of significance or importance upon the items of our descriptions, and instead to treat each initially as having equal value or significance' (Spinelli, 1989: 18). This is really just an extension of the principal of bracketing, in that we try not to impose any assumptions about what is more, or less, important for clients to talk about. For instance, if a client is coming to the end of therapy, and talks about feeling both sad and happy to be saying 'goodbye' to us, our assumption about endings may lead us to focus more on their sadness. From a phenomenological perspective, however, it may be just as important to focus on their feelings of joy or relief.

Verification

Verification is a fourth stage of the phenomenological process whereby we 'keep checking back with [our client] whether our observations and descriptions are true to the actual phenomena perceived and experienced' (van Deurzen, 2012b: 9). Through this process, we can get a firmer sense of how our clients experience their world, while remaining relatively free of our biases and assumptions (Langdridge & Barker, 2013). This has similarities to the classic counselling skill of 'paraphrasing' – restating the meaning of another person's verbal or non-verbal disclosures in one's own words – which is rated by clients as one of the most helpful therapist response modes (Hill, Helms, Tichenor, Spiegel, O'Grady & Perry, 1988). However, verification is less a specific response and more an ongoing process. For example:

Therapist :   So it feels like, when things are difficult for you, your partner gets more distant rather than closer.

Client: It just feels like she runs away. I reach out for her and she's gone.

Therapist: It seems like she's totally disappeared.

Client: Disappeared.... Gone.... But it's that feeling of her running away, like she's slipping through my fingers. I'm trying to grasp her and she's evading me.

Therapist: So it's more than just her not being there. It's that feeling of reaching out to her and, as you do so, she moves away....

Verification can also be seen as a more active, meaning-making process, in which we go on to identify common elements and threads in the client's narrative (Adams, 2001).

Specific practices

In the following subsections, a number of specific therapist activities are described that aim to facilitate this process of phenomenological exploration. It is important to remember, however, that these methods are not isolated techniques or ends in themselves. Hence, whether or not any one particular reflection or metaphor is accurate is less important than an overall journeying alongside the client towards greater reflective awareness. In addition, from an existential standpoint, it is important that these methods are not 'implemented' in a mechanistic way, but are embedded within a fluid, dialogical exchange.

The methods are presented here in an approximate order: from those where therapists are least active and directive (e.g., listening), to those where they are most active and directive (e.g., challenging blocks to exploration). In general, the research suggests that these latter interventions may be particularly helpful in supporting client change (e.g., Greenberg & Rice, 1981; Sachse & Elliott, 2002). That is, while clients have some ability to deepen their own levels of processing, active therapist interventions may facilitate and intensify this work. However, this must be weighed against the likelihood that clients will experience more active interventions as more challenging, such that they may also carry greater risk of harm. Hence, before introducing more active experiential methods, it is almost certainly essential to establish a strong therapeutic relationship, and appropriate training in these methods is also required.

To give an illustration of this process of phenomenological exploration, which will be explored in the subsequent sections, we can consider the following therapist–client dialogue, transcribed verbatim. The client, Claire, was in her early 40s, and came to therapy 'To accept the way that the world is and the way I am' and 'To have some peacefulness'. At assessment, Claire met criteria for severe depression on the PHQ-9, and in session two we started to phenomenologically unpack what this experience of depression was like. Claire began the session by talking about some bad days she had had that week.

Claire 1: I cooked some dinner and then I was – I just felt really bad [*Mick*: Uh huh] my head was just going... just like that, 'What's going on?' and just kind of transferred it down to my stomach [*Mick*: Uh huh] and just went... so instead of me feeling bad in my head just cramps in my stomach [*Mick*: Uh huh] and just, kind of, pissed off and angry. [*Pause*]. It wasn't kind of *down-ness*, no, that kind of... [*Mick*: Yeah]. Almost kind of an anxiety attack or, whatever. And I've noticed that before it just kind of happened. You get up – you try and get up and have coffee, juice and tea and then your work. You're doing things [*Mick*: Yeah] to take your mind off things and then it's just [*sighs*] when you're doing your dishes is when you're thinking.

Mick 1: So tell me what the thoughts were. [*Claire*: I was just, eh...] What were you thinking?

Claire 2: Mostly just frustration ... and annoyance [*Mick*: Ok].... More frustration and annoyance, and...

Mick 2: Ok, tell me what the thoughts were. Tell me as clearly as you can what the actual thoughts going on in your head were. [*Claire*: I was just...] Speak them.

Claire 3: 'There's just no point, I'm useless' [*pause*]. Just kind of, 'Why, why are you fighting it?'

Mick 3: So you are saying to yourself, 'There's no point' [*Claire*: Yeah]. You're standing there doing the dishes [*Claire*: Yeah] and what's going through your head is, 'There's no point'.

Claire 4: I'm just saying 'Why... Why am I fighting this?'

Mick 4: 'Why... Why am I fighting this?'

Claire 5: 'I feel bad' [*Mick*: 'I feel bad'.] Just 'Why?', I just want to release that tension, anxiety, anger, whatever...

Mick 5: So the feelings that go with it are anger...

Claire 6: It's kind of 'Why fight it?' You've got desperation, some kind of desperation ... frustration. And then anger comes in and then you feel sore in your head and you just transfer it to your stomach...

Inviting the client to explore their experiencing

From a pluralistic standpoint, with its emphasis on shared decision making, a first step with any therapeutic method may be to ask clients whether this is something that they want to do. With respect to phenomenological exploration, this might take the form of:

- 'Do you think it would be helpful if we explored that experience further?'
- 'Would you like to look at that in more depth?'
- 'Shall we explore your experiences of...?'
- 'Would you like to talk about what's concerning you, what matters in your life right now?' (Bugental, 1981).

In fact, in the dialogue above, I did not specifically ask Claire whether or not she would like to unpack her experiences of feeling bad. At *Mick 1*, for instance, instead of saying 'So tell me what the thoughts were?' I might have said, 'Would you like to say more about what your thoughts were?' This would have been a more collaborative opener. However, given that Claire had specifically come to therapy to overcome her low moods and experience greater peacefulness, it was probably reasonable to assume that she would want to explore – and understand more about – what was going on for her at these times.

Active listening

ACTIVE
LISTENING

Providing clients with space to talk is probably the single most important means of facilitating their phenomenological exploration (Moja-Strasser, 1996), and is rated by clients as one of the most helpful aspects of therapy (e.g., Paulson & Worth, 2002). At the most basic level, if clients cannot talk, they cannot articulate what is going on for them: their feelings, thoughts and perceptions. Bugental (1981) suggests therapists should talk about one-twentieth of the time, and writes that the best starting point for a therapist is silence. In practical terms, this means not interrupting clients, and ensuring that they have adequate space to talk things through at their own pace. This is important because clients may need time to reflect on their own experiencing; particularly the deeper, pre-reflected levels of feelings and beliefs. If a therapist comes in too quickly, asking questions or offering reflections, it may interrupt clients from connecting at this level. For instance, at *Claire 2*, Claire was beginning to talk about her frustration and annoyance, and if I had not asked her a question at this point, she might have gone on to say more about what these feelings were like. If therapists are talking a lot and clients feel squeezed for space, clients may also respond with sedimented assumptions about what they are experiencing, rather than taking the time to genuinely reflect on what is going on for them. Finally, providing clients with sufficient space to talk may be important in ensuring that they go into the experiences that are most important and salient to *them*, rather than being side-tracked onto those that therapists may assume are most significant.

Of course, listening is much more than just being quiet. It is 'a very complex activity that involves one's whole being including: senses, emotions, thoughts and body awareness' (Moja-Strasser, 1996: 97). This is akin to the holistic listening discussed in Chapter 2, where the therapist 'breathes in' the client's 'emotional-cognitive-physical being' (Mearns & Cooper, 2005: 119). Such holistic listening allows the therapist to respond from a deepened understanding of the client's experiencing; and also conveys to the client – through non-verbal clues and minimal encouragers (see below) – that they are genuinely being received.

MINIMAL
ENCOURAGERS

Minimal encouragers

While providing clients with space to talk is very important, a flow of *minimal encouragers* – brief interjections that let clients know they are being listened to, received and understood – can be very important in supporting this process of phenomenological unpacking. These can help clients feel comfortable enough to go deeper into their experiencing. With Claire, for instance, there are a spattering of 'Uh huhs', 'Yeahs' and 'Oks' throughout the dialogue. Importantly, however, these did not emerge from thinking 'I must say a minimal encourager to Claire now to make her feel more comfortable'. Rather, they just emerged naturally and pre-reflectively from the dialogue, in which my focus was simply on helping Claire understand more about her experiencing.

REFLECTING,
PARAPHRASING
AND
SUMMARISING

Reflecting, paraphrasing and summarising

Another common set of therapeutic methods that can facilitate this process of phenomenological exploration, as noted under verification (see above), are reflecting, paraphrasing and summarising. All these essentially involve saying back to clients what they have said. Reflecting is primarily a word-for-word restatement; paraphrasing involves some rewording of what clients have said; and summaries reflect back to clients, in condensed form, what they have said over some period of time. In the dialogue with Claire, for instance, *Mick 3, 4* and *5* all approximate word-for-word reflections, in which I repeat back to her what she says she is saying to herself and feeling. As with minimal encouragers, these responses can support the process of phenomenological exploration by helping clients feel understood and that their experiences are intelligible, such that may feel safer unpacking their experiencing in more depth and detail. They also provide clients with an opportunity to reflect further on their experiencing, and to consider whether there is a more accurate or nuanced way in which they can articulate what they are experiencing.

To facilitate a phenomenological exploration, however, it is essential that each of these methods put back to clients the *experiential* elements of what they are saying; that is, their feelings, thoughts, bodily sensations and perceptions (see Table 3.1). This is akin to working in a descriptive way, discussed earlier. In the dialogue with Claire, for instance, I try to reflect back to her the thoughts that are going through her mind, and also her feelings; but I do not reflect back the non-phenomenological content, such as the *fact* that she was cooking her dinner. To illustrate this further, below is an example of paraphrasing the experiential content of what a client is saying; and then an alternative response, where only the non-experiential content is being paraphrased.

Client:	I do just feel this distance between myself and my daughter. She's getting to be such a teenager: doesn't wash, spends all her time on Instagram, talks to me like I'm an idiot who's trying to sabotage everything she does. She's so– she's *really* getting arrogant and it gets me really upset; and then I get upset that I'm upset and sometimes I just can't hold back the tears. She told me the other day that I should lose some weight and I– I feel like it's triggering all my childhood stuff about … not being good enough. I wish– I want to try and sort something out with her.
Paraphrasing (experiential):	So you're really experiencing a distance between yourself and your daughter (*perception*), and it upsets you (*feeling*) to the point you sometimes can't stop yourself from crying (*bodily sensation*).

It sounds like, when you feel that she's talking down to you (*perception*), you really feel vulnerable (*feeling*). And I get such a strong sense of you wanting to find a way forward with this (*desire*).

Paraphrasing (non-experiential):

Your daughter is getting more arrogant these days (*external event*), and feels that she is better than you (*other people's experiences*). It sounds like this is about your childhood insecurities (*psychological mechanism*), and you cry when she talks badly to you (*behaviour*). And you're fat (*other people's experiencing*).

ASKING OPEN-
ENDED
QUESTIONS

Asking open-ended questions

It is sometimes said, particularly within person-centred circles, that therapists should not ask questions. And, indeed, the research shows that they can be experienced as one of the least helpful forms of therapeutic intervention (Cooper, 2008a). However, there is other research to suggest that clients *can* experience questioning as helpful (Watson, Cooper, McArthur & McLeod, 2012); and, from a phenomenological standpoint, probably the key issue is whether they come from the therapist's 'nosiness' and agenda, or whether they are a genuine attempt to help clients deepen an awareness of their experiencing. Needless to say, questions also tend to be more helpful if they are 'open-ended' rather than 'closed-ended': inviting clients to expand on their experiencing, rather than giving specific answers. In the dialogue with Claire, she was directly asked at both *Mick 1* and *Mick 2* to say what was going through her head when she was feeling really bad, and there are many other questions that therapists might ask to help clients clarify their experiencing. For instance:

- How did you feel? (*feelings/emotions*)
- What was going on in your head? (*thoughts*)
- How did it feel in your body? (*bodily sensations*)
- What were you wanting? (*desires/intentions*)
- What's your sense of that? (*perceptions*)
- How do you see that? (*beliefs*)
- What were you choosing to do? (*choices*)

Asking clients what they mean by particular terms or phrases can also be a useful means of helping them unpack their experiencing. A client might say, for instance, that they feel 'scared', but what do they really mean by that? No doubt, 'scared' means different things to different people, and might be experienced in quite different ways. In the dialogue with Claire, there are a number of times in which I might have asked her to unpack the terms that she was using. For instance, at *Mick 2* I might have said, 'So what does "frustration" mean to you?' At *Mick 3* I might have said, 'When you say you're "useless", what do you mean by that?'

As with reflections, paraphrases and summaries, from this phenomenological standpoint, questions that ask about non-experiential phenomenon would be considered less helpful. Hence, an existential–phenomenological therapist might be inclined to avoid the following kinds of questions:

- 'What did you do then?' (*behaviours*)
- 'What happened next?' (*external events*)
- 'What's right here?' (*truths*)
- 'What did your husband do after that?' (*other's behaviours*)
- 'What made you do that?' (*psychological mechanisms*)

Highlighting contradictions

Sometimes people say one thing, then something else which seems to imply the opposite. For instance, a client might say: 'I really enjoy spend-ing a lot of time on my own', but in a later session say, 'I find it really difficult not being around others'. Such contradictions can be a valuable way in to a deeper understanding of a client's phenomenological world. It may be, for instance, that a client's primary experiencing is of liking being alone but that, at a secondary level, she feels she should like oth-ers. Of course, the point here is not to catch the client out. Rather, it is to use such contradictions as levers into a more nuanced, detailed and complex understanding of the client's phenomenological world.

In pointing out contradictions in clients' narratives, it is obviously important to do this in ways that are non-critical, and clients may be particularly sensitive here to being shown up or shamed. In the example above, for instance, a therapist might say, 'I can really understand what you are saying about finding it difficult being around people, but I just wonder how that fits with what you said last week, about also enjoying spending time with others?' The point here is to affirm the different statements that clients have made, and invite clients to make sense, for themselves, of how these statements may fit together.

Using symbols and metaphors

Sometimes, it can be difficult for clients to find the right words or phrases to verbalise their experiences. Hence, it can sometimes be very helpful to invite clients to describe their experiencing in alternate

USING
SYMBOLS AND
METAPHORS

ways: for instance, through the use of images, metaphors or move-ments. These may also be used by the therapist to paraphrase what the client has said (see Creative Existential Therapy, Gavin, 2013). For instance, a therapist might say:

- 'Is there an image that could express what that bleakness is like?'
- 'What would your anxiety look like if it were a movement?'
- 'Is there another way of describing your anger – is there some metaphor that would work for you?'
- 'What you're describing sounds like being hit by a runaway train. Is that about right?'

Clients can also be helped to symbolise or represent their experiences through the use of such creative media as drawing, art or clay. For instance, clients might be asked to draw their feelings of vulnerability, or to use sand tray figures to represent how they feel within their family.

In many instances clients, themselves, may spontaneously express their experiencing in metaphorical or symbolic terms. The use of metaphors and representations may also emerge through the collaborative therapist–client dialogue. An example of this comes from work with Claire in our seventh session, which also provides further illustration of some of the methods described earlier. Claire had begun the session reporting on her week, and how she had had some satisfying, as well as dissatisfying, exchanges with friends. About five minutes into the session she then went quiet. The session is reported verbatim, though some segments have been omitted to emphasise the key learning points.

Mick: Do you have any thoughts on what it would be useful to explore today? *[Working pluralistically this is something I often ask clients at the start of a session].*

Claire: Eh ... I don't know. I always think to myself, 'I'm just kind of flat'. Say the session lasted ten minutes or half an hour, I'd be like, 'Whatever...' It's kind of– I don't know... what I can kind of contribute, really.

Mick: 'Cos you're feeling flat?

Claire: Feeling flat, whatever.

Mick: Maybe let's explore the flatness a bit. What is the flatness like? *[Here, I invite Claire to directly explore her experiencing in the here-and-now, see below].* Explain it to me. Cos you've said that a few times *[Claire: Yeah, it's...].* No... no... show it to me, cos you're kind of ... you don't look flat *[Claire: Uh huh].* But actually what you are saying is you feel flat inside. *[I invite Claire to express her experiencing of flatness in a physical way]*.

Claire: I'd say it would just be like that. *[Claire lies right back in chair]*. I'd like to ... lie on the floor, just like that. That's how I feel mentally and physically ....

Mick: So just like that *[I lie back as well, reflecting Claire's experiencing, as expressed non-verbally]*. OK, just– just– as the thoughts come up, so what are the thoughts that go through your head? *[Here, I am asking Claire a question to help her unpack her experiencing]*.

Claire: Nothingness. And then there's a bit of self-loathing there *[Mick: Tell me it?]*. Just float, just float ... that's it. Like your whole, kind of– like, broken eggs or shells. Broken glass and then just– walking on marshmallows, it's just, yeah, that's what it is.

Mick: And what are you feeling in your body? *[Another question]*

Claire: I'm just feeling a weight, a weight there *[Claire points to her stomach]*.

Mick: A weight in your...

Claire: In– in the top of my stomach. And then a weight, see, in my guts, my back. Just a weight.

Mick: And describe that more, that weight *[Another direct invitation for Claire to unpack her experiencing, akin to a focusing intervention (Gendlin, 1996)]*.

Claire: It's just a– just a big, gooey mass, it's like mince or something, or like I've got ten pound of mince inside of each stomach or something, or in the bottom of my guts and back. It's just that kind of fluidy, florishy mess, it's just ....

It's like a cartoon. It's a big– you've drunk ten gallons of water and your belly's on the ground and you're dragging it, that's what it is. You're dragging this belly around.

Mick: So it's a feeling of dragging something? *[Claire: Yeah]* And it's really hard to move forward *[here, I am paraphrasing Claire's description]*.

Claire: You can move, but you're always carrying it and carrying it, and you're always tired. You just get tired of carrying it.

Mick: So there's a kind of tiredness– a tiredness of dragging something *[Claire: Yeah]*. This weight. *[This is a series of reflections]*.

Claire: Yeah, it just ... Over-analysing it, it's myself that I'm dragging, it's my own stupid personality. It's just you're dragging this– it's just all white and a bit grey and your dragging this big belly.

Mick: [*Slowly and softly*] You're dragging this big belly *[I offer another reflection]*. And what's inside of the belly? *[And then a question].*

Claire: It's all kind of– I was saying it's like mince but it's kind of– the mince is alive. It's all just... squirming away [*pause*]. Like when you see, kind of, offal and guts of animals [*Mick:* Mmmmm] whatever it's– that's it.

Here, through the use of physical and visual metaphor – as well as questions and reflections – Claire and I unpack her experiencing of flatness. It is a sense of always dragging something; something that is messy, squirming and alive. For both of us, we have a much fuller and more vivid sense of what it is like for Claire to be in-the-world. Moreover, as May (1975: 15) suggests, such creative expressions may be acts of 'existential courage' in themselves, whereby clients take the risk of discovering 'new forms, new symbols, new patterns' through which to express their experiencing.

BRINGING THINGS INTO THE HERE-AND-NOW

Bringing things into the here-and-now

In the above example with Claire, I specifically invite her to unpack her experiencing *as* she is currently experiencing it: to describe it in to the immediate here-and-now. This can help clients develop a more accurate and vivid awareness of their experiencing, as they are given an opportunity to describe their experiencing as it is actually happening rather than having to recall an experiencing in the more distant past. Clients can be invited to unpack any experiences that emerge within the therapeutic work, whether feelings, perceptions or thoughts. For instance, a therapist might say: 'You talked about feeling anxious in the session today, and I wonder if you'd like to explore that more?' Inviting clients to go into their bodily-felt sensations can be a particularly helpful way of deepening an exploration of their primary experiencing. For instance, a therapist might ask 'When you talk about feeling scared, I wonder where you feel it in your body?' This has many parallels with the experiential practice of *focusing*, developed by Gendlin (1962, 1996), in which clients are encouraged to focus 'in' on their felt-senses, and to describe them as they naturally unfurl within the session (see Madison, 2014).

As with psychodynamic transference work, one aspect of the here-and-now experiencing that many existential therapists will invite their clients to unpack is their feelings and thoughts towards their therapist. How do they perceive, for instance, what the therapist said? What are their expectations? And what is their emotional reaction to the therapist? This may just be when ruptures and difficulties emerge in the therapeutic relationship (Safran & Muran, 2000), or when the client is dealing with specific relational issues (see Chapter 7). However, some existential therapists (e.g., Yalom, 2001) will focus on the therapeutic relationship throughout the work. Yalom (1999: 102), for instance, writes that he will ask clients 'what's happening in the space between us today?' at every session. He also suggests that therapists should always try to find a here-and-now equivalent of the client's 'dysfunctional' interactions to make a focus of the therapeutic work.

DEALING WITH
RUPTURES

Yalom (2008: 227) gives the example of a client, Ellen, who came to a therapy session despite feeling ill. Yalom asked her what happened at home when she felt ill. Ellen replied that she would like her husband to take more care of her, but said that she does not ask for help for fear of 'complaining'. Yalom responded, 'So, tell me, Ellen, how does that work here with me? You don't do much complaining in this office even though I'm officially your caretaker'. Ellen responded that it would feel like begging and whining, but went on to reveal a deeper fear of her 'dirty, concealed parts' leaking out. Yalom reported that this led on to a new, constructive phase of therapy, in which Ellen explored more about her distrust of men. In this respect, Yalom (2001: 62) suggests that immediacy work energises therapy, and allows the client to explore their experiences with greater accuracy. However, it is worth noting that, to date, the empirical research does not provide strong support for the process of working with the immediate here-and-now relationship (Cooper, 2008a).

Personification

Earlier in this chapter, it was suggested that clients can experience their world in different *modes* of being (Box 3.1). To help clients develop a greater awareness of these different modes, it can sometimes be useful to disentangle them through *personification* (Rowan, 2009): symbolically representing and enacting each mode through a person-like form or voice.

As discussed in Box 3.1, numerous therapeutic methods have been developed to facilitate such personification, particularly with the humanistic approaches of gestalt therapy, psychodrama, psychosynthesis and emotion-focused therapy. Across the different therapies, Cooper and Cruthers (1999) suggest that there are three principal categories of methods for facilitating the expression of different modes of experiencing. These overlap somewhat, and are at increasing levels of immediacy and intensity.

METHODS OF
PERSONIFICATION

Descriptive techniques

The first methods of personification are *descriptive* techniques, in which clients are encouraged to express their different modes of experiencing through verbal or written portrayal. Questions that a therapist might ask include:

- Can you tell me more about that 'side'/'part'/'aspect' of yourself?
- What is it like for you when you get into that space/place/way of being?
- How do you see yourself at those times?
- What do you want/need when you are in that mode?

Projective techniques

The second category of personification methods are *projective* techniques, in which 'the individual is not asked directly to describe his or her different selves, but is invited to express them indirectly through a variety of non-self mediums' (Cooper & Cruthers, 1999: 201). This can draw on the many symbolic and metaphorical techniques described earlier – such as visualisations, art media or sand tray characters – and generally involves developing an image or representation for a mode of being and then exploring and developing its characteristics. Questions that clients can be asked include:

- What would that character/image/aspect of yourself look like?
- What would it want/need/do?
- What situations bring it out?

At its most basic, a projective approach may simply involve helping a client to develop an image of that mode of being (see exercise in Box 3.1), and this is essentially what happened in the work with Claire, who spontaneously developed an image for her flatness. However, later on in the extract, she specifically indicated that the squirming mass of bile represented a particular 'part' of her being, 'my own stupid personality'. Hence, over the next few minutes, we went on to explore more about what that 'part' was like and what it wanted. Claire described it as like the Alien, sitting in her guts and striving to poison the host. 'Why does it want to do that?' I asked Claire. 'Because that's its job' she replied.

Around 17 minutes into the session, Claire went on to say that her 'positive side' was trying to fight the big, squirming Alien. My response was to ask her: 'What's your positive side, what's your image for that?'

Claire replied, 'It's just like something tapping me on my shoulder saying, "C'mon, stop it"'. Claire went on to talk more about this 'aspect' of herself, and although she initially described it as a 'good positive voice', it increasingly took the form of an undermining and 'snidy' voice – akin to an 'inner critic' (Elliott et al., 2004) – constantly trying to wind her up and start a fight. Claire gave the image of a sports coach, shouting and prodding at her from the sidelines to do better and that she was never good enough.

Experiential techniques

The third category of personification methods are *experiential* techniques, which attempt to help clients express their different facets by encouraging them 'actually to enter – behaviourally, cognitively, affectively, physiologically – into that mode of Being' (Cooper & Cruthers, 1999: 205). The simplest method here is to ask clients to speak *as* that particular mode. For instance, with Claire I asked, 'If you were that thing in your stomach, if you were that ball, what would you be saying?' She replied, 'Let's keep on going, let's poison the host and take over'. Clients might also be asked to speak *as* the image that they have drawn, or the sand tray character that they have chosen to express an aspect of themselves.

One of the most popular methods for experientially personifying different modes of being, and with good evidence for its effectiveness (Greenberg & Dompierre, 1981; Greenberg & Rice, 1981), is *two-chair dialogue*. Here, clients are invited to put their different modes of experiencing in different chairs, and to speak to and from these different 'sides'. In the following session with Claire, she agreed to try some two-chair dialogue around the different modes that she was describing, and I invited her to start by 'being' the squirming, mince-like bile that was sitting in her stomach. Having spent some moments feeling her way into that mode and describing what it was like, I then invited her to stand behind the chair, and 'be' the voice that was shouting and prodding her to be better. She did so, physically shoving the back of the chair to try and get the squirming mass to move and do something. She was then invited to go back to 'being' the lump in the chair, and to experience what it was like to have that prodding from behind. Claire arched her back against the chair, indicating a resistance to any attempts to move her forward. At this point, I decided to take on the role of the prodding voice, and pushed and shoved the back of the chair, while Claire enacted the resistance of the squirming mass towards it. The harder I shoved, the more determined Claire, as the bile-filled alien, was to resist me.

Towards the end of the session, we sat down in our respective chairs and tried to make sense of what this dramatisation might say about Claire's phenomenological experiencing. What was apparent was that, at times in her life – and particularly when she was tired – there was a voice 'within' Claire telling her that everything was pointless and that she was useless. It felt like an alien, poisonous voice, speaking with bile and self-loathing. Against this, there was another voice 'within' Claire pushing and prodding her to stop being so negative and lump-like, but through critical, snidy and undermining provocation. What also became clear in the dramatisation was that speaking to herself in a critical, snidy way was not motivating her into action. Indeed, it seemed to be having the opposite effect of making her more resistant to change, more determined to stay in that place of gooey, messy, hopeless bile.

This awareness was helpful for Claire because, as discussed above, it then allowed her to find better ways of doing things. Specifically, she looked at ways in which she might soften the critical snidy voice. Indeed, in our next session, Claire came up with the idea of replacing her internal 'football coach' with a 'boxer's trainer', who wipes her down between rounds and gives her a shoulder massage. This 're-deciding' was associated with considerable changes in how Claire went on to relate to herself: a good example of how phenomenological reflection can help clients find more positive, I–I ways of relating to their primary experiencing.

Noting and challenging 'blocks' to exploration

In facilitating this process of phenomenological exploration, it may also be helpful to focus on the ways in which clients may avoid 'staying with', or going deeper into, their experiencing. This 'resistance work' is particularly highlighted by existential therapists of a more humanistic orientation, such as Bugental (1978) and Schneider and Krug (2010). Indeed, Bugental (1978: 74) suggests that the existential therapeutic process is akin to 'peeling an onion', 'as therapist and client expose and make it possible for the latter to relinquish one resistance after another'. Signs of this resistance might be that clients:

- Start to change the topic.
- Become distracted.
- Talk about trivialities.
- Talk in clichéd, polite, formal, abstract or disinterested ways.
- Talk so quickly that they cannot 'hear' themselves.

- Start to intellectualise, rationalise, analyse or try to solve their concern.
- Distance themselves from their experiences and talk about themselves as if they are a different person.

(from Cooper, 2003b: 70)

Schneider (2003) suggests two basic forms of resistance work, *vivification* and *confrontation*. Vivification involves noting and heightening the client's awareness of how they block or limit themselves. For instance, a therapist might say, 'I notice that whenever you talk about your partner you look at the floor'. This can then be pointed out to the client every time it is repeated. Confrontation is a stronger form of challenge: directly encouraging the client to overcome their blocks. For instance, a therapist might say, 'I wonder if you could look directly at me when you talk about your partner'. Bugental (1987) suggests that it is also helpful to explain to clients how their resistance might impede the therapeutic process.

Critical reflections

As we have seen, empirical research suggests that it can be helpful for clients to focus on, and deepen an awareness of, their experiencing (Cooper, 2008a). Given that this association holds across a range of therapeutic practices (Orlinsky et al., 2004), it seems likely that the methods outlined in this chapter can be useful for therapists from a wide variety of therapeutic orientations.

Are the reasons for our behaviour always at the experiential level?

In terms of developing insight into our problems, however, the methods described in this chapter are based on the assumption that the principal 'determinants' of our thoughts, feelings and behaviours exist at an experiential level. Is this true? From a psychodynamic position, for instance, the principal determinants of our behaviours are *unconscious*: processes within our minds that are inaccessible to our conscious awareness (Yakeley, 2012). In support of this, a range of recent studies have suggested that our thoughts, feelings and behaviours *can* be determined by factors outside of our conscious experiencing, such as neurobiological processes (e.g., Marien, Custers, Hassin & Aarts, 2012; also see the companion website).

EVIDENCE AND EXAMPLES CRITICAL OF A PHENOMENOLOGICAL FOCUS: NOTES

Is our primary experiencing always 'right'?

As we have seen, the approach discussed in this chapter also tends to be associated with the assumption that our primary experiencing is an intelligible and meaningful way of responding to our world. Again, though, we can ask if this is really the case. From a cognitive perspective, for instance, our primary experiencing is not some intuitively accurate grasping of the world, but a cognitive construction that is often riddled with biases, errors and dysfunctional assumptions (Beck et al., 1979; Kahneman, 2011). Social constructionist and postmodern thinkers would also challenge the idea that there can be some form of 'pure' primary experiencing (e.g., Derrida, 1974). From this standpoint, how we experience the world will always be filtered and shaped by the social constructs around us.

From a pluralistic standpoint, however, we do not need to reach a definite conclusion as to whether primary experiencing is primarily 'right' or primarily 'wrong': it may be different at different times. Sometimes, for instance, when driving, I have a deep, intuitive sense of where I need to go. In some instances, when I follow that 'inner compass', I find myself exactly at my destination. Other times, however, I follow that deep inner sense and find myself totally and utterly lost: miles away from where I thought I was. So my deep inner sense is sometimes right and sometimes wrong but, either way, what is probably helpful is that I recognise those primary, intuitive feelings. This is so that either I can choose to follow their direction; or so that I can recognise that I am at risk of starting to follow something unhelpful, and should choose to think more rationally instead.

Is there more to existence than experiencing?

From an existential standpoint, itself, the methods discussed in this chapter could also be considered insufficient for a full therapeutic exploration. This is because, from this standpoint, our *existence* is more than just our moment-to-moment experiencing. It is also our *life*: something that is circumscribed, encompassed and defined. Hence, when we inquire into our existences, we are also asking questions like, 'What is the meaning of my life?', 'Why am I here?', 'What kind of person should I be?' And the answers to these questions may, or may not, lie in our experiencing. Similarly, from this standpoint, there are certain aspects of our existences that are *given*, whether or not they feature in our experiential fields. We are mortal, for instance, and whether or not we experience a sense of mortality makes no difference to this fact. From this standpoint, then, to be authentic is not just to be true to our experiencing, but to acknowledge the reality of the human condition. We will explore this much more fully in subsequent chapters.

Personalising practice

Who, then, might phenomenological methods be most helpful for? Based on the analysis presented in this chapter, we can hypothesise that it might be most useful for clients who:

- Have problems in living that they want to understand and address.
- Want to develop a greater awareness of how they feel, and how they experience, their world.
- Feel estranged from their 'true selves', want to know more about who they 'really are', or get more 'in touch' with themselves.
- Have many different areas of their lives that remain pre-reflected.
- Tend to move through a range of different modes of experiencing, and want to understand more about this or achieve greater consistency.
- Have difficulties at the level of secondary experiencing: feeling ashamed, abnormal, isolated, burdened, overwhelmed, confused, or anxious for how they experience their world.
- Find it difficult to articulate their primacy experiencing, and would benefit from being able to express this more clearly to others.
- Are not primarily looking for explanations for their difficulties, or for direct advice on how to improve things.

Summary

In attempting to understand the actuality of human existence, many existential philosophers and therapists have drawn on phenomenology, and the assumption that our *experiencing* is the essence of who we are. Our experiencing is an in-the-moment, ever-changing being-towards-the-world, characterised by feelings, thoughts, sensations and desires. Our experiencing can be primary or secondary; reflective or pre-reflective; and may be constellated around one or more concepts of self. Psychological difficulties may be caused, or exacerbated, by relating to our primary experiencing in negative ways; and developing a reflective understanding of our experiencing can help us develop greater insight and find better ways of doing things. There are many ways that therapists can facilitate this process. Most generally, they can bracket their assumptions, remain at the descriptive level, and try to treat all the clients' experiencing as equally legitimate. More specifically, they can provide clients with space and encouragement to talk through listening and minimal encouragers; and through reflecting, paraphrasing and summaries of the clients' experiencing. They can also facilitate this exploratory process by asking questions, working with symbolic and metaphoric expressions, inviting clients to personify different modes of being, and challenging blocks to exploration.

Questions for reflection and discussion

- 'Experiencing is the essence of human existence'. To what extent, and in what ways, do you agree or disagree with this statement?
- Can psychologically difficulties be understood in solely phenomenological terms, without recourse to a concept of the unconscious?
- To what extent do you think that phenomenological unpacking, in itself, is sufficient for therapeutic change? Does the therapist need to do more?

Recommended reading

Spinelli, E. (2005) *The Interpreted World: An Introduction to Phenomenological Psychology* (2nd edn). London: Sage. Highly recommended. The classic introduction to phenomenology and its implications for therapeutic practice.

Langdridge, D. (2007) *Phenomenological Psychology: Theory, Research and Method*. London: Prentice-Hall. A valuable introduction to phenomenology in the psychological field. For a more concise summary, see Chapter 2 of Langdridge (2012).

Moran, D. (2000) *Introduction to Phenomenology*. London: Routledge. A very rich, complex and thorough analysis of phenomenological philosophy, concepts and traditions.

Spiegelberg, H. (1972) *Phenomenology in Psychology and Psychiatry: A Historical Introduction*. Evanston, IL: Northwestern University Press. Comprehensive and definitive tome on the development of phenomenological and existential thought in psychiatry, psychology and psychotherapy up until the 1960s.

4

Freedom and Choice

This chapter discusses the existential understandings that:

- Human beings are inherently free.
- It can be anxiety-evoking to accept our freedom.
- We tend to deny our freedom, in a variety of ways.
- Denying our freedom can do more harm than good.

It then goes on to describe the existential practices of:

- Using language which construes clients as agentic, intelligible beings.
- Empathising with clients' anxieties around choice and responsibility.
- Helping our clients to acknowledge their capacity to choose.
- Helping clients to identify ways in which they may evade their freedom and responsibilities.
- Helping clients to decide on the best way(s) forward.
- Challenging clients to move from wishes and wills to actions.

'There can be few themes, if any, nearer to the heart of existentialism than freedom' (Macquarrie, 1972: 138). And, indeed, in terms of interventions addressing existential givens, helping clients to face their freedom, choice and responsibility is one of the most characteristic practices of existential therapists (Correia et al., in preparation-b). To be free means that we have the capacity to make choices in our lives.

That is, we can face 'a situation with more than one possibility, considers the options and ends up by saying yes to one of them, thus not choosing something else' (Jacobsen, 2007: 108).

Understandings

The freedom of human being

For Sartre (1958: 25), human beings are fundamentally and ineradicably free. He writes: 'Man does not exist *first* in order to be free *subsequently*; there is no difference between the being of a man and his *being-free*'. By this, he is suggesting that choice is pervasive and omnipresent in our lives (see Exercise 4.1). A client who assaults his wife, for instance, may claim that he was *compelled* to do that – that some red mist, for instance, came over him and he could not help himself – but, from a Sartrean standpoint, there is always some element of choice, some possibility of acting in a different way. The individual is never a 'helpless pawn' (Frankl, 1988: 7).

Exercise 4.1 The omnipresence of freedom

Aim

- To help reflect on the prevalence of choices in everyday life.

The exercise

- Think back over your first hour this morning, and jot down on a piece of paper every choice you made (5 mins). (For instance, 'I chose to have tea rather than coffee', 'I chose to start an argument with my partner'.)
- Now think back over this morning, and jot down everything that you did, or experienced, that was *not* a choice (5 mins). (For instance, 'I did not choose to listen to someone's mp3 player on the underground'.)
- Reflect on this question: What was more prevalent in your experiencing: things that you chose to do, or things that you did not choose to do?

Comment

Most people who do this exercise find it much easier to recognise choices than non-choices. Indeed, many people find it impossible to identify anything they did or experienced that did not have some element of choice.

This highlights the way that choice-making is an integral part of human lived-experience.

Variations

- It is also interesting to try reflecting on choice-making in the here-and-now moment. You can ask yourself 'What choices am I making right now?', and 'What is happening right now that is not a choice?' (For instance, 'Right now I am choosing to think about this question', 'Right now I am not choosing for my heart to beat'.)
- Reflect on this question: 'What, actually, is a choice?' Can you describe, phenomenologically, your experience of choosing? Rollo May (1969a: 218), for instance, suggests that our human freedom is made up of a number of parts: *intentionality*, the basic human tendency to 'stretch' towards something; *wish*, 'the imaginative playing with the possibility of some act or state occurring'; and *will*, 'the capacity to organise one's self so that movement in a certain direction or towards a certain goal may take place'.
- This exercise can be great to do in a training workshop, in pairs. The role of the partner should be to listen, and to make sure the person just sticks to listing choices and not choices. The partner can also count the number of choices and non-choices, and then see which is more prevalent at the end.

Indeed, from an existential standpoint, even to 'not choose' is to make a choice. Keeley, for instance, was a client in her mid-30s who was coming to the end of a teacher training programme, and had a job lined up in a local primary school. The only problem was, as Kelly began to acknowledge in therapy, she really did not like teaching. For Keeley, taking the job at her local primary school – indeed, going on to spend the rest of her life as a teacher – was not something she initially saw as a choice: it was just what was *going* to happen. As we explored it further in therapy, however, it became increasingly apparent that 'going with the flow' was just one of the things she could *choose* to do.

In experiential terms (see Chapter 3), choice can be seen as occurring at the level of secondary experiencing. It is a form of *acting on* our experiencing. Yet, as Exercise 4.1 suggests, we are often making choices at the pre-reflective level (Farber, 2000b). In this respect, from an existential standpoint, 'choice' refers not just to the big, conscious decisions in life, for instance, 'Should I leave my job or not?' Rather, it also refers to the split-second, everyday decisions by which actions take place. In this respect, the existential emphasis on people as choice-making beings is quite similar to the person-centred emphasis on people as active, *agentic* organisms (Bohart & Tallman, 1999). That is, our clients are not just absorbing or passively responding to the world, but intentionally acting upon it – however psychologically distressed or disturbed they may be.

Why does an existential approach emphasise human freedom and choice? In part, this is a consequence of its phenomenological grounding. If we understand experiencing as the essence of human existence (Chapter 3), and if making choices is omnipresent in our experiencing (Exercise 4.1), then freedom and choice are core to our being. In addition, this emphasis comes from an ethic of striving to engage with people in deeply valuing, I–Thou ways (Chapter 2). Here, to engage with our clients respectfully means to see them as people with the capacity to make decisions and alter their lives.

Where is it, though, that choices come from? Surely they must be caused by something? For Sartre (1958), to answer this question would be to betray the very foundations of an understanding of human beings as free to choose. For if we say that choices are *caused* by something, then they are not really choices. Rather, argues Sartre, choices emerge from *nothingness*.

What Sartre is trying to emphasise here is the *ontological primacy* of choices. This means that, in terms of experiencing, choices come first. It is as if, at each moment in time, we are *erupting* into the world as a choice-making being, and only subsequently come to interact with the givens, limitations and determined elements of our world (see Figure 4.1). Another way of thinking about this is that our secondary experiencing is always alongside our primary experiencing. That is, it is not that we experience the world in

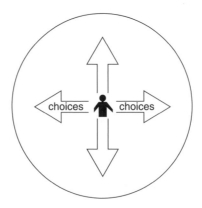

Figure 4.1 Choices in the face of limitations

particular ways; and then come to think, feel and act on that experiencing. Rather, as we experience our world at a primary level, so we have a distance from – and relation to – it: these two forms of experiencing are *equiprimordial* (that is, of equal importance).

This is a very different way of conceptualising human being than our normal, natural scientific one, which assumes that A happens, which then causes B, which then causes C. Take the example of a client with alcohol addiction who is about to open a bottle of wine. One way of understanding this, a natural scientific way, might be to say that that she experienced feelings of loss as a child, which then led her to look for ways of dealing with these feelings as an adult, which then leads her to drink. By contrast, an existential understanding, rooted in a phenomenological worldview, starts with that client in that moment as she stands there with the corkscrew, who has the capacity to either turn it to open the bottle of wine, or put it down to one side and do something different.

From this existential perspective, however, 'to be free is not to have the power to do anything you like' (de Beauvoir, 1948a: 91). As we have seen in Chapter 3, from a phenomenological perspective, there is a certain fixidity to our primary experiencing; and there are also a range of givens and limitations within which we always make our choice (see Chapter 5). So an existential perspective is not suggesting that people's pasts, or other internal and external forces, are irrelevant to their actions. With the client above, for instance, it may well be that her drinking is linked to experiences of abandonment as a child, or to a biological predisposition towards alcoholism. But what an existential understanding suggests is that such factors, however compelling they might be, do not *make* the woman turn that corkscrew. She may feel a desire to drink, to quench a biological aching in her body, but there is something more. There is the woman's *will* or *agency* – 'The defiant power of the spirit' (Frankl, 1988: 73) – that has the capacity to stand over and above the psychological and physical plane.

This inextinguishable capacity to choose towards our circumstances is, perhaps, best illustrated in Frankl's (1986: 157) own account of incarceration in Auschwitz: an incomprehensibly restrictive and oppressive environment. He writes:

> In the concentration camps … in this living laboratory and on this testing ground, we watched and witnessed some of our comrades behave like swine while others behaved like saints. Man has both potentialities within himself; which one is actualized depends on decisions but not on conditions.

Box 4.1 Coming to a crossroads: the existential metaphor for being

Each of the different therapeutic orientations offers different metaphors, or images, for what it is like to be a human being. From a pluralistic stand-point, none of these are 'true'; rather, different metaphors will be more or less helpful for different people at different points in time. From a per-son-centred standpoint, for instance, human being may be seen as akin to a plant, which has the capacity to grow and flourish if it is adequately nour-ished. Cognitive therapy, on the other hand, tends to see people as 'little scientists', who strive to make sense of their worlds, and are helped if they can think about things in more rational and critical ways. By contrast, a Sartrean metaphor for human being might be that of a person coming to a crossroads – or a series of crossroads – and having to decide what path to take. Here, in contrast to the person-centred metaphor (and the human-istic–existential perspective presented in Chapter 3), there is no certainty that any one path is the right one. The person coming to the crossroads may go the right way or the wrong way, and there is no 'process' or 'felt-senses' (Gendlin, 1981) that can be ultimately relied upon. Even rational thinking, contra the cognitive metaphor, has the potential to take a person down a path that may be harmful or damaging to them.

For many people, this existential metaphor for human being may be unsettling; yet some may find it a liberating image, or one that resonates deeply with their experiences at particular times in their lives. What is your response to it?

We are our choices

Given this emphasis on freedom and choice, it follows, from this Sartrean standpoint, that the people we become are shaped by the choices that we make. Sartre (1996: 259) writes, 'Man is nothing else but what he makes of himself'. So a client, for instance, who has developed a deep distrust of other people, would be seen, at some level, as having chosen to engage with the world in this way. This is not to suggest, however, that the client is at fault, or to blame, for his difficulties. Given the principal of intelli-gibility (Chapter 3), there would be reasons why the client made this choice: for instance, to protect himself from re-experiencing hurt. Nevertheless, there remains the possibility of the client re-deciding who he will be, and this is the basis for the methods discussed later in this chapter.

From this existential understanding, it also follows that how we choose to act (at the level of secondary experiencing), has the capacity to change our world, and therefore how we feel towards it at the primary level of experiencing. For instance, a client might choose to leave an abusive relationship, and thereby improve the quality of his or her life. This contrasts with – and can complement – more humanistic understandings, which tend to be based on the reverse assumption: that by changing people's feelings and thoughts, they can make more effective in-the-world choices (e.g., Greenberg et al., 1993). For instance, if we experience social anxiety, an experiential understanding might suggest that we could tackle it by evoking, and trying to 'work through' our emotions: perhaps through focusing or through two-chair work (see Chapter 3). From an existential understanding, however, we might also be able to overcome this difficulty by *choosing* to engage in frightening social situations, such that we discover an ability to tolerate anxiety. Here, an existential approach comes closer to behavioural practices (e.g., Bennett-Levy, Butler, Fennell, Hackmann, Mueller & Westbrook, 2005), with their emphasis on changing the way we think and feel by changing the way we act.

If our choices shape our experiencing, then it is also important that we make choices in the 'right' frame of mind. This might be defined as times in which we are able to consider a range of our different wants, and to consider the medium- and long-term implications as well as the short-term ones. This contrasts with times in which we may be stuck in one very specific mode of experiencing, or skating around on existential black ice and really unable to see up from down (Chapter 3). Stanley, for instance, was a client in his mid-30s who wanted to find ways of moving forward in his life. When we explored this phenomenologically, what emerged was that Stanley would get very interested in jobs or training courses, start them, but then get into a hopeless or despairing mode of experiencing and abruptly give them up. Consequently, he kept on having to start again. For Stanley, one of the most important learnings from therapy was that he should not make big life decisions when he was in his 'dark place'. Rather, he recognised that he needed to 'ride' his feelings of despair, and only make big choices once he was feeling more settled.

Here, we can see how the process of making effective choices is linked in with that of developing our reflective capacity (Chapter 3): being able to stand back from our primary experiencing and holding the potential to choose differently. 'Freedom', writes May (1981: 54), 'is the capacity to pause in the face of stimuli from many directions at once and, in this pause, to throw one's weight towards this response rather than that one'.

The denial of freedom

The anxiety of freedom

When Keeley, introduced earlier, thought about being a teacher for the rest of her life, she felt deflated, sad and hopeless. Nevertheless, when she talked about the other options that might be available for her, she began to feel considerably more anxiety. Here, as existential philosophers have argued (Kierkegaard, 1980), an acknowledgement of our freedom and possibilities may not necessarily be a positive experience but may, in fact, generate considerable anxiety. This can be for several reasons.

First, when we choose one thing, we choose *against* something else: the principle of 'alternatives exclude' (Yalom, 2001: 148). Schopenhauer (1969: 303) writes 'we must in life, if we wish to grasp and possess one thing, renounce and leave aside innumerable others that lie to the right and to the left'. And this is anxiety-evoking because there is always the possibility that what we reject was actually the better option. When I go to a restaurant, for instance, I feel a lot more anxious if there are several things on the menu that I want, rather than just one. If there are several, I'm faced with the possibility that I may make a bad choice, and end up missing out on some delicious dish – perhaps the best dish that I will ever have had! And, indeed, research does suggest that the more choices people are confronted with, the more unhappy they can end up feeling (Schwartz, 2005).

What can make this awareness even more anxiety-evoking is that, when we choose, we are not only choosing for ourselves, but also for others as well. That is, virtually every important choice we make will have a knock-on effect to those around us (Sartre, 1958). So if a client, for instance, has a choice about taking on a new job and moving to a different country, this may have implications for her partner, her children, her friends, her parents – pretty much everyone whose life she currently touches.

Thinking about all our different choices can also make life feel quite overwhelming and uncertain. Imagine if, for instance, you tried to be aware of every choice you were making at every second of your life and all the alternatives: for instance, 'Right now I am deciding to stand up ... but I could also choose to stay seated, or to go for a run, or to ...'. Life would feel impossible; and it would also feel like nothing was grounded or certain: that at every moment, you could go in an infinite variety of directions. For Keeley, then, knowing which way she is going to go for her future, even if she does not like the sound of it, at least feels more comforting, secure and stable than having to (re-) open up all her options.

As Fromm (1942) argues, freedom can also be disquieting because it takes people out of the safety of the crowd, and throws a spotlight on our own individual choices and behaviours. Instead of feeling like we are doing the same thing as everyone else, we have to acknowledge that we are an independent being who could always choose to do otherwise.

Evading and denying our freedom

From an existential perspective, therefore, it is argued that we will often deny our capacity for freedom and choice: we exist in *bad faith* (Sartre, 1958). Existential writers have highlighted a number of ways in which we might do that, for instance:

- Adopting a fatalistic belief system: 'What will happen will happen'.
- Conforming to a crowd, an authoritarian system, or another person; or striving to merge symbiotically with another.
- Taking up a 'victim' position: 'bad things happen to me and I can't do anything about it'.
- Being non-committal: never really opting for one thing over another.
- Being cynical, sarcastic, apathetic or not taking life seriously: 'if everything is rubbish, it doesn't matter what I choose'.
- Trying to be good at everything: so never really opting for one thing over another.
- Delegating our choices to other people, institutions or forces.
- Procrastinating: putting decisions off for as long as possible.
- Acting on whims and impulses: that is, delegating our choices to *internal* forces so that we do not have to think about them.
- Not telling other people what we want or being assertive.
- Behaving in fixed, compulsive or obsessive ways: 'I have to do x'.
- Rebellion: doing the opposite of what everyone else does, which can involve little more volition than conformity.

         (Fromm, 1942; Laing, 1965; May, 1953, 1969a; Yalom, 1980)

Exercise 4.2   You and your choices

Aim

To help you reflect on your relationship to choice, how you might tend to deny this, and how such an awareness can be facilitated, such that you may be more sensitised to these issues in clients.

(Continued)

(Continued)

The exercise

Reflect on these three questions (15 minutes in total):

- To what extent do you fully acknowledge the choice and freedom that you have in your life?
- To what extent do you use the strategies listed above, or other ones, to deny your freedom and choice?
- How might you become more fully aware of the freedom and choices that you do have?

Variations

To relate this to clinical practice, you may find it useful to think through each of these questions in relation to a client you are working with. For instance, choose a client that you might be struggling with at the moment: Is there an acknowledgement of the capacity to choose? Is there a denial of this? How might you help him or her become more agentic?

From an existential perspective, the negative feelings associated with acknowledging our freedom may also extend to an uncomfortableness with accepting the choices that we made in the *past* – i.e., our *responsibilities* – particularly if the outcomes of our actions are negative. If this involves others, we may have a deep and profound sense of guilt. But there may also be a deep sense of 'guilt' towards ourselves (Heidegger, 1962) – or what Yalom (1980) refers to as *regret* or *remorse* – for failing to fulfil our own potential. Marge, for instance, was a woman in her fifties, enormously bright and able, who had dropped out of university in the late 1960s as part of the student protest movement, and had never really gone on to have a satisfying working life. Marge came to therapy wanting to accept her past as it had been and to let go of her regrets. However, as the therapy progressed, she began to recognise a deep rage towards herself for not making the most of her academic potential.

As with a tendency to deny the choices that we face, then, an existential perspective holds that we can also tend to deny the choices that we *have* made: holding other people, institutions or forces responsible for what has happened (May, 1953, 1969a; Yalom, 1980). So while Marge did blame herself for dropping out of college, she was also furious with the leaders of the student protest movement for encouraging her to do so, and with her parents for not being more disciplined with her. 'If only they had pushed me harder', she said, 'I probably would have seen my studies through'. Indeed, from an existential perspective, some of the classic therapeutic explanations for why people behave in the way they do may be seen as a form of denial of responsibility. Bugental (1981), for instance, suggests that therapists may end up colluding with clients that their difficulties are all 'their parents' fault'. Similarly, Sartre (1958) suggests that saying we did things for 'unconscious' reasons can be a way of shifting responsibility away from our own, conscious volition. It becomes, according to May (1983: 171), 'a convenient blank cheque on which any causal explanation can be written': 'It wasn't me, it was my unconscious that did it!' (May, 1983).

The pathogenic consequences of denying our freedom

In the short-term, from an existential standpoint, denying our freedom and responsibility may help us to feel less anxious, less remorseful and more certain about things. In the long-term, though, as with all forms of self-deception (see Chapter 3), it is argued that it generally does more harm than good. Indeed, Fromm (1942) suggests that the denial of free-dom is at the heart of all neurosis. This is for a number of reasons, which closely parallel the reasons why a negative relation to our pri-mary experiencing can cause difficulties (Chapter 3).

First, if we do not acknowledge our capacity for freedom and choice, it is likely to leave us feeling that we have little self-efficacy or self-worth. For a client like Marge, acknowledging that it was *her* choice to drop out of university, and not the responsibility of others, was a painful thing to do. But it also gave her more of a sense of being the power in her life: that she is the one who has – and can – make things happen.

Second, at a pre-reflective level, we may know that we can make choices, and are responsible for our actions. So denying it does not really work, it just leaves us haunted by the possibility that everything really was – or is – our fault. And if we try and shore up our defences further, existential anxiety may transform into the much more problematic neurotic anxiety (Bugental, 1981). Marge might, for instance, construct an even stronger sense of her self as victim – that she has always been at the whim of others, that her parents and her peers destroyed her life – but as these beliefs inevitably falter, she will have to fight harder and harder to defend herself from the existential truth.

Finally, if we do not acknowledge our freedom and choice, and find ways of acting on it, we may be less likely to do the things in life that we really want to do. Keeley, for instance, may feel more comforted simply rolling on to a teaching career. However, over the course of her life, she may be likely to feel more satisfied if she is able to stand back from this, think about what she really wants to do, and then *choose* something that she really does find satisfying and fulfilling. Similarly, while it may be painful to renounce certain alternatives, if we are like 'children at a fair' (Schopenhauer, 1969: 303) snatching at 'everything that fascinates us in passing', we can end up running 'a zigzag path, like a will-o'-the-wisp, and arrive at nothing'.

Authentically facing our freedom

Hence, from an existential perspective, while it may be frightening and unnerving to take responsibility for our freedom and choice, it is only through doing so that we can make the most of the lives we have. This means bearing, resolutely, the existential anxiety that accompanies freedom – having 'the courage to be' (Tillich, 2000) – and making choices that can actualise our ownmost possibilities.

Methods

So how might therapists go about trying to help clients acknowledge and actualise their freedom to choose?

Using agentic language

A very simple initial point is that, in working with clients, it may be helpful to use language which reflects back to them their capacity to choose, agency and intelligibility; rather than constructing them in more deterministic terms as victims of their environment, circumstances or pasts. For instance, rather than saying, 'It sounds like the neglect you experienced *made* you wary of trusting people', it may be more helpful to phrase this as: 'It sounds like you learnt from your childhood that people can't be trusted, and you protect yourself by being very wary of others'. Alternatively, instead of saying 'Perhaps you feel bad about yourself *because* you were bullied', a therapist might say, 'I wonder if you've sensed from your experiences of bullying that there was something wrong with you, and you've carried this belief into your adult life?'

Empathising with the anxiety of facing choices

If existential philosophers are right, and people can sometimes experience high levels of anxiety when faced with choices, a second practical implication of this perspective is that sometimes it can be helpful to simply convey to clients an understanding, and acceptance, of the anxiety they may feel in the face of decisions and choices. This may then help them feel less isolated in their experiencing, more self-accepting (see Chapter 3) and, ultimately, perhaps more willing to consciously think about what decision to make. Dawn, for instance, was a 21-year-old client coming to the end of her college studies, and who spoke one day of her envy towards her friend Kate, who already knew what career path she wanted to follow. By contrast, said Dawn, she just 'didn't have a clue', and was overwhelmed by the variety of options available to her. Here, simply reflecting this back to Dawn and 'staying with' this anxiety seemed of some help – conveying to Dawn that she was not a 'weirdo' or 'spoilt brat' for feeling so envious and uncertain.

As with Dawn, conveying such empathic acceptance may be particularly helpful when, from the 'outside', it may look like someone should be very pleased with all the options available to them. Beth, for instance, had two men very interested in having a relationship with her and, to most of her friends, she was extremely fortunate to be in this situation. To some extent, Beth also felt this; but the other thing she experienced was a real anxiety about what to do: Who should she choose, and what if she ended up getting into a relationship with the 'wrong' man? What made things worse was that Beth – like many people in such situations – felt, *herself*, that she should be more appreciative of the options available to her. Consequently, she experienced a secondary guilt for feeling bad about things. Hearing from her therapist, then, that he could understand why she might be experiencing a lot of anxiety was reassuring for her, and helped her focus more clearly on how to resolve this situation.

Helping clients to acknowledge their freedom and responsibility

Therapists can help clients to acknowledge their freedom and responsibility in a range of ways. These can vary from the firmest, most challenging confrontation; to the gentlest, most exploratory suggestion. (For a training group exercise that can explore the relative merits of firmer and gentler existential ways of working, see the companion website.) The following is an example of the former, with Bugental (1981: 346) challenging a mother, Thelma, to take responsibility for how she responds to her daughter's new boyfriend, John:

FIRM AND GENTLE EXISTENTIAL CHALLENGE

Thelma: I can't do a thing, she's going to go, and that's it.

Bugental: So you decided to let her go with John?

Thelma:	I haven't decided. She's the one who decided.
Bugental:	No, you've decided too. You've chosen to let her go with John.
Thelma:	I don't see how you can say that. She's insisting.
Bugental:	That's what she's doing; what you're doing is accepting her insistence.
Thelma:	Well then I won't let her go. But she'll be unhappy and make life hell for me for a while.
Bugental:	So you've decided to forbid her to go with John.
Thelma:	Well, isn't that what you wanted? What you said I should do?
Bugental:	I didn't say that you should do anything. You have a choice here, but you seem to be insisting that either your daughter is making a choice or that I am.
Thelma:	Well, I don't know what to do.
Bugental:	It's a hard choice.

In this excerpt, Bugental very directly – and persistently – challenges Thelma to take her share of responsibility for what is going on; and to neither blame things on her daughter or her therapist. They get to the point of Thelma acknowledging that she does not know what to do. This is probably a difficult place for her to be, but one that allows her to start realistically considering her choices. By contrast, the following example comes from my own work, and is an example of a much gentler style of existential challenge. The client, Mary, is a mother who came to therapy to talk about her difficulties with her partner, but is baffled by the anger she experiences towards her children.

Mary 1:	I get so frustrated that I'm really shouting at the kids. I don't know why I do it. One moment I'm feeling pretty calm and they're just playing around. And then the next moment I'm so angry. I really want to be more tolerant.
Mick 1:	Can you tell me about a time when you actually shouted at them?
Mary 2:	Take a few nights ago. They were up playing in their room, and I went up, and I saw what a mess they'd made, and– to be honest, I could have swiped the little bastards.
Mick 2:	What was going on for you when you saw the mess? Like, what was going through your mind when you saw the mess and also what were you feeling?

Mary 3: I saw it and I thought, 'You just don't bloody listen to me do you, none of you, you're quite happy to treat me like your slave!' It was just the lack of respect that really got to me.

Mick 3: So although you said earlier that you can't understand why you shout at them, when you talk about what actually happens, it sounds like it feels that there's a pretty good reason for it: that you want them to treat you with respect.

Mary 4: Yeah, I suppose so, but I feel so awful afterwards. It's just so not the kind of parent I want to be.

Mick 4: So it sounds like you're really wanting to get them to listen to you, and you're also not happy with the way that you're currently trying to do that. So I wonder, if– like I wonder if there might be other ways that you could go about doing that. Let's imagine you walking into that room and seeing that mess: How else might you choose to behave?

In contrast to the previous dialogue, Mary is not explicitly challenged to take responsibility for her actions. Nevertheless, through a phenomenological exploration (Chapter 3), the two of us come to see the intelligibility behind her behaviour, and hence Mary's agency in this situation. Mary's angry behaviour is no longer something that *happens* to her, but something that she is actively *doing*. Hence, it also becomes something that she can choose to express in a different way.

Helping clients to identify ways in which they may evade making choices or taking responsibility

On the other side of the 'acknowledging freedom' coin is 'acknowledging strategies of denying freedom'. In the work with Keeley, for instance, it became increasingly apparent that, throughout her life, she had tended to just 'fall' into things, and not really actively decide what she wanted to do. We explored this pluralistically (i.e., trying to bracket assumptions about whether or not this was a bad thing) and Keeley came to the conclusion, albeit reluctantly, that she probably *did* need to be more proactive in how she made choices in her life. As part of the pluralistic work, we also discussed how it was best for me to help her with this. For instance, did she want me to try and focus her down on the choices that she was facing, or would she prefer it if I 'stayed with' her in whatever she wanted to talk about? Again reluctantly, but with a smile, Keeley said that she probably did 'need' me to help her stay focused on her choices. I did so, and at the end of the session, Keeley wrote on her feedback form that it had been helpful to 'keep talking about things' although she had 'felt anxious'. I had helped this, she wrote, by 'guiding the conversation back' when she was 'veering off topic'. Why was it helpful? 'It was unpleasant but nothing negative actually happened, so I may be more likely to think about these things on my own (eventually) rather than avoiding them'.

Another example of helping clients to explore the ways they evade making choices comes from work with Mark, a young man who came in to therapy trying to find some focus in his life. Mark was frustrated by his job, a production manager at a TV company, and longed to do something more exciting and fulfilling. The following dialogue comes from about one year into the therapeutic work:

Mark 1: I just feel that I'm good at everything, but not great at anything in particular. I mean, I do the judo, the swimming, the script-writing, the DJ-ing and I do it all well, but I don't do any of it great. I get so frustrated and fed-up because I can't focus, I just get to a level and that's it, I can't go beyond it. I guess a lot of the problem is that I don't have time to do any one thing well because I never really have time to just focus on one thing – I'm doing so many different things. *[This is a good example of Schopenhauer's (1969: 303) 'will-o'-the-wisp that arrives at nothing', see above.]*

Mick 1: So what would it be like to actually give some of these things up?

Mark 2: I dunno, pretty difficult I guess. I mean, what happens if I stopped doing something and then it turns out that that would have been the thing that I was best at? What happens if I stop doing the DJ-ing and then I realise that actually I would have made a brilliant DJ? It's pretty frightening. That sounds crazy, doesn't it?

Mick 2: No, not at all. I'm thinking of some of these existential philosophers who would say that making choices is so anxiety-provoking for just that reason. That in choosing one thing we are always choosing against something else. So it's a reality that if you choose not to follow your DJ work, it might turn out that that was your best thing, and that would feel pretty awful; but I guess if you don't make some choices about what you want to concentrate on and what you want to drop, then that feeling that you're good at lots of things but not great at anything is going to carry on.

Something else that comes to mind ... I wonder if part of the reason that you don't really focus on just one or two things is that, if you did that, and if you didn't do great then, then you might have a real sense of failure. Like, if you don't really commit to something, and then you don't do great at it, that's ok, because you can say to yourself that you could have always done it better if you had the time. But if you really commit yourself and then don't do as well as you want to, then that can be more difficult to take.

Mark 3:   Yeah, I guess that might be true.

As with much of my work, this is an example of a fairly gentle existential practice. Right up until the last part of *Mick 2*, the emphasis is on empathising with the anxiety that Mark might experience in having to make a choice (see above). Indeed, in *Mick 2*, it can be seen that I am trying to 'normalise' Mark's experiences of anxiety by explicitly drawing on existential ideas. In the second part of *Mick 2*, however, I do suggest to Mark a reason for why he may be avoiding making a choice: because it involves the risk of committing to one thing over another. From a firmer existential perspective, however, this is something that I might have introduced earlier, and in a more explicit and challenging way. For instance, at *Mick 1* I might have said: 'Mark, you're saying that you can't focus and you don't have time to, but it is *you* that's choosing to do all those different things – no-one is making you. I wonder if that's because it feels safer to spread yourself around than to commit to just one thing?'

Helping people re-decide

HELPING
PEOPLE
RE-DECIDE

Helping clients to acknowledge their freedom and their resistance to it may be an important element of existential therapeutic work. Ultimately, however, their value may only be realised through clients actively *choosing* to change their lives in some particular way: the process of *re-deciding* described in Box 3.3.

In practical terms, an important step here may be simply asking clients what they are going to do. In the dialogue with Mary, for instance, I specifically asked her how else she might choose to behave with her children. Other questions might be, 'So what are you going to do?',

'What next?', 'How are you going to take this forward?', 'What choices do you have here?'

It is of little value to help clients make decisions, however, if they are ones that are detrimental to their wellbeing. So how can we help clients to make the decisions that are most likely to benefit them? Unfortunately, there is little guidance from existential writers here. Indeed, much more practical advice is given by behavioural therapists in the field of *problem solving therapy*, who emphasise such practices as helping clients to generate, evaluate and choose the best alternative, implement the chosen alternative, and evaluate its efficacy (D'Zurilla & Nezu, 1999).

It may also be helpful to encourage clients to think about how and when they are making choices, and if they are doing this at the most constructive times. As we saw in the above example of Stanley, for instance, an important part of the work was helping him recognise that he was making choices at times when he had a very unbalanced view of life.

Helping clients move from 'wish' and 'will' to 'action'

Sometimes, clients know exactly what they want to do – or, at least, say they know what they want to do – but find it 'impossible' to put intentions and decisions into action. How, here, might a therapist be helpful?

Again, existential writers do not give any particular guidance; but a useful way in to this question may be through a metaphor suggested to me by a workshop participant. She said that moving from decisions to actions was like standing on a very high diving board, wondering whether or not we should launch ourselves into the water. We know what we want to do, but actively taking the 'leap of faith' (Kierkegaard, 1985) into the unknown can fill us with trepidation and dread. Mostly, if we do eventually dive off, we feel pleased and relieved that we made the leap – and walking back down the steps can leave a real sense of disappointment. However, there is also the slight, but very real, possibility that launching ourselves into the unknown can have disastrous consequences.

So, in terms of therapeutic work, the question becomes, How might we help such a person on a diving board take the next step? (You may find it useful to take a few minutes, yourself, to reflect on what *you* might find most helpful from someone else if you were the person on the diving board). Gentle – or strong – encouragement might be a good idea, though we need to be certain that they want to make that leap. Alternatively, we could help them think through the consequences of whatever choice they make – what could happen if they choose to dive off, and what might happen if they choose to walk down? From an existential standpoint, another strategy might be to remind them that, even if they do not dive off, they are still making a choice; or that any step forward in life involves anxiety. And what about giving the person a great big shove, as a behavioural therapist might do (consensually, of course), when they help someone directly confront their fears (Marks, 1978)? On the one hand, there is the possibility that it could leave the person feeling angry or hurt; but it may also be just what the person needed to get over their fears. And, indeed, research suggests that such exposure-based techniques, applied correctly, are amongst the most effective methods in helping people overcome anxiety problems (Emmelkemp, 2013).

In relation to clinical practice, two further things may be of particular help. First, it may be useful to help clients think very concretely about what it is, exactly, that they need to do. Sometimes, the reason people do not follow through on decisions is that they do not know what actual, specific steps to take next: they just have an amorphous sense of wanting things to change. Hence, phenomenologically unpacking past experiences, and making concrete plans for future ones, has the potential to be of considerable value. For instance, Craig was a young client who wanted to develop more control over his binge eating. I encouraged Craig to describe, in as much phenomenological detail as he could (Chapter 3), the binge eating-as-experienced. Craig talked about going past supermarkets on his way home from work, walking down the aisles of biscuits and chocolates, and being flushed with shame as he bought packets of crisps and hot dogs. As we explored this phenomenologically, he also described how he would end up buying something just to try and stop obsessing over whether or not to buy something; and that he would then end up eating more and more to try and smother his feelings of guilt for having started to 'eat crap'. It was not easy for Craig to describe his experiences at this level of phenomenological detail – he felt deeply ashamed – but it had the potential to be helpful in allowing him to identify things that he could choose to do differently. For instance, he could distract himself by ringing his mum if he felt drawn into a shop, or be more compassionate with himself if he did have one thing to eat so that it did not trigger a whole overeating cycle.

Second, it may be useful to agree with clients that they will do particular things prior to the next, or subsequent, sessions. Overall, the research indicates that homework is associated with modest positive benefit (Burns & Spangler, 2000; Kazantzis, Deane & Ronan, 2000); and, in our own pluralistic research, we find that a majority of clients express a preference for having such tasks to do (Aylindar, 2014). Hence, for instance, if a client has things that she wants to discuss with her husband, it might be agreed that she will try and do that before the next session. Or a client who is thinking of joining a walking club may be encouraged to find out more on the internet.

One particular example of how life-changing such a simple intervention can be comes from work with Peter, who came to therapy experiencing profoundly low moods and social anxiety. Peter was an extremely bright young man who had dropped out of university to look after his grandfather; and was now working, part-time, in an old age people's home. Much of Peter's stress was linked to his job, but he also had a profound sense of hopelessness about his future: no relationship, no pleasures, nothing he really looked forward to. About ten weeks into the therapeutic work, Peter talked about how successful he had been in his academic studies, and how he had often thought about going back to university. He had never dared to find out more, however, for fear that the college would ridicule him if he asked them about coming back. We talked about it, and Peter decided that, after the session, he would contact the registration department at the university to just find out what he might need to do. He did so, discovered that they were much keener to have him back than he imagined, and by that September he had re-enrolled on his course in philosophy and was very happy being back into his studies. When I last heard from Peter, a few years later, he was still loving his academic work and planning to take a Master's degree.

Listing, or writing down with clients, what it is that they need to do can sometimes be a useful means of consolidating this process of moving into action. Around session 18 with Claire (see Chapter 3), for instance, I asked her how she would like to use the remaining seven sessions together. She said that she would like to look at what she might practically do to build on, and sustain, positive change in her life. Consequently, we spent the session together reviewing what we had learnt, so far, about how she could stay out of her despairing and hopeless place. I wrote these down, and gave them back to Claire at the end of the session. Some items were:

- Be bolder emotionally: telling people what I feel and being more up for arguments.
- Talking more supportively to myself, including when I'm feeling down – less harsh and snidy: changing sarcastic self-talk to supportive.
- Challenging myself not to put off decisions, not over-analysing – just doing it.

Critical reflections

Are we really free?

The assumption behind the theory and practice discussed in this chapter is that we are fundamentally choice-making beings, but how free are we really? Recent neuropsychological evidence, for instance, suggests that decision-related brain activity may occur up to ten seconds before a person is actually aware of making choices (e.g., Soon, Brass, Heinze & Haynes, 2008). In other words, as Libet, Gleason, Wright and Pearl (1983: 640) write, 'the brain evidently "decides" to initiate or, at least, prepare to initiate the act at a time before there is any reportable subjective awareness that such a decision has taken place'. So does this mean that our phenomenological sense of choice-making is actually an illusion (Exercise 4.1): that it is determined by non-conscious, a-volitional brain mechanisms? Much more research is needed here, and it may be that choices do exist but predominantly at a pre-reflective level. Alternatively, it may be that human freedom consists of the capacity to say 'no' to non-volitionally initiated activities (Libet et al., 1983). However, neuropsychological research may provide some important insights into choice and freedom in coming years, and much of it may challenge existential assumptions about human agency.

From a more sociological perspective, there is also the question of whether the existential emphasis on freedom and choice ignores the social and political realities that shape people's lives. Can we really say, for instance, that a young black woman, subject to discrimination in education, housing and employment, is really free? Indeed, would it not be insulting to focus on her 'freedom': ignoring (or, worse, dismissing) the external factors that powerfully affect her life? Here, however, it is important to remember that an existential approach always sees freedom as curtailed by a wide range of limitations, and these will be explored much more fully in the following chapter.

Is freedom really good for us?

Another important question is whether a greater sense of freedom and choice does, ultimately, contribute to a greater sense of wellbeing. Evidence here is very limited. On the one hand, as we saw in Chapter 3, people who are more authentic do experience greater wellbeing and less mental health problems, and one aspect of this authenticity is a willingness to act in accordance with one's own beliefs and values (Cooper & Joseph, in press). There is also evidence that a greater sense of control in one's life is associated with greater wellbeing (Spector et al., 2002). On the other hand, however, as we noted earlier, there is research to suggest that the more choices people have, the more overwhelmed and miserable they can end up feeling (Schwartz, 2005; Vohs & Baumeister, 2004). Certainly, as the research demonstrates, making choices requires mental effort and resources (Vohs & Baumeister, 2004). Hence, it may be that some people are genuinely better off with less awareness of the choices open to them.

Is the privileging of autonomy a western cultural narrative?

The existential emphasis on actualising one's freedom could also be criticised for privileging a particular western, patriarchal, late capitalist narrative on how people should be. That is, it prioritises such values as independence and autonomy over the kinds of relational, inter-dependent qualities discussed in Chapter 2. Existential authors like May (1969a: 283), however, *have* tried to give a more balanced account. For instance, he writes that the task of human beings 'is to unite love and will'. Most interestingly, perhaps, de Beauvoir (1948a) suggests that it is only through the relational task of facilitating the freedom of the other (as in the I–Thou stance, Chapter 2), that we can find our own. That is, if others are enslaved, our freedom is meaningless and empty. We need others to be agentic and choice-making to give our own choices meaning.

Personalising practice

From a pluralistic perspective, the methods discussed in this chapter will be more or less helpful for certain clients at a certain point in time. A client, for instance, who feels responsible for the abuse that he experienced as a child, may find it very damaging to be encouraged to think about his own choices in relation to this event.

Based on the analysis presented in this chapter, we can hypothesise that exploring freedom and choice may be most helpful for clients who:

- Want to work out what to do for the future, or specifically want to look at the choices that are available to them.
- Are facing choices, and have the potential to change how things are for the future.
- Have a belief in free will, want to take responsibility for themselves, and are aligned with the idea that how they live their lives is up to them.
- Are stuck in their lives, and are avoiding – or afraid of – making choices.
- Would welcome being pushed by their therapist (even given a proverbial 'kick up the backside').
- Do not understand, or do not like, how they are responding to circumstances.

Summary

From an existential standpoint, we are fundamentally choice-making beings, and the choices we make profoundly influence the way we have – and can – develop. However, acknowledging this can create anxiety, such that people may develop strategies to avoid an acknowledgement of their freedom and responsibility. This may have short-term benefits, but can ultimately lead to psychological difficulties. Hence, existential therapists aim to help clients recover their sense of freedom and possibility, and act on it. This may simply involve using agentic language and acknowledging the anxiety of making choices. It can also involve challenging clients to acknowledge their freedom, and the ways in which they may tend to evade an awareness of it. Clients can also be helped to make constructive decisions, and to move from decision-making to action.

Questions for reflections and discussion

- 'An individual who abuses alcohol has a choice about whether or not to do so'. Discuss.
- To what extent do you agree with the existential hypothesis that psychological difficulties are brought about by the choices that we make in our lives?
- How important do you think it is, in therapy, to help clients acknowledge their capacity for freedom and choice?

Recommended reading

Yalom, I. (1980) *Existential Psychotherapy*. *Part II*. New York: Basic Books. Definitive exploration of freedom and responsibility and its role in therapy.

May, R. (1981) *Freedom and Destiny*. London: W.W. Norton and Co. Existential exploration of freedom and its relationship to the concept of destiny.

Fromm, E. (1942) *The Fear of Freedom*. London: Routledge. Classic exploration of freedom and our fear of it.

Farber, L.H. (2000) *The Ways of the Will* (exp. edn). New York: Basic Books. Profound existential insights into the nature of the will and its relationship to anxiety and relatedness from one of the sages of existential psychotherapy.

Sartre, J.-P. (1996) Existentialism. In L. Cahoone (ed.), *From Modernism to Postmodernism: An Anthology* (pp. 259–265). Cambridge, MA: Blackwells Publishers Ltd. Useful, accessible summary of Sartre's existentialist position.

5

Limitations

This chapter discusses the existential understandings that:

- Human freedom is always constrained by a range of unavoidable limitations, including mortality, tensions, paradoxes and embodiment.
- Wellbeing comes from facing the limitations of existence.

It then goes on to describe the practices of:

- Empathising with the anxiety of facing limitations.
- Helping clients to acknowledge their limitations.
- Helping clients to identify ways in which they may evade facing their limitations.
- Helping clients to make choices within their limitations.

Halfway through writing this chapter, I realised that I was really struggling with it. When I thought about why, I realised that I really do not like limitations: they make me feel bored, depleted and powerless. Perhaps it is because I am a youngest sibling: for me, limits are like a bossy older sister telling you what to do – 'You can't do this', 'There's not time to do that', 'You need to be sensible and prioritise what you want to do'. I tend to rail against limits, and always hope and believe that there's a way around them. Often there is; but, from an existential perspective, sometimes there is not; and denying the immovable limits of life is like coming up against a wall and continually trying to walk through it. Few of us like to meet walls in life, particularly when we are trying to get somewhere. However, from an existential stance, if we can acknowledge them and reassess the situation, we have the possibility of making the most of what we can within those boundaries.

Like me, for instance, you may be someone who wants to think that there are 48 hours in the day; or that you have an invisible duplicate self who is able to do all the things that you are not able to do yourself (to explore your own relationship to limitations, see Exercise 5.1). So you take on more and more, say 'yes' to whatever is asked of – or offered to – you, and live in the delusion that somehow it will all get done. But the harsh, unforgiving reality is that a day only has 24 hours, and out of those you need to sleep for about eight. And then you may want to see friends, or spend time with children, or have an intimate evening with a partner, or relax in front of *Game of Thrones* – as well as all the work tasks that you have taken on. So things do not get done, people get let down, and you experience a constant stress in your life that you are not doing as much as you should be.

A few years back, I came to terms with the fact that I just could not do it all. I needed to acknowledge what the boundaries were, and that I had to start saying 'no' to things. I made it my mission in life to say 'no' to three things before breakfast. I did not like it – still do not like it – but at least I felt saner and that life was a bit more in control. What is more, the things that I was left doing were more the things I really wanted to do – I had prioritised and made better use of what time there really was. So, just as an existential perspective encourages us to face up to the reality of our experiencing (Chapter 3) and our freedom (Chapter 4), so it encourages us to face up to the reality of our limitations, and to make the most of the life we have within them. Sometimes (but only sometimes), bossy older sisters may just be right.

Exercise 5.1 Your relationship to limitations

Aim

- To explore how you feel, and respond, to limitations in your own life.

The exercise

Take a few minutes to answer the following questions:

- How do you relate to limitations in your life? Do you find it easy to accept them? Do you rail against them? Do you tend to deny they exist?
- What limitations do you find most difficult to acknowledge?
- What do you imagine your life would be like without any limitations?

Understandings

The limits of existence

As we have seen in Chapter 4, from an existential perspective, we are fundamentally free, but existential thinkers also hold that that freedom is 'hedged in' in innumerable ways. These are the inescapable *limits, givens, existentials* or *boundary conditions* of existence: our *facticity*, the things that we cannot choose or change (Jacobsen, 2007; Jaspers, 1986; Langdridge, 2012). Some of the key givens that existential thinkers have highlighted are:

- Mortality: the fact that we are beings-towards-death.
- Tensions: that we are always pulled in different directions by competing wants.
- Paradoxes: that the more we try to get something, the more we may undermine its attainment.
- Embodiment and sexuality.
- Uncertainty and ambiguity.
- Social, economic and political givens.
- Being-in-the-world: that we always exist in relation to the world around us (see Chapter 3); and also inhabit a natural world and universe that is not of our making.
- Thrownness: that we are born into a world that is not of our making.
- Temporality: that we live 'in' time.
- Chance: the 'huge tide of accident' surrounding our lives.

(Barker & Langdridge, 2013; Cohn, 1997; Heidegger, 1996; Jaspers, 1932b; Milton, 2010a; Spinelli, 2015)

We can also consider our being-with-others (Chapter 2) as an existential given (though Yalom, 1980, places more emphasis on our aloneness);

along with our freedom (Chapter 4), and our being-towards-the-future (Chapter 6).

The relationship between freedom and givens, as understood existentially, is presented in Figure 5.1. From this perspective, we always have freedom, but the choices and options available to us – and the consequences of our choices – are always determined by factors beyond our control.

More than that, though, from an existential standpoint, it is the limitations of life that give meaning and significance to our choices. If we were not to die, for instance, it would not really matter whether we chose a career as a banker, miner, or astronaut – we could do them all. But the finitude of life means that a choice for one thing is a choice *against* something else, and that means that our choices *really are* choices, and not like some computer game where we can re-spawn if we get ourselves killed. From an existential perspective, then, 'Freedom and determinism give birth to each other' (May, 1981: 84). We exist as freedoms-towards-limitations, and we live out our lives suspended between these two poles of existence (Schneider & May, 1995).

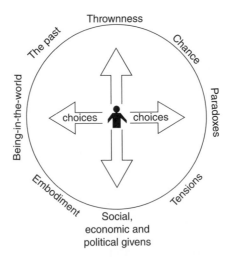

Figure 5.1 Freedom within limitations

Mortality

Our being-towards-death is perhaps the most fundamental limitation of human existence. Unavoidably, inexorably we are moving towards the ending of our lives. Death is like the last stop on the train line that we have to get off at, with no possibility of a return trip. It is also a journey that we must make alone. As Heidegger (1962: 284) argues, death 'is in every case mine', for no-one can die our deaths for us, or save us from this possibility. And even if we believe in an afterlife, *this* existence is still moving towards its ending: the life that we have here and now in the context and with the people around us.

Of course, if we were like an ant to which termination simply happened, death would not be an issue. We would exist; and then no more. So the key point for Heidegger (1962) is not simply that we *die*, but that we know – at a pre-reflective level – that we are moving towards death. It is this knowledge of our *mortality* that is the given of existence (see Exercise 5.2).

Exercise 5.2   Facing mortality

Aim

- To explore how it feels to consciously focus on your mortality.

The exercise

- Draw a line on a piece of paper. At the start of the line, mark your birth, at the end of your line, your death.
- Now mark where you feel that you currently are on this line (see example, below).

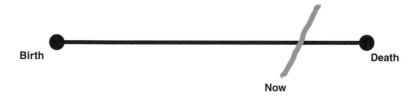

Birth   Death

Now

- Take five minutes to reflect on this line. What feelings and thoughts does it evoke in you looking at it?

Comment

In my experience, people have very different responses to this exercise. Some feel quite shaken by bringing this awareness of their mortality to the

(Continued)

(Continued)

fore, others are indifferent. Some people are surprised by where they put themselves on the line: realising that they are further along than they assumed they were, or noticing that they have been fairly optimistic about the time they assume they have left.

Variations

- Having time to talk these questions through with a partner, say for 10 minutes each, can be a very useful exercise within a training group context.
- For an exercise that you may find much more challenging, to the point that you may really not want to do it (and please do not if you feel uncomfortable doing so), consider doing this line for someone you love, like a partner or a child. How does it feel to reflect on *their* mortality, and how does this feel compared with reflecting on your own?

There is also the existential reality that those we love will die: our partners, our friends, our children. This is discussed far less in the existential literature. Indeed, Yalom (1999) suggests that we are concerned by the death of others because it reminds us of our own. In my experience, however, the fear of others dying is often of far greater concern than of our own demise (see variation in Exercise 5.2). This is the indignity, absurdity and meaninglessness that those around us are also making their own individual journeys towards extinction (Orange, in Friedman, Carel, Hassan & Orange, 2012). And, just as no-one can stand in for our deaths or save us from it, so we cannot do this for others. We are powerless to interfere with the ultimate mortality of those we love.

Tensions

Another given of existence that has been highlighted by existential authors is that we always exist within a web of *tensions,* or *dilemmas* (Spinelli, 2001; van Deurzen, 2012a; Wahl, 2003). This means that, in our lives, we are intrinsically and unavoidably pulled between competing wants (see Figure 5.2). For instance, we may want to be independent of the demands of others, but also to feel safe and comfortable in close relationships. Or we want to be healthy and fit, but also to enjoy life and gorge ourselves on unhealthy foods and alcohol. Some examples of the tensions that have emerged in my therapeutic work with clients include the following:

- Jane wanted desperately to be approved of by others and be part of 'the group', but at the same time she believed passionately in being authentic and did not believe it was morally right to conform to others' opinion.
- Sofia wanted to be there for her friends and support them, but at the same time did not feel she had the 'mental space' for others and wanted to focus on her own difficulties.
- Henrik wanted a job that provided routine and structure, but at the same time felt bored and limited when he worked within a highly organised environment.
- Petra wanted to spend her time watching TV and smoking marijuana, but she also wanted to be active, get on with things, and prepare for the future.

Here, the key point from an existential perspective is not simply that people have tensions in their lives, but that people will *always* have tensions in their lives – and often the same ones, resurfacing in different guises at different times. In other words, it is a given of existence that we will always be pulled in different directions by competing wants; with no possibility of final integration, harmony or resolution. So, from this perspective, Sofia may always want both to support her friends and to focus in on her self; and there may be no means by which she can ever entirely transcend this tension. In other words, contrary to the new age mantra, you *cannot* have it all. Get one thing you want and, by the very nature of existence, you will be losing out on something else you desire (see Exercise 5.3). As Spinelli (2001) puts it, you cannot overcome tensions; you can only live through them.

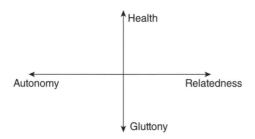

Figure 5.2 Tensions of existence: an illustration

Exercise 5.3 Exploring tensions in your life

Aim

- To help you become aware of the tensions in your life.
- To help you reflect on the usefulness of the concept of tensions.

The exercise

- Take 10 minutes to think about the tensions that exist, currently, in your life. These are desires that are pulling against each other: for instance, the desire for closeness to your children versus the desire for development at work.
- Take 5 minutes to reflect on how it is to think about yourself in terms of this web of tensions. Does it fit your lived-experiences? Do you find it helpful or unhelpful? What feelings does it evoke?

Comment

In my experience, many people find that this way of thinking about their lives fits closely with their own lived-experiences. Some also find it reassuring to think that these tensions have always been, and will always be, there – they can ease up on battling to resolve them. Others, however, find it quite a 'static' model which does not allow for personal development or change.

Variations

- You may find it useful to draw, or map out, the different tensions, as with Figure 5.2.
- Having time to talk these questions through with a partner, say for 15 minutes each, can be a very useful exercise within a training group context.
- Try mapping out the tensions for a client of yours: perhaps one that you are struggling with. What do you learn about doing this?

Understanding human existence in terms of unavoidable tensions has resonances with a psychodynamic approach, which also tends to construe human beings in terms of ineradicably competing wants. This stretches right back to Freud (1923), whose model of human being pits the *id*, the cauldron of seething desire, against the socially and morally sanctioned needs of the *superego*. From a psychodynamic perspective, this conflict can be tamed through the mediating forces of the *ego*, but – as with an existential perspective – can never be entirely transcended:

awareness and conscious control is the best we can hope for. What this model does contrast with, however, is a more humanistic understanding of being (e.g., Rogers, 1961; Stiles et al., 1990; Vargiu, 1974), which tends to emphasise 'growth' and the possibility of synthesis and integration of wants. This reflects the generally greater optimism of the humanistic approaches as compared with the existential or psychodynamic stances.

Paradoxes

Paradoxes, like tensions, are contradictions in the very fabric of being that makes a final state of 'perfection' unattainable. Jaspers (1932a; 218) writes 'They are not resolved but only exacerbated by clear thinking, and solutions can only be finite, can resolve only particular conflicts in existence, while a look at the whole will always show the limiting insolubilities'. While tensions, however, are conflicts that are unique to the individual, paradoxes have a more universal quality. They are conflicts in being that we all must face. Furthermore, while tensions refer to a pull between opposing ends of a polarity, with paradoxes, it is the very striving for one thing that undermines the possibility of its achievement. For instance:

- The more we strive for happiness, the more frustrated and miserable we can become.
- The more we know, the less we may understand.
- The more we try to be something different, the more we may stay the same.
- The more we accept how we are, the more we may change.
- The more we want people to like us, the less likeable we may become.
- The more someone pushes us away, the more we can want them; the more we know we can 'have' someone, the less we may want them.
- The more we care about life, the more we may fear losing it.

Stella was an example of someone struggling with the paradoxes of life. She was in her 60s when she came to therapy, and had recently been through a cancer diagnosis and treatment. She sensed that she did not have long to live. As a consequence, she felt that she wanted to make the most of the time that she did have. However, in therapy, Stella recognised that the more she strived to make the most of every day, the more anxious and stressed she actually became. In other words, paradoxically, the more she tried to live her life to the full, the less she actually did so; yet if she just tried to relax and take each day as it came, she felt she was wasting what precious time she had. Later in this chapter, we will look at how an existential approach may help clients to address such paradoxes of being.

Embodiment and sexuality

Contrary to a Cartesian position, which separates mind from body, existential authors have emphasised the fundamentally *embodied* nature of human existence (Cohn, 2002; Merleau-Ponty, 1962). 'That is, we are inextricably bodily beings, we *are* our bodies, and it is only through our bodies that we can engage with, encounter, and "rise towards" our world' (Cooper, 2003b: 21). In this respect, we can think of being-in-a-body as another inescapable given of existence. We have a physical form and even if we try to entirely cut ourselves off from it (as Laing, 1965 suggests some people diagnosed with schizophrenia attempt to do) we cannot escape our bodily confines. We also have physical qualities such as height and levels of attractiveness that may not be easily modifiable. There is also our health status. Illness can come to us whether we want it or not – arthritis, cancer, high blood pressure, chronic fatigue, and ultimately death (see above) – and we must make our choices in relation to it (Jacobsen, 2007). Indeed, as suggested earlier, when we are brought face-to-face with such severe limitations as bodily illness, our capacity to choose and the consequences of those choices might be brought into much sharper relief.

As embodied beings, we also have a particular psycho-physiological constitution that is not of our choosing. Research suggests, for instance, that genetic factors account for around 29% of the total variance along a range of personality traits (Plomin, DeFries, McClearn & McGuffin, 2001). This means that our choices are circumscribed by a range of hormonal or neurochemical processes beyond our control: the *genetic given* (Cooper, 2001b, available on the companion website). So, for instance, in the face of loss, one person may be more biologically predisposed to experience sadness than another. From our evolutionary heritage, we may also come into the world with particular innate wants: for instance, for food, or attachment to others (Milton & Gillies, 2007).

EXISTENTIAL
THERAPY
AND
GENETICS

A closely related given of existence is that we are sexual beings (Cohn, 2002; Milton, 2014), even if that is in the form of asexuality. We have sexual organs, sexual desires, and exist in a world-with-others where sexual arousal and contact are always a possibility. In this respect, sexuality permeates our being, it is 'always present like an atmosphere' and 'spreads forth like an odour or like a sound' (Merleau-Ponty, 1996: 168, in Smith-Pickard, 2014: 81). Sexuality is much more than just the sexual act; it is the ever-present ground from which sex emerges (Smith-Pickard, 2014).

Spinelli (2015: 21) has joked that, when dividing up the topics of interest, 'the "gods of psychotherapy" bequeathed psychoanalysis with "sex" while the existentialists got "death"'. However, in recent years, there has been much more interest and debate in the existential field regarding the sexual dimension of being: for instance, whether our sexual orientation is a choice or a given, and whether gay-affirmative therapies are consistent with existential practice (see, in particular, Milton, 2014).

Uncertainty

De Beauvoir (1948a: 9) describes existentialism as a philosophy of ambiguity; while Spinelli (2015) suggests that uncertainty is one of the key existential themes. This, then, is another existential given: that nothing is ever certain, that meanings are never fixed but must constantly be 'won' (de Beauvoir, 1948a: 129). As we saw in Chapter 3, for instance, I might describe myself as a particular kind of person, or claim that I had a particular background, but these 'narratives' are never static realities. Reflectively, or pre-reflectively, I know that there are always other narratives, other possible accounts.

Here, as discussed by Spinelli (2015), we can see parallels with a wider pluralistic worldview, which holds open the possibility of multiple co-existing 'truths'. And, of course, we reach the paradox that these existential and pluralistic views, themselves, should be held with uncertainty. We need to be uncertain about uncertainty – and even uncertain about that. Life, from this standpoint, is a complex, interconnected web of possibilities, with no ultimate ability to stand outside of this nexus to see how things 'really' are.

Social, economic and political givens

As beings who inhabit a world with others, we also exist amongst a multitude of social, economic, political, cultural and historical givens (de Beauvoir, 1948a; Langdridge, 2012). We are thrown into a world, for instance, that has particular laws, economic circumstances and power structures, all of which may determine the possibilities available to us. Our socio-cultural circumstances may also be very different depending on our social grouping. Black existential writers, for instance, have described how racism becomes a powerful frame within which black people must make their choices (Gordon, 1997; Henry, 1997).

Being as in-the-world

In many respects, as discussed in Chapter 3, what this existential perspective on limitations comes down to is an understanding of human being as always *in-the-world*. That is, we cannot simply modify or re-envision our existence at will. Rather, who and how we are is shaped by the world around us: a world of brute *facticity* with givens that are not of our making. This, as discussed in Chapter 3, is at the level of primary experiencing. However, it is also at the level of secondary experiencing, in terms of the particular conscious choices that we are able to make. I want to eat a tub of ice cream every meal time without putting on weight; I can't. I'd like to work three hours a day and become the most respected psychologist of my day; it is not going to happen. At every moment of my existence, I am face-to-face with a cold, unflinching reality that is indifferent to my particular choices and wants. It is not *my* fantasy world, it is a world that is fundamentally other; and however much I rage or grieve at it, it remains unmoved.

An example: Paul wanted Nancy to be with him. He was a young man in a loveless marriage, and his affair with Nancy – an old school friend – was the one thing that he described as giving him a sense of excitement and passion in life. Paul desperately wanted to begin a new relationship with Nancy, but he knew that Nancy would never commit to him. She travelled widely, had several other romantic relationships, and had made it clear to Paul that, however fond she was of him, she would not want to settle down together. Paul tried hard to think his way around this given of the situation: maybe Nancy would come round, maybe his marriage was not so bad, maybe Nancy was not so great after all. But the existential reality was this: he wanted to be with her, she did not want to be with him, it really hurt.

The denial of limitations

The pain of limitations

To face limits in life, then, means to experience disappointment, sadness and hurt. It also means to experience the anxiety of not being totally in control of our lives (Wolfe, 2008): that we can be profoundly impacted by such givens as uncertainty, illness or bodily desires. And, indeed, there is a large body of rigorous empirical research in the field of 'experimental existential psychology' and 'Terror Management Theory' to show that people do become more anxious – and strive for a more constant sense of self – when they are reminded of the given of mortality (Pyszczynski, Greenberg & Koole, 2004). These limitations may be particularly painful in contemporary western culture, where we are led to believe that every portion of our lives is within our control (Farber, 2000b). But the reality is very different. We cannot always get what we want.

Evading and denying our limitations

As with our freedom (Chapter 4) and our experiencing more generally (Chapter 3), therefore, we may try to deny or evade an awareness of the limitations of our lives: ignoring the walls or pretending that they do not exist (Cohn, 1997). With respect to mortality, for instance, Heidegger (1962: 295) writes that, 'Proximally and for the most part', human being 'covers up its ownmost Being-towards-death, fleeing in the face of it'. That is, as the evidence suggests (Arndt, Cook & Routledge, 2004), we tend to deny our own mortality: keeping it at the level of primary experiencing. Indeed, Yalom (1980: 41) argues that the terror evoked by death is so 'ubiquitous' and 'of such magnitude', that 'a considerable portion of one's life energy is consumed' in its denial. Ways in which we might try to do this include:

- Seeing death as something that happens to others, but never to ourselves.
- Believing that we are so special that death could never happen to us.
- Trying to 'rationalise away' death: for instance, by reassuring ourselves that when we are dead we will be dead, so we will not feel anything.
- Believing in an afterlife.
- Conforming: if we stay within the safety of the crowd, death cannot get to us.
- Striving to produce things that will live on after our physical ending, such as children, books or notoriety (an 'immortality project').
- Believing that we have an *ultimate rescuer* – a person, spirit or force – that can save us from death.
- Adopting a frivolous, carefree or risk-taking attitude towards life – pretending that life does not really matter to us.

(Baumeister, 1991; Becker, 1973; Heidegger, 1962; Jaspers, 1932a; May, 1999; Yalom, 1980; adapted from Cooper & Adams, 2005)

Similarly, clients may tend to deny, or evade, an awareness of other limitations. Femi, for instance, was an ambitious young solicitor who came to therapy because she was having problems with her boyfriend, Pete. Femi described how much she loved Pete and really wanted to make the relationship work. However, she said that she found Pete distant, unloving and critical, and was upset about an affair he had had some months before. At the start of session four, Femi described a big argument that they had had the previous evening. 'Pete was irritable from the moment I walked in', she said, 'he complains that I'm never about and treat the flat like a bed and breakfast'. When we unpacked this further (Chapter 3), it turned out that Femi had been at work until nine in the evening, when she had promised Pete she would be home by six. 'I love my work', said Femi, slightly defensively, 'and I know that at my age, if I'm going to do ok, I need to really put all my energies into it'.

'Given all the energy you want to put into work', I asked Femi, 'Do you think you can also put the energy you want into your relationship?'

Femi smiled wryly. 'Hmm...' she said, 'Can we talk about something else!' Femi laughed and I laughed, but the point was a serious one and something that we came back to several times. Femi, entirely understandably, wanted to have it all. She wanted to be a committed, successful lawyer; and she also wanted to spend lots of time with her partner in a romantic, intense relationship. But the reality was, her time and energies were limited. If she was spending 12 hours a day, seven days a week, on her work, she was not going to be able to spend the time with Pete that she wanted to.

The pathogenic consequences of denying our limitations

For Femi, a denial of life's limitations brought some short term relief. But, in the long term, as with primary experiencing and freedom, the costs of denying such limitations are likely to outweigh the benefits (Strasser & Strasser, 1997). This is for two key reasons.

First, when we deny the limits of life – as with any aspects of reality – they do not go away. Rather, they continue to haunt us, tucked away in the corners of our pre-reflected experiencing. So we know that death is still lurking, or that time constraints are impossible to meet; and this can leave us feeling unsettled, fragile and on edge: anxious that, at any moment, we may be pounced on by the realities of our situation. What is more, as we have seen previously, because our defences against reality will inevitably falter, we can end up developing increasingly neurotic strategies to try and shore them up. For instance, we might try to protect ourselves from an awareness of our own mortality by believing that we are special: that we are such a unique and inimitable person that death could never happen to us. But when that illusion is temporarily shattered and reality breaks through – perhaps by a serious illness, perhaps by the death of someone close to us – we can experience intense anxiety, and fight to reconstitute our defences. So specialness becomes narcissism, and narcissism becomes morbid self-interest; and, for Yalom (1980), it is these defences that we build – and then have to fight to protect and rebuild – that is the root of all neuroticism. Far better, then, to look such givens as death in the face – *Staring at the Sun*, as Yalom (2008) titles his recent book – and deal with the anxiety at its original source, rather than investing huge amounts of energy in constructing, reconstructing, and fearing the collapse of, our psychological defences.

Second, as Femi found out, if we deny the reality of the situation that we are in – with all of its limitations – then we are less able to find effective, appropriate and satisfying ways of moving forward within it. Instead, we live in a world of 'extravagance' (Binswanger, 1963): of false hopes, optimism and ideals that do not allow us to genuinely tackle life. And, in attempting to 'will what cannot be willed' (Farber, 2000b: 79), we may experience a constant frustration and anxiety.

Hence, from an existential perspective, an inauthentic life is one in which we deny our limitations as well as our freedom. Indeed, for Sartre (1958), 'bad faith' is a constant weaselling between seeing ourselves as all-determined ('I *have* to do X') and all-powerful ('I can do whatever I want'); as opposed to an authentic acknowledgement of our freedom-within-limitations.

Authentically facing our limitations

Acknowledging the limits of life may be painful, but it can also act as a wake-up call (Martin, Campbell & Henry, 2004), that helps us focus on realistically working out which way to go. So once Femi came to terms with the fact that she could not commit 100% to her work *and* 100% to her relationship, she could start looking at realistic and work-able ways forward: for instance, by making sure she always left work by 8pm, and by trying to take Pete on work trips with her. Similarly, as Heidegger (1962) has argued, if we face our mortality with open eyes, and contemplate what time we really have left (see Exercise 5.1), we are forced to acknowledge that we cannot postpone living: 'that our procrastinations, excuses and attention to trivialities eat in to the very limited time that we have. Hence, we are motivated to take charge of our lives (Koestenbaum, 1971), and to focus on those things that really matter to us' (Cooper & Adams, 2005: 80). And, indeed, research suggests that facing the given of death does sharpen personal concerns (Martin et al., 2004) and lead to greater growth (Yalom & Lieberman, 1991); with people who are more accepting of death having higher wellbeing (Neimeyer, 1997–1998).

To be authentic, then, means to acknowledge that we can choose, but we cannot choose everything; we are shaped by our circumstances, but we always have possibilities within that. From an existential standpoint, being authentic means being willing to inhabit the world in all its complex, messy, disorientating reality; and to take responsibility for our choices and actions within it. 'To live the tension of the world is the highest test of our being' (Buber, 1964: 143).

Methods

So how can clients be helped to come to terms with the limitations of their existences and make the most of the lives that they have within them? Many of the methods here are similar to those that can help clients to face the given of their freedom.

Empathising with the anxiety of facing limitations

Just as we can empathise with the anxiety that our clients can feel when faced with their freedom so, from an existential perspective, we can stay with, validate and normalise the feelings that clients may experience when facing the limitations of existence, such as despair, hopelessness or frustration. If a client is expressing fear at the thought of their death, for instance, or regret at the fact that they cannot change their past, this may be something that a therapist can acknowledge, reflect and legitimise. For instance:

Client: It's so stupid of me to be so worried about getting older. I should just accept it.

Therapist: I can really see how frustrated you are with all that worry, but it also does kind of make sense to me. Like you say, it does seem that you've got less options open to you now, and that you've got less time left.

Client: I keep on changing my mind about this guy I'm seeing. I'm driving myself crazy as well as everyone else.

Therapist: You hate being really torn about it, but I guess there's a reality that the two things you're feeling really strongly are both legitimate. You love him, and I can really see your passion; but you also don't want to mess up things with your kids. I have to say, if it was me there, I think I'd be struggling with that tension too, and I think you're doing brilliantly in the middle of it all.

A more extended example of empathising with the anxiety of facing limitations is given in the companion website.

In helping to normalise clients' feelings about facing the limitations of existence, it may also be useful for therapists to self-disclose their own struggles and difficulties in the face of these givens (Spinelli, 2001: 167). For instance:

EMPATHISING WITH THE ANXIETY OF FACING LIMITATIONS: NOTES

- 'There's a real hopelessness, isn't there, about getting older and older; and I guess I know for myself that that can sometimes feel really difficult and out of control.'
- 'What becomes clear, the more we talk about it, is how complex and uncertain the reality is. And I know that when I'm facing that I can also try and make things more black-and-white, which then makes things even more confused.'

Used judiciously, such self-disclosures may help to create 'a *mutual* acceptance of our shared powerlessness and uncertainty in the face of the "impossible dilemma of being human"'(Spinelli, 2001: 168).

Helping clients to acknowledge the limitations of existence

A step on from validating the feelings associated with limitations is to actively invite clients to acknowledge them. At the least directive end, this may simply involve 'nursing the shudder rather than anesthetizing it' (Yalom, 1980: 166). An extended example of this comes from 19 year old Petra, introduced earlier, who had been encouraged to attend therapy by her father. Petra's father worried that she was doing nothing with her life, and Petra worried too: she had little sense of where she wanted to go in life, spent most of her time smoking marijuana and watching TV, and felt very envious of her friends who were all progressing in various directions. At the start of our work together, Petra indicated that her primary goal had been to live independently from her parents and, to be able to fund that, she had recently taken on an apprentice role at a local estate agent. However, a few weeks into therapy she had quit the job, and subsequently moved back in with her parents. In our ninth session together, the dialogue proceeded along the following lines:

Petra 1:   I just– I know I should be looking for a job, looking on the internet, but I just– once I start thinking about it and I sit down at the laptop and I– there's so much other things to do, like I check my Facebook, and then I– you know, stupid games and things. And then– like it's eight o'clock and I just want to watch TV, go out for a smoke. Just goes so quickly.

Mick 1:   So can you take me through that. Just say again. So there's you– you're sitting at the laptop... *[this is an invitation to Petra to phenomenologically unpack her experiencing, Chapter 3].*

Petra 2:   Yeah, I'm sitting there and I'm looking– I might be like starting with Facebook, then YouTube, then I go to some of the job sites and I'm looking– searching... *so* boring, and, you know, that's even before I've started thinking about filling anything in. So, like, five minutes if I'm doing good, and then... I've probably got something else from Facebook by then– on my mobile– so it's maybe– probably another hour or two before...

Mick 2:   ... Before you go back to the jobs. And what's that like– like I get a sense it's almost– like it's painful for you to be staying on those job sites.

Petra 3:   *[Laughs]* Yeah– yup– It's so– I just think, 'Jeez, I just can't be arsed.' You know, it's so– it's such a mountain to climb and I ... You know, one thing I was thinking about was how things used to be *so* easy when I was little. It was no effort, nothing was any effort. Like if I wanted to– and I just think, these days, like if I want to do something, you know, I've probably got to put so much effort in; and I do sometimes think, 'What the *beep*', you know, like I just can't be arsed. And that's probably why– with the estate agent– who wants to spend all day looking up pricing codes and that.

Mick 3:   So I can see you– you really hate making that effort but it sounds like– you seem to be saying that maybe if you want to get on with things and get somewhere in your life that's something you *do* need to do.

Petra 4:   Yeah, it's probably the reality is that if I am going to do something with my life I need to get off my arse and do something. I'm not going to get very far just sitting on my couch watching TV and getting stoned. Not unless I want to star on Jeremy Kyle *[laughs]*.

In this vignette, Petra is beginning to recognise one of the givens of existence: that if you do not put much in to something, you are unlikely to get much out. Petra – quite understandably, perhaps – would love to be able to move forward in her life through smoking marijuana, watching TV, and chatting with her friends on Facebook. The existential reality, however, is that if she wants an income and to live independently, she is going to have to do more than that. In this vignette, Petra was recognising this given for herself, and my role, at *Mick 3*, was simply to reflect and validate this learning.

However, as a firmer existential practice, it may also be appropriate to directly suggest to clients that they are facing particular limitations or givens of existence. The following dialogue, for instance, comes a few sessions later with Petra, as we continue to explore her process of looking for jobs:

Petra 1:   ... and I look at it and I just think, you know, I just think– Christ– Jeez– like, who's going to do that? What a crap job. I'd rather be getting stoned even if I don't have any money.

Mick 1:   So it sounds like most of the jobs you look at– all the jobs you look at, you look at them and they really don't– just don't seem to be something you want to do.

Petra 2:   Yeah, totally, well... you know, like a few of them are ok, but I never look at a job and think, 'That's *definitely* what I want to do'. A few of them look ok but there's never definitely *the* job. You know, the one that I get really excited about and think, like, I *definitely* want to do that.

Mick 2:   Ok, so what would that be?

Petra 3:   [*Pause*] I dunno. [*Pause*] I dunno. Clown... furniture tester... [*laughs*] professional dope smoker [*we both laugh*]. *What?*

Mick 3:   [*Smiling*] You know, I know you're joking here but– I just think– you know, I do get a sense that your line here is a bit 'I won't go for a job until the perfect one comes up,' and I just wonder if that's realistic. I guess there is a reality that you're 19, you're recently out of school, and it's going to take a while ... before you get to do what you really want to do. And, I think– you know, even if you've got a hundred PhDs there's maybe not likely to be ever the perfect job. Maybe it's one of the things about life that the chances of the perfect thing being out there ... for any of us ... is pretty slim. And if you're waiting for it to turn up you could– you know, there's a risk– you could be waiting for ever. [*Pause*] Mm...

Petra 4:   [*Long pause*] I dunno, you know, like furniture tester sounded a lot better! [*laughs*]. Yeah, yeah, I know what you mean. It's just... Yeah, I mean I've been kind of looking for ages and the reality is that nothing perfect has shown up at all, and given that– I don't really know, what it is I can't really see– you know, it's not that likely that I'll suddenly find the perfect job. But I do keep on waiting.

Mick 4:   Yeah, I know you do. And I can really understand that. But at the same time there's a reality, isn't there, that while you're waiting for the perfect job to come up you're also feeling really frustrated and unfulfilled and perhaps losing the time when you could be setting something up. And I guess, you know– if I'm honest, I just worry– and you also do too– that you could end up waiting forever.

In this vignette, at *Mick 3*, Petra is directly encouraged to consider whether she needs to acknowledge a given of existence: that there is no perfect life just around the corner waiting to present itself to her. At *Mick 4*, another given is introduced, albeit more implicitly: that time is limited, and that therefore a choice for one thing is a choice *against* something else. Hopefully, this is communicated with some warmth and even humour, but there is also some degree of firmness: 'These seem to be the boundaries of your existence, what are you going to do within them?'

Helping clients to identify ways in which they may evade facing limits

As with helping clients to see how they may evade their freedom, it may also be useful to help clients consider how they evade or deny an awareness of life's limitations. Do they deny it, for instance, or try to act in ways that reassure them of their omnipotence? Yalom (1989), in his classic series of existential case studies, *Love's Executioner*, gives several examples of this, and how he uses interpretation to help clients identify such defence mechanisms. In one of the cases, for instance, he helps a client with advanced cancer to consider how his attempts to be loved by beautiful women may be a way of trying to buttress his belief that he is no different from anyone else, and thereby not mortally ill. In another case study, he helps a woman to consider whether her obesity is a means of defending herself against the reality of death. Her father became very emaciated before he died and Yalom suggests to her that, perhaps, this is her means of not being like him.

Helping clients to look at how they deal with boundaries and limitations in the therapeutic relationship may also be a useful way of helping them reflect on how they meet limitations in their extra-therapeutic lives (Strasser & Strasser, 1997; Yalom, 1980). Does a client, for instance, rail against the time limits of a session, or avoid thinking about the fact that the therapy will inevitably come to an end?

Helping clients to make choices within their limitations

In some instances, helping clients to acknowledge the limitations of their existence – or the ways in which they evade an awareness of them – may serve to defuse such secondary feelings as shame or guilt. In many other instances, however, the real value of this work is to then support clients to re-evaluate the ways that they are living their lives, and re-decide ways of doing things within the boundaries that do exist. For example, having discussed with Petra the possibility that she may really need to put work in to get a job, and that no perfect job may be attainable at this point, we then went back to looking at what she might actually do. This was in very practical, concrete terms.

Mick 1:   So, ok, you're sitting there at the laptop. And you're thinking, 'Right, an hour on Facebook to start with'.

Petra 1:   No [*laughs*]. No, I'm thinking, 'Right, I need to start looking for some jobs.' And then I maybe try a few sites ... and then I think, 'Ok, just a bit of time on Facebook' and then it ends up hours later.

Mick 2:   Ok, so what we're saying is– what you're acknowledging is that, if you go down that route, you do then end up– you do spend most of the rest of the day on Facebook or playing games. That does happen, doesn't it? *[Here, I am gently pointing out to Petra another unacknowledged given of her existence: that if she starts looking at Facebook, she almost inevitably spends the rest of the day on social media sites.]*

Petra 2:   Yes, I guess mostly, but– I guess I need to just keep myself focused on work and– like, no Facebook until seven in the evening.

Mick 3:   And, can I just ask, Is that– Do you think that's realistic? Are you actually going to be able to do that? *[Again, I am introducing a given here: that she really struggles to do work-related things, and would much rather be on social media sites].*

Petra 3:   Ok, ten in the morning then [*laughs*]. No, seriously, I– I reckon– say, an hour? Like if I'm realistic, I could do an hour, maybe a bit more, then onto Facebook. Then maybe back again for another hour.

Mick 4: Ok, so– and what– like, supposing you're sitting there and five minutes later– because, realistically, that's quite possible isn't it [*Petra:* yeah] that five minutes later you're going to be wanting to go onto Facebook [*Petra is being called back, again, to another reality of how she does things*]. Ok, so you're sitting there and...

Petra 4: I guess it's about saying to myself some of the things that, you know, we discussed. Like, 'If I want to get a job and get away from my parents, I'm just going to have to do this.' I know– it's– that it's not going to happen if I'm messaging and messing– spending all day with friends.

Mick 5: And I guess there might also be something about– about the thing that the perfect job may not be out there, and maybe you need to be a bit wider in what you are– what you're looking for. [*Petra:* mm].

Petra 5: And I think, you know– if I start saying to myself 'Let's have a quick look on Facebook,' I could– I was thinking I could do something like count to 10: '1... 2... 3...' So I don't, you know– so I give myself a bit more time.

In this dialogue with Petra, I am consistently calling her back to make choices within the reality of her situation. She *does* love social media sites, she *does* need to get away from them if she wants to find a job, she *is* unlikely to find the perfect job straight away ... so what is she going to do? These challenges are uncomfortable for Petra, but without acknowledging the reality of her situation, the choices she makes may be unlikely to have any real purchase. She can decide in therapy, for instance, to spend seven hours a day looking at job sites and filling in application forms (*Petra 2*), but if this ignores the fact that she has never managed this in her life before, and that she struggles to do this more than anything else, she may be unlikely to succeed.

Similarly, for Paul, the choices that he had to make in relation to Nancy needed to take into account the fact that she did not want to be with him. It was a painful, brute reality – a bitter disappointment – but after one particularly rejecting conversation with her, he decided that the best way forward was to break contact with her. Paul made this decision outside of therapy, but the therapy had helped him voice – and come to terms with – the reality of her feelings towards him. Therapy was also a place where Paul could talk through this decision, express his feelings of loss, and remind himself that it was the best decision he could make within his given circumstances.

Critical reflections

The *Serenity Prayer*, written by the American theologian Reinhold
Niebuhr, and adopted by Alcoholics Anonymous and other twelve-step
programmes, reads as follows (in its original form):

> God, give me grace to accept with serenity
> the things that cannot be changed,
> Courage to change the things
> which should be changed,
> and the Wisdom to distinguish
> the one from the other.
>
> (en.wikipedia.org/wiki/Serenity_Prayer)

In many respects, this articulates the essence of an existential approach
to working with both freedom and limitations: helping clients to
improve what they can in their lives, but within the context of acknowledging and accepting what they cannot.

How do we know what is a limitation?

However, perhaps the most challenging aspect of this work is the third
component of this prayer: having the wisdom to know the difference.
Is it really a given, for instance, that Nancy does not want to be with
Paul. She says she does not, but maybe she will change her mind in a
year or two. And perhaps Petra *will* find herself the perfect job through
messaging on Facebook. In this respect, *maybe the greatest limitation of
existence is the uncertainty that we can never know what is a limitation and
what is not.*

An implication of this is that, as therapists, we need to be very
cautious in suggesting to clients that there are certain givens or
limitations of their lives. We may be wrong, and we may be
encouraging clients to come to terms with something that they could,
actually, change. So it is probably best to introduce limitations in a
tentative way, through phrases such as 'I wonder if...', 'It seems
like...', 'Do you think that...' rather than 'It is...', 'You are...' or 'You
can't'. Also, and particularly from a pluralistic standpoint, it would
seem important that any understanding of limitations emerges
through a collaborative client–therapist dialogue, as was the case with
Petra. A third implication is that it may be better to think of limitations
and freedom as existing on a spectrum, rather than being all-or-nothing.
So, for instance, with Petra, it may be more appropriate to suggest

that she is 'very unlikely' to find a job through Facebook messaging, as opposed to this being impossible. Indeed, as suggested above, to convey to clients that there are absolute givens in their lives would seem to contradict one of the most basic existential givens: the uncertainty of being.

Is everyone afraid of death?

Closely related to the above point, some of the understandings and methods presented in this chapter are based on the assumption of a universal fear of certain givens, in particular death. But is that really the case? Although, as we have seen, there are case studies and empirical research to show that this is true for some, it may not be true for everyone (Farber, 2000a). Some people, for instance, may just not worry about it, or see it as a welcome relief from suffering. This may be particularly dependent on cultural factors. Kaufman (1978: 224), for instance, writes: 'To a large extent, the fear of death, or the anxiety associated with death, is a product of Christianity, and we encounter very different attitudes as the burning ghats in Varanasi in India and in Buddhist lands'.

Is an unrealistic optimism really that bad?

Contrary to the existential perspective presented here, there is also little research to show that unrealistic optimism, on average, leads to disappointment, disillusionment or endangerment (Armor & Taylor, 1998). In fact, what it suggests is that some degree of unrealistic optimism may have a number of benefits, including helping people to persist at tasks, successfully adjust to threatening events (Armor & Taylor, 1998), and steer away from depression and low self-esteem (Baumeister, 1991). From the psychological evidence, it would also seem that *hope* is a key predictor of psychological wellbeing (Snyder, Michael & Cheavens, 1999). Based on the data, Armor and Taylor (1998: 362) conclude that:

> Substituting relatively pessimistic (or conservative) assessments for unrealistically optimistic ones may simply make people more unhappy and less enthusiastic about their undertakings, less persistent in pursuing them, and more concerned about the future, without necessarily improving the accuracy of their assessments.

Personalising practice

Despite these critiques, from a pluralistic standpoint, it is still possible that some people are denying or evading their limitations in unhelpful ways. More generally, we can hypothesise that exploring limitations may be most helpful for clients who:

- Want to look at, or are facing, particular limitations in their life, such as mortality.
- Would welcome being challenged to face up to particular limitations.
- Believe that it is important to come to terms with the limitations of life.
- Have not spoken before about the feelings generated by these limitations.
- Are unrealistically optimistic in unhelpful ways, such as a naïve passivity or very extreme levels of unrealistic optimism (Armor & Taylor, 1998).

Summary

From an existential standpoint, human freedom is always curtailed by certain givens of existence, such as mortality, tensions and being-in-a-body. It can be painful and discomforting to accept these givens existence, but by denying them to reflective awareness we can fail to make the most of the *actual* circumstances we encounter. From an existential standpoint, we can empathise with the anxiety that facing the givens creates; and we can also help clients acknowledge the limitations in their lives, and ways that they might avoid an awareness of them. Ultimately, we can also work with clients to make the best choices that they can within the circumstances that they face.

Questions for reflection and discussion

- What do you consider the most significant limitations that people face in their lives? Is it the same as the ones that the existential writers emphasise?
- To what extent do you agree with Yalom that much of our psychological difficulties stem from a denial of death?
- Under what circumstances do you think it might be helpful to support a client to acknowledge their limitations? Under what circumstances do you think it might be unhelpful?

Recommended reading

Yalom, I. (1980) *Existential Psychotherapy (Part 1: Death)*. New York: Basic Books. The definitive review and analysis of working with death in psychotherapy.

Van Deurzen, E. (2012) *Existential Counselling and Psychotherapy in Practice* (3rd edn). London: Sage. An approach to existential therapy which particularly emphasises the need to come to terms with the limitations and challenges of life. For a more specific critique of the contemporary belief in having it all, see van Deurzen, E. (2009) *Psychotherapy and the Quest for Happiness*. London: Sage.

Wolfe, B.E. (2008) Existential issues in anxiety disorders and their treatment. In K.J. Schneider (ed.), *Existential-Integrative Psychotherapy: Guideposts to the Core of Practice* (pp. 204–216). New York: Routledge. Written by a leading figure in the field of anxiety problems, and showing links to existential themes.

6

Purpose and Meaning

This chapter discusses the existential understandings that:

- Human beings are fundamentally purpose-orientated.
- We have a basic need for purpose and meaning, and experience psychological distress if we do not have this.
- Life is inherently meaningful.
- Life is inherently meaningless.

It then goes on to describe the existential practices of:

- Keeping the clients' futures in mind.
- Reflecting back future dimensions of existence.
- Goal-setting.
- Helping clients find purpose and direction in their lives.
- Helping clients to make sense of their live.
- Empathising with clients' feelings of meaninglessness.

What is the meaning of life? This is, perhaps, 'the most persistent and important question ever asked' (Wong, 2013: xxix). So important, in fact, that Monty Python made a film about it.

As with the previous two chapters, when we focus on the question of life's meaning and purpose, we move away from a strictly phenomenological approach (Chapter 3). Now, we are not just focusing on existence as experienced, but as a circumscribed phenomenon with qualities and characteristics. We are asking, 'What does my existence mean, what is its purpose?' Here, the answers may or may not reside in the realm of our experiencing.

What does meaning mean? In an existential sense, it can be understood as the 'web of connections, understandings, and interpretations' that help us comprehend our lives (Steger, 2013: 165). It is the *sense* that we make of our existences, the *rationale* we have for being, the reasons we may hold for why our lives *matter* (King & Hicks, 2013).

Meaning also has a future-oriented and motivational component. This is the plans, projects and goals which actualise the sense that we make of our lives, and to which we devote our time and energy (Tengan, 1999). This can be described as our *purposes*. All purposes are meanings, but not all meanings are purposes. A meaning, for instance, may be about making sense of past events: why my life *was* worthwhile, rather than what I intend to do with it now.

In this chapter, we will focus primarily on purposes. This is because it links with the existential emphasis on the future-oriented nature of human being, which will be discussed in the next section. It is also the area in which there is most empirical research and one that is, perhaps, most amenable to clinical change.

Understandings

The future-orientated dimension of human being

For many therapeutic orientations, and particularly the psychodynamic ones, the way that we think, feel and act is seen as being primarily determined by our *past* experiences. For instance, if a client tends to put up barriers towards others, that might be understood in terms of early experiences of hurt and rejection. Humanistic approaches like gestalt therapy add to this an emphasis on the here-and-now *present*: for instance, that the person pushes others away because they experience very powerful feelings of anxiety at moments of intimacy. From a pluralistic standpoint, both of these focuses can be of considerable value. An existential perspective, however, introduces an additional understanding. This is that how we think, feel and act may also be strongly influenced by our perceived futures (see Exercise 6.1), and their relationship to our meanings and purposes. From this standpoint, then, the person might be seen as pushing others away because they *want* to make sure they do not experience deep feelings of hurt again, or because they want the other person to know how hurt they feel.

Exercise 6.1   The influence of past, present and future

Aim

- To explore the influence of different temporalities on how you presently feel.
- To introduce the idea that the future may have an influence on how you are.

The exercise

- Reflect on, and perhaps write down, exactly how you feel right now (2–3 minutes).
- Next, ask yourself this question: Is how you feel right now primarily related to what has happened to you (the *past*), what is happening to you (the *present*), what you feel is to come (the *future*), or some combination of all three?
- In asking yourself this question, see if you can really unpick what your feeling is related to: for instance, you might feel worried because you had an argument with your partner this morning, but is this because of what recently happened, or because you are not sure how you can address it in the future?
- Some 'phenomenological variations' may help here. For instance, imagine that the present was the same but the future was different, or vice versa. Would the feeling still be there, or would it be different?

Reflections

In doing this exercise, some people find that their present feelings are primarily related to their past, others to their present, and others to their future (see Box 6.2). Some people also find that they cannot really disentangle the three temporalities: their feelings are past–present–future combined. From a therapeutic standpoint – and particularly one informed by pluralistic values – this suggests that different clients may need to explore all three temporalities at different times; and that an existential emphasis on the future can be a useful complement to therapeutic approaches that focus on the past or present (and vice versa).

This existential emphasis on the future comes from a radical, phenomenologically based revision of how we think about time, developed by both existential (e.g., Sartre, Heidegger) and neo-existential (e.g., Henri Bergson) philosophers. Typically, we think of time as existing on a straight line, from past to present to future (see top half of Figure 6.1). But if we start from a phenomenological standpoint (Chapter 3), giving ontological priority to the way in which we actually experience the world, things can look very different. Right now, for instance, I do not experience myself as being *caused* to eat my toast because of any past event. Rather, I experience myself as eating my toast because I *want* something to happen: for instance, to experience the pleasurable combination of marmalade–butter–crunchy toast. Phenomenologically, then, we might suggest that it is not the past that precedes the present and future, but the future that comes first. As Sartre (1996: 259) states, 'Man, first of all, is the being who hurls himself towards a future [e.g., his toast] and who is conscious of imagining himself as being in the future'. Heidegger (2001: 159) puts this even more succinctly when he writes: '*Everything begins with the future!*' Indeed, Spinelli (1994) suggests that even the way we understand our pasts is shaped by how we act towards our futures. For instance, if I want others to feel sorry for me, I may tend towards remembering and embellishing more negative past events.

Of course, this is not to suggest that the past is irrelevant. For instance, if I had not previously experienced eating toast as pleasurable, I would not be eating it now. However, an existential approach rejects a deterministic understanding of the past, just as it rejects any other deterministic understanding of being (see Chapter 4). In this respect, the past can be seen as something we *draw upon* as we choose towards our future. That is, it is a *tool of being* (Cooper, 2001c; and Cooper, 1998 on the companion website). This is depicted in the lower half of Figure 6.1, which presents time as an existential therapist might see it: with the present acting towards the future by drawing on the past.

EXISTENTIAL
PERSPECTIVES
ON THE PAST

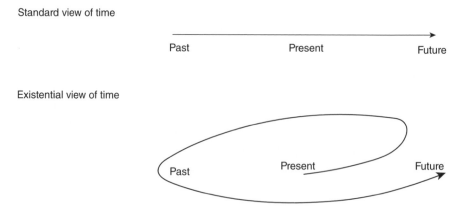

Standard view of time

Past   Present   Future

Existential view of time

Past   Present   Future

Figure 6.1   Standard and existential views of time

From a pluralistic standpoint, however, it makes little sense to argue over which comes first: the past, present or future. Clearly, all are interlinked in complex ways. This is certainly how existential philosophers have conceptualised it (e.g., Heidegger, 1962; Sartre, 1958), such that any exploration of a person's past will inevitably bring in issues of their present and future, and vice versa. The contribution of an existential perspective to a pluralistic approach, then, is not that it prioritises the future *instead of* the past or present. Rather, what is useful is that it invites us to consider our clients' futures *as well as* their pasts and presents; and to see the role that this might play in their psychological difficulties and development.

Exercise 6.2   Your relationship to time

Background

A phenomenological approach does not focus on time as an objective phenomenon, but as something that is subjectively experienced (see above). Developing this further, the phenomenological psychiatrist, Eugène Minkowski, suggested that different people may be more or less focused on different *zones* of experienced time (Ellenberger, 1958). Here, psychological difficulties are associated with particular zones becoming blocked off or distorted, such that the person is not fully open to their lived-world (cf. Daseinsanalysis, see Chapter 1). Minkowski suggested seven zones:

- The remote past ('zone of the obsolete').
- The mediate past ('zone of the regretted').
- The immediate past ('zone of the remorse').
- The present.
- The immediate future ('zone of expectation and activity').
- The mediate future ('zone of wish and hope').
- The remote future ('zone of prayer and ethical action').

So, for instance, a client may experience psychological difficulties because she is always focused on the present, and never learning from the past or thinking about the future consequences of her actions. Alternatively, a person might always be fantasising about the distant future, but never making the most of his present.

Aim

- To explore the idea that different people have different relationships to time.
- To develop an understanding of your relationship to the different time domains.

(Continued)

(Continued)

The exercise

- Reflect on this question: In your life, how *focused*, or *blocked*, are you to each of Minkowski's zones of experienced time (see above) (10 mins).

Variations

- Think about this question in relation to a client that you are working with. Which time zones does he or she tend to focus on, and which does he or she tend to block off?

Purposelessness and distress

If our present experiences are shaped by our perceived futures, then having a positive sense of where we are going in life is likely to be an important element of our psychological wellbeing. More broadly, our wellbeing may be dependent on having some understanding of what our life *means*. This is both so that we can have a positive orientation towards the future; and also so that we have some sense of worth, understanding and order in our lives: a coherent narrative of who we are (Baumeister, 1991). Conversely, if we do not have a sense of purpose or meaning in our lives, we may fall into despair, hopelessness, low self-worth and suffering. This is a viewpoint expressed by many existential, as well as humanistic (e.g., Maslow, 1971), psychologists and psychotherapists. For instance, van Deurzen (2012c: 176) writes, 'Many people become desperately confused and depressed when they lose the northern star of the passionate purpose of their life'. To explore your own sense of purpose in life, try Exercise 6.3.

Exercise 6.3   Purposes in your life

Aim

- To explore the importance of purpose and goals in life.
- To experience reflecting on, and articulating, your own personal goals.

The exercise

- For each of the following questions, write down the immediate answer that comes into your head:

  o What are your principle goals in life?
  o What is your relationship with these goals like? (For instance, do they feel achievable or unachievable; desirable or uninteresting?)
  o How does your relationship with these goals affect how you feel in the present?

Variations

- It can also be very interesting to ask yourself the reverse of these questions:

  o What is your most *feared future*? (i.e., the thing that you would least like to have happen in the years ahead.)
  o What is your relationship with this feared future like? (For instance, does it feel very possible or very unlikely; awful or unbearable?)
  o How does your relationship to your feared future affect how you feel in the present?

- Think of a client that you are working with: How might they answer the above questions?

This understanding of distress is advocated most strongly by Victor Frankl (1984, 1986) and the meaning-oriented therapists (see Chapter 1). They argue that human beings' most fundamental need is for meaning and purpose and that, without this, we fall into hopelessness and despair. 'The loss of meaning in life is a hidden killer', writes Ventegodt and Merrick (2013: 573), 'it is like a worm eating the apple from within'. Without meaning, it is argued, we experience an *existential vacuum*, which we may then attempt to fill through such *existential neurosis* as addictions, compulsions or obsessive behaviours. 'During the day', writes Fabry (1980: 119), we may plunge ourselves into meaningless activities, such as phone calls, children and television. But at night we are plagued by 'existential sleeplessness', as the lack of any genuine meaning in our lives returns to haunt us. According to Frankl (1986), 20% of neurosis in clinical practice results from a lack of meaning and Yalom (1980) suggests that this figure may be somewhat higher. (For an alternative, psycho-social model of being based around a hierarchy of purposes, see Cooper, 2012d, available on the companion website.)

INTEGRATED
PSYCHO-SOCIAL
MODEL OF WANTS

There are good evolutionary grounds for arguing that human beings need purpose and meaning in their lives (Aron & Aron, 2013; Steger, 2013), and that we are naturally oriented towards goals (Klinger, 2013). Klinger (2013: 31) writes:

> The human brain cannot sustain purposeless living. It is not designed for that. Its systems are designed for purposive action. When that is blocked, its systems deteriorate, and the emotional feedback from idling these systems signals extreme discomfort and motivates the search for renewed purpose, renewed meaning.

In this respect, our emotions can be seen as arising in response to our goal striving (Klinger, 2013). We feel satisfaction, for instance, in achieving our goals; anxiety out of a fear that we will not reach them; and despair when they seem beyond our reach (Cooper, 2012d).

Consistent with this, research suggests that people do seem to have a need for purpose in their lives (Baumeister, 1991). For instance, if people's goals become blocked, they may pursue that goal even harder or become obsessed with them (Baumeister, 1991). Moreover, there is abundant evidence of links between meaning in life and a wide range of other indicators of psychological wellbeing and distress (see Steger, 2013 for an excellent overview, also Exercise 6.4). A recent summary concluded: 'Individuals with a sense of purpose and meaning report greater life satisfaction, more positive emotions, higher levels of optimism, and better self-esteem' (Park, Park & Peterson, 2010: 2). Concomitantly, several studies have shown an association between meaninglessness, negative affect and various forms of psychological distress, including alcoholism and depressed mood states (Klinger, 2013; Schulenberg, Hutzell, Nassif & Rogina, 2008). Indeed, finding meaning and purpose has even been prioritised in national government health agendas (Department of Health, 2009).

From the evidence, it also seems that simply *having* goals may be as important to wellbeing as *attaining* them (Emmons & Diener, 1986); provided that they are perceived as being attainable (Brunstein, 1993). For purposes to contribute towards our psychological wellbeing, they also need to be based on our genuine needs, values and interests; rather than on extrinsic, externally derived standards and expectations (Sheldon & Elliot, 1999). Keshen (2006) refers to this as *authentic purposes*.

Exercise 6.4   The Meaning in Life Questionnaire

Background

Over the years, several measures have been developed to help assess the extent to which individuals have meaning and purpose in their lives, such as The Purpose in Life Test (Crumbaugh & Maholick, 1964) (see Guttman, 1996). Most recently, however, Steger, Frazier, Oishi and Kaler (2006) have developed the Meaning in Life Questionnaire, a brief psychological test with excellent levels of reliability and validity.

Aims

- To develop an understanding of how a measure of meaning operates.
- To develop insight into your own sense of meaning in life.

The exercise

Complete the Meaning in Life Questionnaire, as outlined below.

Scale

Please take a moment to think about what makes your life and existence feel important and significant to you. Please respond to the following statements as truthfully and accurately as you can, and also please remember that these are very subjective questions and that there are no right or wrong answers. Please answer according to the scale below:

Absolutely Untrue	Mostly Untrue	Somewhat Untrue	Can't Say True or False	Somewhat True	Mostly True	Absolutely True
1	2	3	4	5	6	7

1. I understand my life's meaning.
2. I am looking for something that makes my life feel meaningful.
3. I am always looking to find my life's purpose.
4. My life has a clear sense of purpose.

(Continued)

(Continued)

5. I have a good sense of what makes my life meaningful.
6. I have discovered a satisfying life purpose.
7. I am always searching for something that makes my life feel significant.
8. I am seeking a purpose or mission for my life.
9. My life has no clear purpose.
10. I am searching for meaning in my life.

Scoring

Item 9 is reverse scored.

Items 1, 4, 5, 6, & 9 make up the Presence of Meaning subscale.
Items 2, 3, 7, 8, & 10 make up the Search for Meaning subscale.

Scoring is kept continuous.

Comment

Consistent with previous research (see above), Steger and colleagues (2006) found that higher scores on the presence of meaning subscale were associated with higher scores on many other indicators of psychological wellbeing. Indeed, as Steger and colleagues suggest, this 5-item subscale could serve as an excellent existential alternative to diagnosis- and pathology-oriented outcome tools, such as the Patient Health Questionnaire (PHQ-9). However, higher scores on the search for meaning subscale were not associated with greater wellbeing. In fact, there were some indications that they were associated with greater fear, sadness and depression. This might be because the harder someone is searching for meaning, the more frustrated they might be with the meanings and purposes they currently have.

A clear example of the psychological difficulties that can be associated with a lack of purpose comes from Peter, who was introduced in Chapter 4. At the start of therapy, when Peter was working in an old age home, his low mood seemed closely linked to his hopelessness about the future: that all he had to come was years of drudgery, boredom and frustration. Once he started university, his mood dramatically changed, and this seemed closely linked to a whole new realm of possibilities opening up for what lay ahead. He could be a researcher, an academic, a journalist: there were possibilities in his future that he now looked forward to, and he acted in his life with an entirely renewed sense of hope and optimism.

Alongside helping clients to identify future possibilities and goals, it may also be important to help clients find meaning in the lives that they *have* had, or *are* having. This might be particularly relevant to certain groups of clients, such as people nearing death, older adults, or people who cannot change their external circumstances (for instance, someone with a severe disability). Here, argues Frankl (1986, 1988), while we may not be able to change our circumstances or our suffering, we can still change our attitudes towards it: and, in doing so, find a degree of resolution, dignity or coherence to our lives. This echoes Erikson's (1998) model of psychosocial development, which suggests that, as people move towards older adulthood, they can either develop an integrated sense of meaning for their lives, or fall into despair and hopelessness. It may also be important for us to have a sense of significance in our lives (see Box 6.1).

Box 6.1   The search for significance

Frankl and the logotherapists argue that the most basic human need is to have a sense of meaning in our lives: that we have a reason and purpose for why we do what we do. In my personal and clinical experience, however, I have found that also what is very important to people is a sense of *signif-icance*: that we make a difference to the lives of others, matter to them, and have a place in *their* worlds. This may be the motivating force behind many of our actions. Yalom (2008: 87), for instance, writes 'my desire to be of value to others is largely what keeps me pecking away at my keyboard long past the standard time for retirement'. What would it feel like to believe that our lives have made no difference to anyone; that we could just as well have not existed and the world would exactly be the same? Indeed, Laing (1969) suggests that the essence of paranoia is the belief that one's life has no importance to anyone but ourselves. For some of my clients, that seems to have been their deepest existential fear: not that they don't have a reason for existence, but that the world has no reason for them.

Meaning or meaninglessness?

Across existential philosophers and therapists, there is a general agreement that human lives are oriented to meaning and purpose and suffer if they do not have it. Where there is radical disagreement, however, is on whether human beings have some kind of given, ultimate, 'super-meaning' to their lives; or whether human lives are inherently and ultimately meaningless.

In the former camp tend to be the more spiritual existential writers, such as Buber (1964: 57–58). He states: 'For as the needle of the magnet has chosen from all the points of the compass north ... so the soul from the beginning has chosen its direction'. In other words, each of us come into the world with a given meaning and purpose, unique to us, which we can realise 'out of the infinity of possibilities'. Furthermore, each situation has a particular meaning that we are called on to actualise (Frankl, 1986). So, for instance, as I sit on this train, watching the young girl next to me being criticised and harangued by her mother, *I* may be being called on to intervene. Here, at the level of primary experiencing-in-the-world, each moment is seen as containing an invocation for *us* to respond in a particular way.

In this respect, as Frankl (1984, 1986) argues, our meanings in life are not things we *invent*. Rather, they are things that we *discover*. From this standpoint, we have an intuitive, immediate understanding of what we are called on to do; and we can either reflectively acknowledge and actualise this calling, or we can fail in our response-ability. Pre-reflectively, then, we might say that Peter experienced the work at the old age person's home as empty and meaningless. He 'knew' that it was not right for him. Equally, when he started to learn about the world of education, he had a powerful sense of 'this is what I was meant for': passionate, enthused, alive. From this standpoint, then, the aim of therapy is to help clients rediscover their missions in life (Ventegodt & Merrick, 2013). In the terms of Chapter 3, it is about helping clients to be true to their primary experiencing, but with the assumption that that primary experiencing contains a calling to respond in a particular way.

In contrast to this viewpoint are the more atheistic existential writers (e.g., Camus, 1955; Sartre, 1958) who hold that 'life has no meaning *a priori*' (Sartre, 1996: 264). That is, 'there exists no "meaning", no grand design in the universe, no guidelines for living other than those the individual creates' (Yalom, 1980: 423). This is not to suggest that we cannot experience feelings of meaning or purpose in our lives (or, indeed, that we should not). Rather, it means that if we trace the meanings and purposes that we have in our lives 'all the way back', we find that they have no solid foundation. We are 'interpretation all the way down' (Dreyfus, 1997: 25); or, as Camus puts it 'absurd'. So, for instance, we might want to learn about existential therapy because we want to be a better therapist, and we want to be a better therapist because we want to help more people. However, from this existential standpoint, this goal of wanting to help people is just one, fairly arbitrary rationale for doing things, which has no ultimate justification. Indeed, for Heidegger (1962), our most powerful 'socialisation' is that we come to believe that the meanings and purposes of the world around us – for instance, that we should strive for happiness, growth or social justice – are 'truths', as opposed to foundation-less social constructions. It is as if we find ourselves thrown in a world of others racing headlong towards goals, and feel compelled to run alongside them, never stopping to ask where we are going or why. Here, for Heidegger, moments of *authenticity* come when we stop running and see the race for what it is: a headlong chase that has no ultimate purpose or objective.

Box 6.2   The absurdity of existence: *Waiting for Godot*

Samuel Beckett's play, *Waiting for Godot,* can be considered a classic allegory for the human search for meaning in an ultimately absurd and unforgiving world. Two men, Vladimir and Estrangon, wait endlessly and futilely for 'Godot' to arrive. All hopes and expectations are rested on Godot's appearance, yet it is never clear who Godot is, nor what salvation he could ever bring to these men should he appear. The absurdity of human existence, and our deadness to this reality, is emphasised throughout the play. Vladimir states: 'Astride of a grave and a difficult birth. Down in the hole, lingeringly, the gravedigger puts on the forceps. We have time to grow old. The air is full of our cries. But habit is a great deadener. At me too someone is looking, of me too someone is saying, he is sleeping, he knows nothing, let him sleep on'. Towards the end of the play, the two men are told that Godot will not come that evening, but are assured he will come the next day 'without fail'. They consider hanging themselves, but cannot find a suitable rope. 'I can't go on like this' says Estragon. Vladimir replies, 'That's what you think'. In the last lines of the play, Vladimir says to Estragon, 'Well? Shall we go? And Estragon replies: 'Yes, let's go'. The play ends with the stage direction: *They do not move.*

For Yalom (1980), as for Heidegger, an acknowledgement of the true absurdity of our existence has the capacity to evoke powerful feelings of dread, despair and nihilism. For this reason, as with acknowledging our freedom (Chapter 4) and limitations (Chapter 5), Yalom argues that we may develop a range of strategies to defend ourselves against the anxiety that this ultimate given elicits. For instance, we might commit ourselves to an ideology; throw ourselves into mindless pursuits; or assume that other people can be relied on to know what life is 'really' about (as with Godot, Box 6.2). We might also crave fame and notoriety (for instance, auditioning for the *X-Factor* or appearing naked on *Big Brother*) as a means of staving off a pre-reflective dread of our own meaninglessness and insignificance (Fromm, 1942). As with other forms of denial, however, it is argued that these defences generally do more harm than good. Existential anxiety becomes neurotic anxiety, as we fight to shore up our defences. And because our awareness of the ultimate meaninglessness of life cannot be quelled, we are constantly haunted by an awareness of this absurdity. Better, then, it is argued, to courageously face up to the ultimate meaninglessness of existence, and find ways of living *despite* this: towards *local* meanings and purposes if not ultimate ones. As Camus (1955) puts it, we can still live and create in the very midst of a desert.

Interestingly, then, while some existential writers argue that we should courageously face up to our meanings in life, others argue that we should courageously face up to our meaninglessness! Here, a pluralistic standpoint sidesteps this dichotomy by suggesting that both positions may be true: that for some people, finding some 'ultimate' sense of meaning may be very important while, for others, it may be very useful to accept that there are no ultimate meanings. In the work with Peter, for instance, it seemed enormously helpful for him to move towards a greater sense of purpose in life. Had I suggested to him that, ultimately, his newfound direction was ultimately meaningless, it would almost certainly have been counter-productive. On the other hand, as will be explored later in this chapter, for clients who have a profound sense that life is meaninglessness, a therapist's empathic understanding of this worldview may be experienced as validating.

Box 6.3   What is the meaning of counselling and psychotherapy?

At a metatherapeutic level, the Heideggerian analysis of being as foundation-less raises the question of the meaning of therapy. Is it really a purposeful activity or it is also some headlong race that covers up the ultimate mean-inglessness of life? Consistent with a pluralistic perspective, such question-ing can be helpful in that it allows us to 'stand back' from the assumption that therapy is inherently helpful, and to consider that it may be more or less meaningful for different people at different times. It also encourages us to be wary of falling into *therapeutic* meanings and purposes in an unreflective and uncritical way. That is, within each of our therapeutic schools lie certain assumptions about what it is meaningful to strive for – whether actualisation (Rogers, 1959), happiness (Layard, 2006), or meaning itself (Frankl, 1984) – and we may end up simply taking on these goals as if they were ultimate truths. From this standpoint, then, *authentic* therapists are those who can recognise their own assumptions about what makes for a meaningful life, and allow this certainty to be challenged. This is not just at the level of con-tent (for instance, 'it is meaningful to enjoy going to the theatre') but in terms of our most deeply held, orientation- or ideologically-grounded beliefs (for instance, that we should be happy or face our mortality).

Methods

So what can therapists do to help their clients develop a more positive and authentic relationship to their purposes and meanings?

Keeping a client's future in mind

First, in reflecting on clients and the difficulties that they are experiencing – whether in supervision or in the session itself – it may be useful to be mindful of the future dimension: their sense of where they are going, and how that might affect how they are now. For instance, you may find it useful to explore the questions of purpose in Exercise 6.3 with respect to your clients (for instance, in supervision): that is, what are their goals in life/feared futures? How do they relate to these future possibilities? How might this affect them now? Here, as with Peter, you may find that some or all of the distress that clients are experiencing can be linked to their perception of their future, for instance, that their feared future is bound to happen; or that they have no real sense of what they want; or that they do know what they want, but believe that they can never attain it. You may also find it useful to think about your clients' relationships to the different temporal zones (see Exercise 6.2), and whether they are more open, or more blocked, with respect to some time zones than others.

Reflecting back future dimensions of being

A step on from keeping the client's future in mind is to bring a more future-oriented perspective in to the therapeutic encounter. At the gentler end of existential practice, this may involve simply reflecting back to clients the more future-related elements of what they are saying. Here, person-centred psychotherapist Bohart (2001) distinguishes between *present-centred* and *future-oriented* empathy responses, and presents evidence that the latter lead clients to feel a greater sense of power and ability to solve problems. Bohart (2001: 107) writes that future-oriented empathic responses refer clients 'down the road', reflecting back hopes for the future, fears for the future, what the client wants, and what the client thinks might happen if they act in a certain way.

Take the following example: A client is talking about his problems in relationships:

Client: I feel very close to some women, but I get a sense that, ultimately, they are always going to let me down. I don't think I really trust them– like they'll end up doing something to hurt me and I won't be able to cope with it.

Here, a present-centred response might be:

Therapist: You experience closeness with some women, but you also feel some distrust around them.

By contrast, a future-oriented response might be:

Therapist: So there's a worry that if you get close to a woman, they'll let you down and hurt you.

From a pluralistic standpoint, neither of these is a better response, *per se*. However, for some clients at some points in time, a more future-orientated empathic response may help them develop their sense of why they experience the world in the way they do, as well as where they are going in life.

At the firmer end of the continuum, therapists may then begin to bring in more of their own understandings and interpretations of how clients' relationships to their future are affecting their present. The following example (reconstructed from therapist notes), comes from about three months into therapy with a client in her late-50s, Lily. Lily was recently retired and came to therapy diagnosed with depression. Her husband, Bob, was experiencing a lot of health problems, and she had a deep sadness about a 'loveless' relationship with her daughter, Sophie.

Lily 1:   I wish Sophie would phone. She said to me she'd ring me last Wednesday and she didn't. She never comes to visit. She said that she's going to come down next weekend but I just don't know if she will or not. She didn't come down last time she said she would. And if she does come down this time, I'll be so angry with her about last time and how she ignores me and Bob that I'll probably have to be out of the room for most of the time she is here.

Mick 1:   So either way you won't get much out of it: if she doesn't come down you'll feel resentful, and if she does come down, you won't actually spend that much time with her.

Lily 2:   I just wish things were easier between me and her. When she was little, I so much wished that she'd be the person I could really talk to and share things with. I don't have a lot of friends– not close ones, anyway. I guess my expectations of her were too high. Now, I just don't know what's going to happen.

At this point, I felt very moved by what Lily was saying. It felt like she had had such great hopes for her relationship with Sophie, and I sensed an overwhelming feeling of disappointment and sadness for the way things had turned out. A present-centred empathic response would have reflected this back. However, what I also sensed in that moment was that, with her hopes of closely relating to Sophie gone, there was really nothing for Lily to look forward to; nothing that made living feel worthwhile. At that point, this felt to me like the crux of her distress.

Mick 2:   You know, as you're talking, what I'm thinking about is that the future for you is feeling pretty bleak: it doesn't feel like there's a lot for you to look forward to. It's like, you don't think things are going to end up particularly positively with you and Sophie, and then you talk about the way that Bob is just getting worse and worse.

Lily 3:   What have I got to look forward to? Sophie never calls, never bothers to turn up when she says she will. What am I supposed to do?

Mick 3:   How would you like things to be? What kind of future do you want?

Lily 4:   I want to feel close to Sophie. I want her to talk to me. I want Bob to stop criticising me and for him to find someone else to take him to the clinic sometimes. I want to go out with friends a bit more. I don't want to be coming to therapy for the rest of my life telling you how awful I feel.

Goal-setting in therapy

Some existential thinkers and practitioners (see Critical reflections, below) would see goal-setting as antithetical to existential therapy, with its emphasis on *being* rather than *doing* (Chapter 2). However, if we understand human beings as fundamentally purpose-oriented, then it makes sense to explore, and make explicit, their goals for the therapeutic enterprise itself. Questions that clients might be asked, for instance in an initial session, could include:

- 'Do you have a sense of what you want from our work together?'
- 'What do you hope to get out of therapy?'
- 'What kind of things would you like to change in your life?'

(from Cooper & McLeod, 2011b: 72)

This, then, becomes an ongoing site for metatherapeutic communication, and Chapter 4 of *Pluralistic Counselling and Psychotherapy* focuses in detail on how therapists can work with clients on what they want from the therapeutic enterprise.

Helping clients find purpose and direction

In the above dialogue, at *Mick 3*, I specifically went on to ask Lily what kind of future she wanted. Here, from an existential standpoint, helping clients to envisage and think about how to create a more desirable future for themselves may be an important element of the therapeutic work.

As with a person-centred approach, a key part of this process may involve helping clients to identify what it is that they *really* find satisfying, rewarding and fulfilling in their life, at the level of primary experiencing. When we explored her feelings towards teaching, for instance, Keeley (introduced in Chapter 4) said that there was something around being in a position of authority that she really did not like: 'I find it much more comfortable to relate to people on an equal plane.' We explored this further, really trying to unpack what it was that she experienced as most rewarding. 'I think it's when I am in an exchange with someone', she said, 'they say something, then I build on their ideas, then we come out at the end of it both feeling that we have really learnt something'. From this, we went on to talk about what kind of career might be most facilitative of this. I asked her if teaching adults in a Further Education (FE) college might feel more like 'her thing'; she wondered about being a family therapist. We agreed, at the end of the session, that she would find out more about training in family therapy.

Another example of helping to clarify these basic *wants-for-the-future* is work with Dorak, a young Turkish man who had travelled for many years before training as an occupational psychologist, and carried with him a deep sense of failure and worthlessness. In our first session, we talked through what Dorak wanted from therapy, and agreed three main goals: 'To feel positive about where I've been and what I've done', 'To not feel overwhelmed or defeated by a sense of unfairness', and 'To have a clear sense of what work I want to do and feel OK about that'. As Dorak had indicated at assessment that he would like homework, we agreed at the end of the session he would spend some time, before the next session, thinking about what he was grateful for in his past. He did this and found it very helpful in developing a more nuanced sense of how his life had been so far; along with becoming more aware of the skills and strengths that he had developed along the way. Towards the end of the session, I suggested to Dorak that he might want to spend some time before the next week thinking about what he was good at. Dorak replied that, for him, this was not such a useful question – it reinforced a feeling of pressure that he *should* be good at something – and what was more important to him was to think about what he liked and what he enjoyed.

At the beginning of the next session, Dorak brought in some drawings that he had done over the week. One of these was of a triangle, an image that Dorak said he had had in his head for many years, and on the three points of the triangle were the three areas of his life in which he felt that he needed fulfilment: academia/theory, personal development, and culture/creativity/arts. 'And I want them all', he said, laughing. We talked about whether Dorak felt his impending career in occupational psychology would meet all these needs. Dorak felt that it met his desire for personal development and reflective work; but that it was also an 'easy option' because he was letting go of his need also to be theoretical and creative. From this discussion, we began to talk about ways in which he might also be able to meet these other needs: for instance, by looking towards delivering training and teaching work as well as direct psychological input, and to developing his creative abilities in music and writing. As with Keeley, therefore, the work with Dorak involved helping identify what he really wanted from life; but it also went on from here, to look at practical steps in which he could move closer towards his desired future.

There are also a wide range of more structured techniques that can be used to help clients identify, and develop, more positive meanings in life. For instance:

- *Existential attribution* (Wong, 1998). This involves asking clients 'Why?' questions that help them track back to their most fundamental meanings and purposes. For instance, 'Why is it important for you to relate to people on an equal plane?', 'What is it about being in an exchange with someone that feels good to you?', 'Why is it so important to you to help others?'
- *Fast-forwarding* (Wong, 1998). Asking clients to depict likely future scenarios given a particular choice. For instance, 'How do you imagine your life would be if you left your husband and children?'
- *Magical thinking* (Wong, 1998). Like the 'miracle question' of solution-focused brief therapy (Bannink, 2007), this involves asking clients questions that help them transcend their present situation and consider new possibilities. For instance, 'If you could do whatever you wanted right now, what would it be?', 'If you woke up in the morning and everything was just right, what would it be like?'
- *The movies exercise* (Schulenberg et al., 2008). This invites clients to develop a film of their life, focusing from the past to their present life, and then from their present to their future. Clients can be asked a range of questions to deepen this exploration, for instance, 'What would the film's genre be?' 'Who would play the lead roles?', 'What would happen in the ending?'
- *Goals Form* (Cooper, 2014). This is a simple, freely available form that invites clients to to record their goals for therapy, or for life more generally (available on the companion website, also www.pluralistictherapy. com). It can be used in a first session of therapy, and/or at regular intervals to help clients track their progress towards their personal goals.

GOALS FORM

Helping clients to make sense of their lives

As well as helping clients move towards a positive future, it may also be important to help them make meaning of their lives to date, and of their present being-in-the-world. At the gentler end of the existential continuum, this may involve supporting clients to explore their pasts, and consider what they have learnt and can take from it. For instance, Daryn was a slight, 30-year-old man of Afro-Caribbean origin, who came to see me after six years of moving in and out of psychiatric institutions with a variety of diagnoses (see full client study in Cooper, 2008b). Daryn was extremely bitter about his time in the psychiatric system, and the abuse and de-humanisation that he felt had been meted out to him by the psychiatrists and mental health nurses. For much of our early work together, the priority seemed to be to give Daryn space to talk about these experiences – for the first time – and to feel that someone really understood how awful and de-personalising it had been. After many months, however, Daryn began to wonder whether he could *do* something with these experiences: for instance, write about them as a book or article so that other people could see what the psychiatric system could really be like. I encouraged Daryn to think more about this, and talked to him about mental health survivor organisations that might be interested in hearing more about his story. As far as I know, Daryn never went down this track, but the idea that there was something meaningful he – and others – could take from his experiences in the psychiatric system seemed to be useful in itself. This transformed a wholly negative experience into something that could, potentially, be of some ultimate value.

At the firmer end of the existential continuum, there are methods such as *Socratic dialogue*, which was developed by Frankl (Fabry, 1980), and is now commonly incorporated into CBT (Dryden, 1999). Here, the therapist enters into a dialogue and debate with the client, and 'poses questions in such a way that patients become aware of their unconscious decisions, their repressed hopes, and their unadmitted self-knowledge' (Fabry, 1980: 135). Firmer still is the *appealing technique*, which consists of directly proposing to clients ways of making sense of their lives. For instance, Joyce Travelbee (1979), who incorporated logotherapy into her nursing work, gives the example of working with a middle aged woman who had spent much of her life caring for her elderly parents, and consequently felt depressed that she 'had wasted her life'.

Travelbee: Suppose you had *not* cared for your parents. What would have happened to them?

Client: [*After some thought*] I guess they would have had to go on welfare. They would have had to go to the free hospital for

	medical care. It would have killed my father. He was such a proud man.
Travelbee:	You spared your parents much suffering by your sacrifices. Have they really been in vain?
Client:	I don't regret what I have done. They had only me. They gave me life. In return I was able to give more years to their lives. It *does* count for something.

Travelbee (1979) reports that after several such conversations the client's depression began to lift, and she no longer experienced bitterness towards her life.

Empathising with a feeling of meaninglessness

While some clients may benefit from being helped to find meaning and purpose in their lives, for others, it may be more useful to have their questioning about life's meaning validated. Indeed, Frankl (1986: 26), himself, states that 'Challenging the meaning of life can ... never be taken as a manifestation of morbidity or abnormality; it is rather the truest expression of the state of being human, the mark of the most human nature in man'. Of course, for clients who are not wondering about the meaning of their lives, it would almost certainly be extremely unhelpful to say something like, 'Well, that's all very well, but did you know your life is meaningless anyway!' But for the many clients who do wonder what it is 'all about', it may be helpful to know that they are not alone in this thought; or that they are crazy or self-indulgent for thinking in this way.

The following example of this comes from my work with Andreas. This illustrates the validation of a client's feelings of meaninglessness, and also a pluralistically informed approach to existential therapy. Here, the existential understandings and methods are brought in to *support* the client's wants, as established through metatherapeutic dialogue.

Andreas was a young man of Swiss origin, who came to therapy wanting to like himself more; have more fun in his life; and understand what caused his unhappiness, pessimism and detachment from others. Arriving for session 26, he seemed very low. I invited him to talk about it: something that he tended not to do with others, preferring to shut himself away. What became evident as we did so was just how guilty Andreas felt about feeling bad: 'I'm meant to feel happy, grateful,' he said, 'I'm constantly told how lucky I am, "think of all the starving children in Africa". And yet I feel desperately sad'. I reflected this back to Andreas: that whatever people told him about how he *should* feel, the reality was that he felt terrible a lot of the time. We agreed that it was probably better to acknowledge that, than to pretend otherwise.

As with much of our previous work, what became evident to me, at this point in the session, was just how bad Andreas felt about feeling bad (a negative secondary experiencing, Chapter 3). It occurred to me, therefore, that it might be useful to talk through with Andreas about different understandings of why he might feel so low: each of which suggests that there is intelligibility for why people feel down, rather than some moral or personal failing. Indeed, previously, Andreas had told me that it was helpful to hear about different theories, because it helped him feel less like these feelings were *his* fault, but something more universal, generic and normal. The transcript is given verbatim.

Mick 1:   And we don't know why you feel *that* sadness. It could be ... biological ... it could be ... existential ... it could be cognitive ... [*Pause*].

Shall I tell you what the different theories are and you can tell me– [*Andreas*: Yes, ok].

OK, biological theory: that there's some biochemical imbalance. That means that ... um ... you– you're more likely to experience low moods than other people.

Cognitive: there's something about the way that you think: that you tend to interpret things–er– your future, your self– in very negative ways ... *negatively automatically thinking.*

Existential: the world is basically a miserable place, and you're just very good at seeing it, and everybody else is denying the truth that actually you see in a much better way than other people.

Humanistic: that ... being miserable, to some extent, is a given but the more you, kind of, deny who we are... the... more miserable we feel. Not to say that we can always feel good, but at least we can not feel miserable about being miserable.

[*Pause*]. Existential number two: don't have a sense of meaning and purpose in life, and that we feel miserable when we don't have a sense of meaning. [*Pause*].

Sure there's others, but those are the– oh, interpersonal: not satisfying relationships.

Integrative: a bit of all of those. [*Andreas*: Mm]. What do you think?

Within a pluralistic approach, this is an example of initiating a metatherapeutic dialogue over an *understanding* of the client's difficulties. My own assumptions, here, was that the client's problems were primarily related to difficulties with establishing close relationships with others, and this is something that I had discussed with Andreas several times. I had a genuine sense, however, of not fully understanding where his sadness was coming from, and felt it would be helpful to explore this with him.

Andreas 1:   I think I relate to ... parts of the ones that you said the most: existential one and two, and also interpersonal. *[Andreas goes on to discuss his desire to find answers for himself.]*

Mick 2:   But I mean the existential view would be that the sadness that you feel is a very, kind of, intelligent and appropriate reaction to what it means to be a human being. That, to exist in this world is, by definition, full of dread and unsettledness, and, you know: for Heidegger, to be authentic is to be living in dread at the realisation of the groundlessness of our being. And that most people spend their lives ... preoccupied with *little* meanings that they believe are meaningful to give them a sense of hope and purpose, and are– which he called inauthentic; because the authentic truth is that it's pretty miserable. You know, that there's moments of joys and happiness, but, as one existential therapist put, 'it's the exception rather than the rule' *[Andreas*: yeah]. And some of the existentialists would say that there is a– you know, that we can find meanings that really work for us, but I think most would say that we can– they're temporary, and we fall back into meaninglessness again and again because that's the way the world is. And that actually people like you who feel that, are... are– maybe not happier, but maybe more authentic than all the– *das mann* ['the they'], running round trying to have– have a sense of meaning.

Almost certainly, I am talking much too much here, and in highly abstract terms. I very much doubt it was useful to bring in Heidegger by name (though Andreas was familiar with his work); but my intention was to validate and normalise Andreas' sense of the fundamental meaninglessness of existence.

Andreas 2:   Yeah. *[long pause]* I think, um, I was speaking to someone about this the other day. I was saying to them that my, kind of, understanding of life is that it's the– 'life is brutality, and occasionally interspersed with moments of kindness, which make them beautiful' *[Mick: Mm]*. But everything about life is brutal: birth is brutal, death is brutal, existing is brutal. Um … But at the same time, whilst I do believe that, I can't help but feel … that I want it to be– you know, I want to see hope, and I do feel like I have the capacity for hope, but at the same time– it's kind of like a– I think that's what makes me unhappy.

Mick 3:   Is what, the *hope*?

Andreas 3:   Yeah. *[Pause]*

Mick 4:   Some existentialists *[I am referring to Binswanger's concept of extravagance here (see Chapter 5), and off again on a theoretical tack]* would say that's the thing that makes us most miserable, is the hope and the belief that it's gonna get better and *[Andreas: Mm]*, you know– rather than acknowledging the– the–

Andreas 4:   But then, I feel like if you don't question things you may as well be dead, because *[Mick: Mm]* you've done it already. Where is the growth, where is the development if you just repeat the same thought for the– the rest of your life *[Mick: yeah]*, you have to *challenge* yourself. So maybe that's what my challenge is: to kind of– the testing of the theory, I don't know.

Mick 5:   Testing of which theory?

Andreas 5:   That maybe– although life is brutality you can still seek out hope and meaning.

Interestingly, in this dialogue, it was an affirmation of Andreas' sense of meaninglessness that seemed to help him move towards the possibility of hope and purpose. This is very consistent with the existential understanding (e.g., Yalom, 1980) that if people are really supported to go down into their sense of meaninglessness, they will not get lost or collapse, but come back up with a renewed sense of vigour and purpose. Viewed pluralistically, however, this is unlikely to be true for all clients for all times. One young man I worked with, for instance, spent much of a session describing those times in his life where he felt that life lacked any meaning. When he had finished,

I spoke – eloquently and reassuringly, I thought – about Heidegger's belief that such times may actually be 'moments of insight' into the true nature of our existence. The young man reflected, looked at me, and then replied softly: 'Heidegger ... is such a dick!'

Critical reflections

Does greater meaning and purpose create greater wellbeing?

Generally, as we have seen, the hypothesis that wellbeing is associated with the presence of meaning and purpose in life is very well supported by the empirical research. However, it is important to note that this evidence is *correlational* rather than *causal*. That is, it does not *prove* that finding meaning in life reduces psychological distress (Steger, 2013), because 'the causal arrow might run in the other direction' (King & Hicks, 2013: 127). That is, people might experience a greater meaning in life *because* they are feeling happier, and there is some evidence to suggest that this is the case (King & Hicks, 2013). And, indeed, in my own experience, I know that questions and anxieties about the meaning of life rapidly dissipate (albeit temporarily) after a pint or two of beer. It may also be that some third variable, such as feelings of hope, lead to greater feelings of both wellbeing and meaning.

Can the search for meaning create greater distress?

Furthermore, as we have seen, the search for meaning, *per se*, does not seem to be predictive of psychological wellbeing (Steger, 2013). Indeed, there may be instances – for example, in people with cancer – where attempts at meaning making are 'indistinguishable from rumination' (Park, 2013: 528). Moreover, from an existential or humanistic standpoint, it could be argued that this drive towards meanings, goals and purposes is indicative of a pathogenic need to *do*, rather than just to *be* (e.g., Fromm, 2005). Along these lines, and consistent with much Eastern philosophy, Schopenhauer (1969: 309) argues that our willing and striving are actually the source of our suffering, for 'no satisfaction ... is lasting'. On the contrary, 'it is always merely the starting-point of a fresh striving'. Hence, for him, wellbeing comes not through identifying and pursuing our goals, but through an ascetic 'will-lessness, which alone stills and silences for ever the craving of the will' (1969: 362).

Do we have just one super-meaning?

Empirically, the logotherapeutic assumption that people have a single, ultimate meaning to their lives would also seem to be problematic. Rather, what the research suggests is that, 'meanings of life are actually built up in small chunks', and that 'people make sense of their lives one day at a time' (Baumeister, 1991: 60). Furthermore, there is very little evidence to support the logotherapeutic hypothesis that each particular situation has one, and only one, correct interpretation. 'Whether you attribute your suffering to God's will, what you deserve, the driver of the other car, or fate does not seem to make a big difference to how well you adjust', writes Baumeister (1991: 249). 'But if you can't find any satisfactory explanation', he adds, 'then you adjust poorly'.

Are existential therapists consistent on meaning?

This critique of logotherapeutic assumptions, however, would be shared by many in the existential field, and this points towards a further limitation of existential work around meaning and purpose. Nowhere, perhaps, are existential thinkers and practitioners so explicitly divided. As we have seen, for instance, while some aim to help clients accept the ultimate meaningless of existence (e.g., Yalom, 1980), others vigorously challenge clients to 'overcome' this belief (e.g., Frankl, 1986). Here, as Steger (2013) suggests, a 'unifying theoretical framework' might help to bring together these understandings; and there is certainly a need for a more nuanced, complex and detailed understanding of the relationships between meaning, purpose and wellbeing. What is it specifically, for instance, that helping someone to find meaning in their lives can do; and is this the same as helping them find purposes or goals?

Is there evidence for meaning-oriented practices?

Despite these difficulties, recent research on the effectiveness of meaning-oriented practices – particularly in the care of patients with chronic physical diseases – suggests that they may be a very promising form of existential intervention (e.g., Fillion et al., 2009). Indeed, in our recent EXIST review of both individual- and group-based existential therapies (Vos et al., 2014; see Box 1.2) we found that these were *the* best-evidenced form of existential practice. Meaning-oriented therapies significantly increased clients' sense of meaning in life; and brought about modest improvements in levels of self-esteem and self-efficacy, as well as modest reductions in hopelessness and anxiety. This suggests that the understandings and methods discussed in this chapter may be of considerable value to the wider therapeutic field.

Personalising practice

Based on the analysis and practices discussed in this chapter, we can hypothesise that meaning-oriented methods may be most helpful for clients who:

- Want to look at questions of meaning and purpose in life, or are asking these questions already.
- Have negative secondary feelings (e.g., shame, isolation) about asking questions of meaning and purpose.
- Are at a time-point in their lives where questions of meaning or purpose may be particularly salient, such as facing a serious disease.
- Have a deep sense of meaninglessness or purposelessness in their life.

Summary

Existential theory suggests that our lives are fundamentally oriented towards the future. Hence, having a positive sense of where we are going in our lives, and what our lives mean, is considered integral to psychological wellbeing; and there is some good empirical evidence to support this. According to some existential approaches, the meaning of our lives is given to us in our primary experiencing; but others hold that there are no given meanings to life – only those that we construct. Practically, there are a range of ways in which therapists can help clients develop a more positive relationship to their meanings and purposes in life. Most basically, this may involve understanding the client in terms of their future orientation, and reflecting this back to them. Clients can also be helped to find purpose, direction and meaning in their lives through a range of methods and therapeutic techniques. For some clients, however, it will be most important to empathise with, and help normalise, their feelings of meaninglessness. Although meaning-oriented understandings and interventions are amongst the most contested in the existential field, the research suggests that they are also amongst the most promising.

Questions for reflection and discussion

- To what extent do you agree or disagree with the assertion that life is inherently meaningful? What are the implications of your stance for your therapeutic practice?
- Which kinds of clients might benefit most from being encouraged to find purpose and meaning in their lives? Which might benefit most from being encouraged to accept a fundamental meaninglessness?
- Is therapy a meaningful activity, or is it a socially sanctioned charade that covers up the ultimate meaninglessness of life?

Recommended reading

Frankl, V.E. (1984) *Man's Search for Meaning* (revised and updated edn). New York: Washington Square Press. The most accessible of Frankl's books, detailing his harrowing experiences in the concentration camps and the basic principles of his meaning-orientated logotherapy.

Frankl, V.E. (1986) *The Doctor and the Soul: From Psychotherapy to Logotherapy* (R. Winston & C. Winston, Trans., 3rd edn). New York: Vintage Books. A more comprehensive introduction to logotherapy, and the various principles and techniques associated with it.

Yalom, I.D. (1980) *Existential Psychotherapy, Part IV.* New York: Basic Books. Definitive exploration of how people may avoid the dread of meaninglessness, and implications for therapy.

Bohart, A.C. (2001) Emphasising the future in empathy responses. In S. Haugh & T. Merry (eds), *Empathy* (pp. 99–111). Ross-on-Wye: PCCS Books. Accessible introduction to the principles and practices of a future-orientated therapeutic practice.

Wong, P.T. (2013) *The Human Quest for Meaning: Theories, Research, and Applications* (2nd edn). New York: Routledge. An excellent collection of contemporary chapters on meaning, aimed at advanced clinicians as well as researchers. Stand-out chapters include Steger's 'Experiencing meaning in life' (Ch. 8), which gives a succinct, comprehensive and accessible review of the evidence linking meaning to wellbeing; and

Klinger's 'The search for meaning in evolutionary goal-theory perspective and its clinical implications' (Ch. 2), which considers meaning and purpose in an evolutionary context.

Klemke, E.D. & Cahn, S.M. (eds) (1999) *The Meaning of Life: A Reader* (3rd edn). New York: OUP USA. Collection of key academic reflections on the question of meaning in life, particularly contrasting theistic and atheistic views.

7

Interpersonal Perceptions and Metaperceptions

This chapter discusses the existential understandings that:

- Our perceptions of others' experiencing may not match their actual experiencing, and that this may be a source of psychological distress for us.
- Our *metaperceptions* (how we think others experience us) may not match their actual perceptions of us, and that this may be a source of psychological distress for us.

It then goes on to describe the practices of:

- Helping clients to explore, and test out, their perceptions of others' experiences.
- Helping clients to explore, and test out, their metaperceptions.
- Encouraging more assertive and transparent communication.
- Exploring, and testing out, our own metaperceptions as therapists.

Understandings

Throughout my undergraduate years at university I had a crush on a fellow student. Let's call her Subi. She was someone I perceived as beautiful, intelligent and cool and, being awed by her attractiveness, avoided her entirely! In my very last weeks as an undergraduate, however, I met Subi at a party and, after a few drinks, summoned up the courage to talk to her. I no longer remember the exact details of that conversation, but I do remember feeling amazed to discover that, over all this time, she had been feeling pretty much the same way towards me as I had been feeling towards her. That is, far from feeling superior to me, she had seen me as distant and cool, and had never really made the effort to get to know me because she assumed I would never have been interested. What I perceived as her disinterest in me, then, was actually her response to perceiving me as disinterested in her!

I often reflected on that exchange with Subi, and the opportunity that was missed as a consequence of that misperception. And when I embarked on my counselling training, participating in a range of personal development groups and 'community' meetings, it became apparent to me how rife – and how painful – interpersonal misperceptions could be. In particular, I began to recognise that even though I could feel intensely vulnerable and fragile in an encounter with a peer, that other could actually be experiencing me in a very different way: mostly as confident, assertive and domineering. It hurt me, and could leave me feeling misunderstood, confused and angry. But the reality was, even in instances when I explicitly stated how vulnerable I was feeling, people could still perceive me as experiencing something very different.

For me, this interest in interpersonal perceptions came several years before beginning an existential training, and it is something I have written about in relation to a broad range of therapeutic orientations (Cooper, 2005b; 2009a (available on the companion website)). However, the dynamics of interpersonal relating have been at the heart of many existential philosophies (e.g., Buber, 1958; Sartre, 1958); as well as existential therapeutic practices, some of which have drawn explicitly from the field of interpersonal psychotherapy (e.g., Farber, 2000b; Yalom, 2001).

EXPLORING THE
INTER-PERCEPTUAL
WORLD

Across the existential approaches, the field of inter-perceptual dynamics has been most extensively explored by Laing (see Chapter 1). In his early work, Laing tried to understand psychosis in terms of an intelligible response to an 'insane' environment (1965). Drawing on the work of the anthropologist Gregory Bateson (Bateson, Jackson, Haley & Weakland, 1956), Laing argued that psychosis could result from growing up in a particularly deceptive, entangled and double-binding family environment (Laing, 1965, 1967, 1969, 1970; Laing & Esterson, 1964). In his later work, Laing (e.g., 1970) extended this analysis to the wider population, describing the interpersonal knots and entanglements that all of us may experience. Laing (1969: 174) saw interpersonal life as a 'nexus of persons, in which each person is guessing, assuming, inferring, believing, trusting, or suspecting, generally being happy or tormented by his phantasy of the other's experience, motives, and intentions'. He described the study of this field as *social phenomenology* (Laing, 1967): extending the analysis of experiencing (as discussed in Chapter 3) towards an analysis of the *inter-experiential field* (Cooper, 2005b).

In 1966, Laing published *Interpersonal Perception: A Theory and Method of Research* (with psychologist Herbert Phillipson and researcher Robert Lee) which specifically focused on the complex web of self- and other-perceptions that inhabit any relationship. Here, they coined the term *metaperception*, to refer to one person's perception of how another person perceives them. Subsequent research into metaperceptions has primarily been in the social psychological field (e.g., Carlson, Vazire & Furr, 2011; Kenny & Depaulo, 1993), with little explicit attention from existential therapists. However, there may be much that therapists of all orientations can take from the work in this field.

Interpersonal perception

In looking at the field of interpersonal perceptions, we can start by asking how much do we know of what others experience? Reflect, for instance, on the last person you talked to: What do you think they were experiencing when you were talking to them, and how accurate do you think your perception was? For Laing (1969: 28), the fact that we 'cannot see through the other's eyes and cannot hear through the other's ears' means that our perception of another's experiencing will always be, at least to some extent, inaccurate and incomplete. That is, however empathic or intuitive we may be, there is never the possibility of fully experiencing the experiencing of the other – it will always lie beyond our grasp.

If, as human beings, we simply accepted the unknowability of the other's experiencing, then the potential for interpersonal entanglements might be slight. However, human beings have a powerful tendency to read intentions and meanings into the activities of others. Indeed, anyone who has ever glared at their alarm clock for waking them up will know that even inanimate objects can be ascribed motivations. So although, objectively, we may have very little evidence on which to base an assessment of another's experiencing, this may not stop us from making inferences about what is going on for them and what they are trying to do. I see my partner frowning, for instance, and I can read into it a whole host of emotions and thoughts: 'She is annoyed with me ... because I left my socks lying around the house again ... and she wishes she hadn't married a slob ....' Of course, I might be entirely right, but I might also be entirely wrong (actually, I was right!); and the more I infer from 'public' actions to 'private' intentions, the more off-track I may be liable to go.

Furthermore, as with this example, not only are our perceptions likely to be inaccurate, but they are also likely to be biased in the direction of the other's manifest, public behaviour and appearance. We know, of course, that how people look on the 'outside' is not always how they feel on the 'inside', but in the absence of any further data, the other's observable behaviour and appearance are likely to strongly influence any inferences we make (for instance, Storms, 1973). Take a look, for instance, at the two fish in Figure 7.1 and ask yourself, which one feels more contented? Of course, objectively, we know that there is no reason to assume any differences in how the fish are feeling: indeed, as fish, they may not be feeling anything at all. But how easy is it to imagine that the 'sad' fish on the right is experiencing just as much contentment as the 'gently smiling' fish on the left? Similarly, for instance, if I see someone looking very calm and relaxed when they are speaking in public, I can find it almost impossible to believe that they are feeling shaky and nervous inside, even if that is what they subsequently tell me. Have you ever had that experience of finding something really terrifying, only to have that denied by people on the grounds that you looked so calm?

Figure 7.1 Which fish is more content?

From a cognitive perspective, this tendency to be overly influenced by how things appear can be seen as part of a wider *perceptual salience*, or *availability*, phenomenon, whereby our inferences about things tend to be biased by the data that is most present at that time (Kahneman, 2011). For instance, is the letter 'k' most likely to be found at the beginning of a word or as the third letter in a word? In fact, the answer is the latter, but because it is easier for us to call to mind examples of words beginning with 'k', there can be a tendency to over-assume its prevalence at the start of words. For Daniel Kahneman (2011: 20), Nobel prize winner and author of *Thinking, Fast and Slow*, this tendency towards cognitive errors comes from the 'part' of our mind which operates in automatic and quick ways – our primary experiencing – 'with little or no cognitive effort and no sense of voluntary control'. So we just automatically tend to assume that a fish that is smiling must be happy, or that someone who looks calm must be calm, and it is only if we consciously activate our effortful, agentic mind – our reflective awareness – that we can consider these questions in more rational, balanced ways. For Kahneman, the basic principle of our automatic thinking processes is that 'What you see is all there is' and this is the essence of the tendency to perceive others *as* they appear. You look cool so you must feel superior to me; you seem calm so you cannot be experiencing panic. From this perspective, it is only in the instances when people invoke a more deliberate, measured and systematic analysis of the other's experiencing that they can come to a more accurate perception of how they are thinking and feeling.

Here, we can see considerable divergence from the model of primary and secondary experiencing outlined in Chapter 3. There, it was argued that our primary experiencing is an intuitive, intelligible grasping of the world, as it exists for us, and that psychological difficulties tend to emerge at the level of secondary experiencing. Here, the model of primary experiencing is much less positive: that our intuitive grasp of the world is actually pretty distorted and inaccurate. This has implications for practice: in particular, a need for more proactive and psycho-educational interventions to challenge the validity of primary perceptions. However, in both approaches – indeed, perhaps in all therapies – the route towards wellbeing is seen as coming through reflective awareness, in which we can stand back from our immediate ways of engaging with the world, and find alternative, and potentially more constructive, modes of engagement.

Although all of us may be biased, to some extent, in our interpersonal perceptions, research suggests that some people may be more biased than others (Wellman & Lagattuta, 2000); and high levels of interpersonal misperceptions may lead to psychological difficulties for a range of reasons. First it may lead to the development of interpersonal conflicts, which are known to be a key source of psychological distress (Segrin, 2011) (see Chapter 2). Take the following example (adapted from Cooper, 2009a). Ismail, a 40-year-old man, came to therapy saying that he has had problems relating to women, and was having particular difficulties with his current partner, Maureen. Ismail reported that Maureen constantly criticised him for being insensitive and uncaring, but he could not understand why she was accusing him of this, because he felt that he was trying as hard as he could to be thoughtful towards her. As his experiencing was unpacked (see Chapter 3), what emerged was that Ismail spent a lot of time away at work, and when he did come home, he tended to keep out of Maureen's way, because he experienced her as hostile and critical. Maureen, reported Ismail, talked about feeling useless, unwanted and abandoned in the relationship, but Ismail said he just could not see this – she was such a powerful, dominant and critical force.

Through exploring his experiences in therapy, it became apparent that Ismail struggled with relationships for a number of reasons. However, with Maureen, one of the key ones seemed to be that he just could not 'see' her vulnerability and insecurity, even when she was directly expressing this to him. Rather, along the lines of 'What you see is all there is', he perceived her as she behaved – as dominant, critical and aggressive – and this contributed to a vicious interpersonal cycle: he withdrew, she got more critical, he withdrew further to avoid her 'wrath'. By contrast, had Ismail been able to perceive – and acknowledge – some of Maureen's vulnerabilities, she may then have felt more understood by him. This may have led her to express more intimate and affectionate feelings towards him, helping to unwind the vicious spiral entrapping both of them.

There is a second, more elliptical reason why misperceiving the experiences of others may be detrimental to our own wellbeing. As we have seen, interpersonal misperceptions tend to go in the direction of how people present themselves, and people will tend to present themselves in a relatively positive light – what social psychologists refer to as *impression management* (Goffman, 1971). Hence, if we rely too strongly on how people present themselves, we will tend to infer that others are more confident, able and happy than they actually are. The problem here is that, as social psychologists have demonstrated (Festinger, 1954), our conceptions of ourselves tend to be relative to our perceptions of others. In a classic social psychological study, for instance, participants who filled in a job application form next to a pristine 'Mr. Clean' experienced reductions in feelings of self-esteem, whilst those who completed the application form next to a dishevelled 'Mr. Dirty' experienced increases in their sense of self-worth (Morse & Gergen, 1970). This means, then, that the more we perceive others in terms of their outward appearances, the more we may end up perceiving ourselves in a negative light.

Anton is an example of this, whose experiences of failure and hopelessness seemed intimately tied up with his assumptions about how others were experiencing their world. Anton wanted to be 'normal': he wanted to be able to go out and have a good time 'like other people' without feeling insecure, scared or 'down'. In many respects, however, what distressed Anton the most was not his feelings of sadness, *per se*. Rather, at the level of secondary experiencing, it was the fact that this left him feeling different from – and inferior to – others. But all this was based on his assumptions about what others felt: an assumption based much more on what he saw than what he had found out to be true.

Metaperceptions

Think back to that last person you spoke to. In that interaction, as we have explored, you will have had perceptions of his or her experiences, and he or she will have had perceptions of yours. But you will also have had a perception of how he or she perceived you (just as he or she will have had a perception of how you perceived him or her). What was your intuitive, felt-sense of what that was? Do you think, for instance, that he or she perceived you as funny, or anxious, or friendly?

As well as forming implicit perceptions of others' experiences, therefore, we will also form an implicit sense of how others perceive *us*, our *metaperceptions* (Laing, Phillipson & Lee, 1966). This is illustrated in Figure 7.2, where the straight line represents A's perception of B, and the dotted line represents B's metaperception of how A perceives them. So when I talked, for instance, to the receptionist at my doctor's surgery this morning, I not only had some sense of her experiencing (caring, busy, attentive) but also some sense of how she was experiencing *me* (rushed, disorganised, demanding). And this metaperception, as well as my perception of her, was critical in determining my response to her. Here, for instance, I was apologetic and a bit obsequious, to compensate for her 'perception' of me as pushy and aggressive. But had I assumed she experienced me in a different way – for instance, foolish and ignorant – I might have responded quite differently: perhaps with anger or irritation.

Metaperception

Person B

Person B

Perception

Figure 7.2 B's metaperception of A's perception

As with perceptions of others' experiencing, we can also ask how accurate our metaperceptions are likely to be. I assumed, at a pre-reflective level, that the receptionist saw me as rushed and anxious, but is that really the case? For instance, when I handed in my new registration form, I put quite clearly that I was a 'professor' (my metaperception that health professionals see me as an idiot otherwise), and I also happened to be wearing a suit for a meeting later that day. Is it possible, then, that she perceived me as someone with quite high status, someone *she* needed to be obsequious to? Indeed, is it possible that her metaperception of me was that I saw *her* as foolish and disorganised, and that this was determining her way of responding to me?

Research in the social psychological field has tended to suggest that, as with perceptions of others' experiences, our metaperceptions can be highly inaccurate. Numerous studies, for instance, have shown that individuals' metaperceptions correlate very poorly with the others' actual perceptions of them (see reviews of the empirical evidence by Kenny & Depaulo, 1993; Shrauger & Schoeneman, 1979), and this is particularly the case for people who have low self-esteem (Langer & Wurf, 1999) or high social anxiety (e.g., Depaulo, Hoover, Webb, Kenny & Oliver, 1987). Indeed, correlations between metaperceptions and others' actual perceptions are generally only either non-significant or small (e.g., Depaulo et al., 1987; Kenny & Depaulo, 1993). More specifically, what the research has demonstrated is that while people do seem to have some insight into how others, *in general*, tend to perceive them (e.g., 'Most people see me as fairly friendly'), they have 'just a tiny glimmer of insight into how they are *uniquely* viewed by *particular* other people' (Kenny & Depaulo, 1993: 151, italics added). In other words, people tend to assume a greater homogeneity in how they are seen by others than there actually is (Kenny & Depaulo, 1993).

In terms of why people tend to be such poor judges of others' perceptions of them, social psychological research has come up with one very plausible explanation: people's metaperceptions 'are based primarily on their perceptions of themselves' (Kenny & Depaulo, 1993: 154). So I, for instance, felt rushed and anxious when I met the GP receptionist, and my natural tendency was to assume that she perceived me in the same way. Again, what we have here is a manifestation of the perceptual salience phenomenon: my own, 'inner' experiences are so salient to me that I simply assume other people are experiencing them as well.

Clinically, this belief that others see us as we see ourselves – the 'myth of self-transparency' (Depaulo et al., 1987) – has been associated with a range of psychological problems. Cognitive psychotherapists, for instance, have suggested that it is a key distortion associated with avoidant and paranoid 'personality types' (Reinecke & Freeman, 2003) and interpersonal psychotherapists have identified it as a common factor in marital disputes (Stuart & Robertson, 2003). Indeed, to some extent, it could be argued that this metaperceptual error is a key factor in any interpersonal conflicts. In the example of Ismail, for instance, the problem is not just that he feels criticised; the problem is that he feels criticised and berated, *and, at some level, assumes that Maureen knows how awful he feels.* 'Why does she go on criticising me all the time?' he says. So one of the key disjunctions here seems to be between Maureen's perception of Ismail (as self-contained, confident and oblivious to her criticisms), and Ismail's metaperception of how she sees him (as vulnerable and feeling criticised). Were Ismail able to recognise how Maureen really saw him (i.e., his metaperception matched her actual perception), his response to her might have been much more conciliatory in the first place.

In the example of Maureen and Ismail, both parties seemed to assume that the other saw them as more inadequate than they actually did and, in my clinical and personal experience, this is nearly always the direction of metaperceptual errors. Perhaps the reason for this is that, at a phenomenological level, we have such an 'insider's view' of our own doubts, uncertainties and vulnerabilities that it is very difficult to believe that others cannot see them too (again, the perceptual salience bias). Yet, as argued above, observers are often much more influenced by our public self, in which we tend to present ourselves as more competent and able than we are. It is a bit like putting on a mask and then forgetting that we have put it on. This means that others' responses to us seem consistently out of kilter to what we are actually experiencing. It is only when we remember that we are wearing a mask and that this is what others are responding to that things can start to make sense again.

This assumption, that other people can see our vulnerabilities, can then do much to further reinforce a person's feelings of low self-esteem. Not only do they see themselves as inadequate, but they believe others see them as inadequate, and this further compounds their sense of not being good enough. As symbolic interaction theory suggests (Mead, 1934), how people see themselves is highly dependent on how they imagine others see them; but if how they imagine others see them is dependent on how they see themselves, then it can be very difficult to escape from a vicious circle of low self-esteem. Indeed, going back to our discussion of an I–It relationship in Chapter 2, a person's interactions here can become entirely solipsistic and self-reinforcing. There is no place for an other because people are responding to a perceived perception which then confirms that their metaperception is correct!

What can also make this circle particularly vicious and pervasive is the fact that many people compensate for these feelings of vulnerability by putting on a more invulnerable 'mask', which then heightens the others' feelings of relative inadequacy, *ad nauseum*. In this respect, interpersonal relationships can be likened to an escalating series of bluff and counter-bluff in a poker game, in which each player senses a worthlessness in their own hand, fears others can see it too, and consequently raises the stakes higher and higher in an attempt to convince others – and themselves – of their worth.

Methods

This analysis of interpersonal perceptions and metaperceptions points to the value of a range of therapeutic practices.

Helping clients explore, and 'test out', their perceptions of others

If clients' misperceptions of others' experiences are a potent source of psychological distress, it would seem important for therapists to have strategies to help clients reflect on and, if necessary, revise, their perceptions of others' experiences. At its most basic, this might simply involve a therapist asking their clients to articulate what they imagine others to be experiencing. For instance, a therapist working with Ismail might ask: 'What do you think Maureen experiences when you are away from home?' More actively, therapists could also invite their clients to role play a dialogue with themselves and others. For instance, Ismail could be asked to talk from Maureen's position and articulate what she might be experiencing. In both instances, the point here would not be for Ismail to come up with the 'right' answer or to take him away from his own experiencing, but to encourage him to reflect on his perception of Maureen's experience, and thereby to stand back from it and consider it in different ways. In a sense, the aim is to help clients get to a place where they can *empathise* more fully with others: where they have a more accurate understanding of how others experience their world, and hence are less likely to fall into misunderstandings and interpersonal conflicts. Indeed, from an intersubjective standpoint, it has been argued that psychological well-being is not only associated with the experience of being empathised with (cf. Rogers, 1957, 1959) but also of being able to extend that empathy to others (cf. Yalom, 2001). We might call this the development of *other-awareness*, a corollary to the more familiar process of evolving self-awareness.

Clients can also be encouraged to reflect on how others, more generally, may experience their world; and to have their myths or fantasies about others' wellbeing challenged. As with a cognitive-behavioural approach, this might involve inviting them to review the evidence on which such a judgement is based, or some psycho-educational input based on some of the research and theory presented above. For instance:

Mick: Anton, you're assuming that others are happy when you're all out in the pub [*Anton*: right]; but do you know that that is actually the case? What's the basis for assuming that?

Anton: Cos they're sitting there, laughing, having a good time. They're smiling and laughing and chatting.

Mick: Ok, so they look like they're having a good time, but one thing you've said yourself is that a lot of the time when you're feeling miserable you join in and try and have a good time and that, actually, you get frustrated because people then just think you're happy and don't see how sad you're feeling. So how d'you know other people aren't doing the same thing?

Anton: [*Laughs*]. They ain't as good actors as me. [*pause*] Yeah, I know what you mean, I suppose that's possible, but it just doesn't look that way.

Mick: Yes, I know, you might be right, but you also might be wrong, and maybe something worth finding out about.

Of course, such challenge needs to be given in a sensitive, empathic and non-critical way. But if a strong therapeutic alliance exists, and if a client has indicated that they would welcome being challenged, then it may be very helpful to encourage them to re-think their assumptions about what others are experiencing. Indeed, given the human tendency to evaluate ourselves relative to others, it might be suggested that there are two basic paths to wellbeing: one is to recognise our own strengths and abilities, and the other is to recognise how vulnerable many other people feel inside.

Drawing on cognitive-behavioural theory and practices, in particular 'behavioural experiments' (Bennett-Levy et al., 2005), clients can also be encouraged to actually test out whether their assumptions about how others experience their worlds are actually true. For instance, Ismail's therapist might explore with him whether it would be useful for him to ask Maureen more about how she is feeling; and to directly learn about her experiencing, rather than making assumptions about it. Similarly, if clients believe that everyone else feels happy and confident, as with Anton, they could be encouraged to consider actually checking this out with others – in some safe and appropriate context – to see if it is really true or not.

One context that may be particularly safe and appropriate for clients to explore their interpersonal perceptions is the therapeutic relationship itself. As Spinelli (1997: 146) writes, the therapist is 'both a representative of all others in the client's world and *at the same time* the exception to the role regarding the client's percept of others'. He goes on to state that this may be 'one of the most significant offerings that therapists can make to their clients', because the therapist can give the client feedback about how they are experienced by others, in an honest, immediate and non-critical way. Through self-disclosure, therapists can also help clients develop a deeper understanding of how others might actually experience the world.

Paul, for instance, was a young teacher who came to therapy to try and overcome the anxieties and panic attacks he was experiencing in the school environment. For him, it was a mark of shame that he could feel so vulnerable and so 'different' from his fellow teachers. In the early parts of therapy, we phenomenologically unpacked Paul's moments of terror: the situations in which they emerged, the thoughts and feelings that he experienced, and the kinds of things he might do to lessen their prevalence and impact. When Paul returned to the subject of how alone and isolated he felt in this fear, however, it seemed appropriate to share something of my own experiencing:

Mick: Paul, I get such a strong sense of how awful these moments are for you, how terrifying it is, and I don't want to take away from that, but when you talk about your isolation here, it sounds like you feel like you're really on your own experiencing this.

Paul: Totally, I just see everyone else getting on with it ... no-one else starts sweating when they have to stand up in front of a class. I do think, deep down, it's just pathetic.

Mick: I don't know if this is helpful, but I guess what I'm aware of is that, for me as a lecturer and trainer, it's certainly something that I've also struggled with, and do still experience some times. Is it ok– shall I say a bit about that? [*Paul*: Yeah... yeah... it's fine]. Like, I can get really scared in front of a lecture room. I can feel panicky and awful.

Paul: Yeah ... that's quite surprising, actually, mmm ....

Mick: Yeah, I can get really scared. And, actually, a lot of the things that you talk about, like the trembling and the shakiness .... I really know what you mean.

Paul: Ok... So... um... What do you do to deal with it?

Mick: Well I guess, like you, I can find it really difficult and really hate it. But I guess the kinds of things we've talked about– about ways you can deal with it are also what's helped me, like around making sure I'm prepared, having strategies in place if I do feel wobbly ....

Disclosing these personal experiences to Paul felt like an opportunity to challenge some of his assumptions around experiencing panic – that he was alone with this, and that he was weird, abnormal or 'less than' other people for feeling scared. If his therapist shared some of these experiences, maybe others did too, and maybe he was not quite so alone with this as he experienced himself to be. In this respect, as both Farber (2000) and Spinelli (2001) have argued, it can sometimes be useful for a therapist to disclose their vulnerabilities to a client: helping to challenge the client's perception that they are less than others. Indeed, given the authority, status and psychological healthiness that clients may ascribe to therapists, hearing that therapists can also experience psychological difficulties may have a powerful de-pathologising effect (see Box 7.1).

Box 7.1   How 'sorted' are therapists?

In my own experience, one of the most important factors in helping me develop a more positive sense of self-worth was getting to know many of the 'gurus' of the psychotherapy world ... and realising how profoundly dysfunctional many of them were! Yes, they were sometimes more self-aware than the average person (though sometimes not even that!); but when you put together the narcissism, competitiveness, sense of failure, and inability to relate to others, I really did not seem to be doing so bad! Now that I have achieved some recognition in this field myself, I can confirm that being a known author on therapy is no guarantee of psychological sort-edness!

Yalom (2001: 8) states something similar when he writes: 'During my training I was often exposed to the idea of the fully analysed therapist, but as I have progressed through life, formed intimate relationships with a good many of my therapist colleagues, met the senior figures in the field, been called upon to render help to my former therapists and teachers, and myself become a teacher and an elder, I have come to realise the mythic nature of this idea. We are all in this together and there is no therapist and no person immune to the inherent tragedies of existence'.

At the same time, there is no doubt that the kind of self-disclosure that I made with Paul regarding my own anxieties can be 'risky': will clients simply come to the conclusion that the therapist is as damaged as they are and lose faith in their ability to help? In this instance, from Paul's feedback, it seemed like the disclosure was helpful and normalising. However, in Paul's case, this was probably because it came some weeks after we had established a good therapeutic alliance, such that I could afford to show some vulnerability without undermining Paul's trust in me. In addition, as supported by the research (Hill & Knox, 2002), I only very sparingly self-disclosed with Paul, such that Paul would be unlikely to feel that his time was being usurped.

Helping clients explore, and test out, their metaperceptions

If metaperceptual errors, like errors in interpersonal perceptions, are a potent source of psychological distress, then helping clients to reflect on, and challenge, their metaperceptions, can also be a useful therapeutic task. An example of this comes from Graeme, a young man who met criteria for moderate depression at assessment, and who came to therapy to feel more positive in his life and to achieve more of his potential. Graeme was also very keen to improve his relationships with others. He wanted to stop withdrawing from people; to get on better with them; and to be more spontaneous, open and authentic in his encounters.

From the start of our work together, I had experienced Graeme as an articulate and cultured young man, but it soon became apparent that he saw himself in a very different way. Graeme had been one of a few working class children at a middle class school, and had subsequently developed a sense of himself as uncultured, brutish and coarse. This seemed to be a key source of his interpersonal difficulties, and his metaperceptual assumption was that others also saw him in this way. Consequently, if people did not respond positively to him, he would interpret this as others rejecting him because of his 'brutishness', which would then further compound his sense of self-worthlessness.

One example of this had happened some time before we started therapy together. He had been taking some evening classes in sculpture. Graeme had begun to feel bored after a very long lecture by the tutor, and had summoned the courage to express this in the class. To his horror, the tutor had scolded him for expressing such negative feelings. Then, a few weeks before our 14th session, Graeme had had a few drinks and jokingly called one of his colleagues at work a 'numpty' [i.e., stupid]. Again, to his horror, the colleague had not laughed along but instead had seemed genuinely insulted, and had subsequently avoided Graeme. Graeme experienced both of these events as major rejections, and 'proof' that others saw him as uncouth, loud-mouthed and worthless. In session 14, this was something I challenged (transcribed verbatim):

Mick 1:   … This might not resonate, but is there something about your *authority*, in the sense of, like, I experience you as quite a– I don't know if 'powerful' is quite the right word but just, you know, there's quite a lot of *weight* of what you say and how you experience things, and how you word– how you communicate things. And I wonder if you– like, I take what you say seriously [*Graeme*: Mm hm], and I wonder if you sometimes underestimate how seriously people take you or….

Graeme 1: Probably [*pause*]. Um ... Yeah, I don't have a good sense of my power ... Yeah, I have difficulties estimating, like, how far I can reach or really how far my– [*Mick*: Yeah] my power will reach on people .... In real life experience they get offended [*Mick*: Yeah] they get upset [*Mick*: Yeah, yeah] they think that you're an arsehole because you said things to them. So....

Mick 2: Well, I mean– Because, if you take that example of calling someone a numpty, someone's only going to be upset by that if they gave you some kind of power. I mean, if they didn't take seriously what you said or it wasn't important [*Graeme*: Un huh] it wouldn't affect them [*Graeme*: Un huh]. So that seems to me, actually– your words are really reaching out [*Graeme*: Mm hm]. And my experience of you is that, yeah, you– your words and your perception does reach out and I imagine people take that....

Graeme 2: It's difficult to make sense of it. Um... I had a similar conversation with my sculpture tutor, and– that I don't think I am being taken seriously. Because I said that one group session that I was bored, and I didn't take a– I wouldn't have been taken seriously [*Mick*: Uh huh, yeah] and she said that, er– 'No, you are an intellectual and you are sitting in this class with people who are not that educated and you make them [*Mick*: Yeah, yeah] feel little' [*Mick*: Yeah]. But I didn't see that way, because my general experience is that eventually they never really listen to me....

Mick 3: Well I can really... I– I think there is something about being taken seriously, and I can really see people taking you seriously, and I can definitely see a gulf between what you imagine and what you actually get back from people. And I think one of the really interesting conversations we've had recently is this sense of your self as uncouth [*Graeme laughs*] and uncultured, because I think– if that's in your head [*Graeme*: Mm hm] how you imagine people see– perhaps not taking you seriously, I think that is *so* different from how people would experience you. I think it's just– I mean, my experience of you– I think if you went out and did a straw poll and you had a list of words about how people perceived you, I think that is just– [*Graeme laughs*] that would just be the last one, and I think you're expecting that– imagining that, and actually people are seeing something very different. I think that's going to create a lot of confusion and a lot of difficulties in situations because I can imagine– Yeah, I can imagine that if you're saying something like 'I feel bored' [*Graeme*: Mm hm]– I mean, if no-one cared about what you thought and saw you as uncultivated [*Graeme*: Mm hm] then it would be like 'What the hell?' But I imagine that people take what you say seriously– concerned about what you think about them, see you as intelligent [*Graeme*: Mm] and intellectual [*Graeme*: Mm hm] and quite powerful [*Graeme*: Mm] and actually that therefore does have quite a big impact on people [*Graeme*: Mm].

In this dialogue, Graeme was challenged with the possibility that others were reacting negatively to him, not because they saw him as uncouth and worthless, but because they saw him as articulate and powerful. This had the potential to fundamentally challenge Graeme's low sense of self-worth, and it also gave him some new possible means of dealing with interpersonal difficulties. More specifically, rather than buffing himself up when he ran into interpersonal conflicts, it might be that what he sometimes needed to do was to acknowledge, and respond to, the vulnerabilities of the other.

As is evident in this extract, and as discussed earlier, a key element of this interpersonal work was bringing my own perception of the client 'into the room' (or, as Yalom (2001: 52) describes it, bringing the dysfunctional interaction into the immediacy of the here-and-now). This provides the therapist with a valuable touchstone from which to challenge clients' metaperceptions. We cannot say for certain how other people experience our clients, but we can say what *our* experiencing is. Such challenges can be a powerful point of therapeutic leverage, as the client's metaperceptual assumptions are clearly and categorically disputed. On the companion website there is a further example of helping clients explore their metaperceptions in the immediate therapeutic relationship.

CHALLENGING CLIENTS'
META-PERCEPTIONS IN
THE IMMEDIATE HERE-
AND-NOW: NOTES

In the work with Graeme, a negative metaperceptual assumption was challenged with a positive self-disclosing statement (cf. affirming dissensus, Chapter 2). And, generally, the research suggests that such kinds of positive 'self-involving statements' can be helpful to clients (Claiborn et al., 2002; Hill & Knox, 2002). This compares with negative self-involving statement (e.g., Yalom, 1989) – for instance, sharing with a client that one feels bored or irritated by them – which do not seem to be so helpful (Cooper, 2008a). If the therapeutic alliance is very strong, it may be that such feedback can be taken constructively. However, given the power that therapists tend to hold, they also have the potential to be deeply destructive. Indeed, I have worked with several clients who were still disturbed by the negative self-involving statements that previous therapists had made. In many instances, then, the benefits of brutal honesty may be outweighed by the risks to the alliance that negative self-involving disclosures have. From a pluralistic standpoint, however, perhaps the crucial question is one of what clients want. If clients, for instance, want to understand why their relationships go wrong, and/or ask for totally honest feedback, it may be appropriate to give it; but much less so for clients who are primarily wanting a sensitive, compassionate listening ear.

Assertiveness training

If interpersonal misperceptions are problematic because they have a negative impact on clients' interpersonal (as well as intrapersonal) relationships, then it is not only corrections to the clients' interpersonal perceptions that could facilitate the clients' wellbeing. Equally, if those in relationship with the clients, such as Ismail's Maureen, could be helped to perceive the clients' experiences more accurately, then this could also have a positive relational, and thereby psychological, impact. Of course, psychotherapists working on a one-to-one basis are not able to have a direct impact on significant others in a client's life, but they can help clients to express their experiences and wants more directly to those others, such that those others may then be more fully aware of what the client is experiencing and wanting. Furthermore, if the therapist is modelling an authentic way of being, this may also help clients to develop more transparent modes of relating.

In some instances, however, it may also be helpful for therapists to directly encourage or challenge clients to be honest with others about what they are feeling or thinking (a strategy also sometimes advocated in Interpersonal Psychotherapy, Stuart & Robertson, 2003). For example, in one session with Ismail, I gently asked him whether he had ever actually told Maureen how he felt towards her. I assumed he had, but just wanted to check out this assumption. Ismail thought about it and said, 'Probably not'. Whilst he acknowledged that he had expressed his anger towards her in various indirect ways, he noted that he had never really told her about this, and his other feelings, directly.

A few sessions later, Ismail came in to say that he had started to tell Maureen how he was feeling, and that it seemed to be improving things a bit. He added, however, that it was also really frightening to talk to her in this way, because he was very scared that she would exploit his vulnerabilities at a later date. In the session, we explored these fears. The next session he came in to tell me that things were really so much better in the relationship, and that he was amazed at how well Maureen had heard how he was feeling towards her. Rather than retaliating when he had told her his feelings about the relationship, she had expressed warmth and concern for him, and the two of them felt much closer than they had been for some time.

Helping clients to communicate their experiences and perceptions more transparently and directly to others is just one part of a larger process of helping clients to be more *assertive*. In my experience, this is often one of the most important and helpful parts of the therapeutic process for many clients. Assertiveness training is usually associated with more behavioural approaches to therapeutic change, where it has been shown to bring about positive outcomes (Sanchez, Lewinsohn & Larson, 1980). However, the principles embedded within it are closely related to the phenomenological and relational understandings and practices outlined in Chapters 2 and 3 of this book, respectively. Indeed, to a great extent, the practice of helping clients to be more assertive is probably incorporated into every orientation of therapeutic practice.

For some clients, the term 'assertive' can be equated with being insistent or demanding of what you want. However, it is probably best understood as a broad set of guidelines for communicating effectively with others. It is based on direct communication, so that both parties can maximise their wants and reduce the kinds of misperceptions, entanglements and confusions discussed in this chapter (see, also, Cooper, 2012d; and Cooper, 2009a (available on the companion website)). As psycho-education, some of the key principles that can be communicated to clients are:

EXPLORING THE
INTER-PERCEPTUAL
WORLD

- If you want someone to know your experiencing – your feelings, thoughts or wants – *tell them*, as clearly and as honestly as you can. Don't assume self-transparency: that others will know what you are experiencing without you having to communicate it. Indeed, given that the other will have their own biases, wants and assumptions, you may need to communicate your experiencing a few times before the other really begins to understand it.
- Try to communicate in terms of your *subjective* experiencing, rather than in terms of *objective* facts; for instance, 'I felt hurt' rather than 'you hurt me'; 'I *thought* you were really angry' rather than 'You *were* really angry'. This helps to bypass an argument about what *really* happened, or about who was right or wrong.
- Try to avoid blaming the other, or communicating to the other that they were wrong, even if subtly (for instance, 'I know you tried your hardest but I guess it's really difficult for you to be sensitive to others'). Instead, try and recognise the feelings behind your desire to blame the other – for instance, anger, hurt or disappointment – and try and communicate those instead.

- Accept that two people can experience the same situation in very different ways, and that this is an opportunity for greater understanding – not an indication that someone must be wrong. As part of that, it is very important to distinguish between *intention* and *effect*: someone's behaviour may have had the effect of really hurting you, but this does not mean that that was the intention behind it.
- Try not to attribute intention to the other's behaviour, or get into arguments about why they did what they did. You can never really know for sure. What's much more incontrovertible is what effect it has on you.
- Being assertive means listening to the other as well as expressing yourself. Try and take in what they are saying, and understand how they experience their world. Try not to be defensive: what they experience is what they experience, and it is not a reflection of who you are as a person.
- Try to remember that, in most instances, both you and the other person are trying to do your best in this situation; and neither of you are deliberately out to hurt the other.
- If necessary, talk about how you are talking, and agree the basic principles of how you are going to communicate. You might use the principles laid out here, or some other ones. One of the main reasons why dialogues may break down is because there is not agreed 'rules' of communication.
- Communicating your experiences to others – and hearing their experiences – can be anxiety-evoking, and not always easy. You may feel hurt, and you may hurt the other. So be prepared to experience strong emotions when you talk and, if you do so, try to come back to these guidelines – simply describing your experiences to the other – rather than acting or reacting on the basis of your emotions.
- And finally, just because you want – and are prepared – to talk assertively, it does not mean that the other will too. Other people may just not have the skills, or maturity, or interest in communicating in this way: for instance, they may be much more interested in blaming you and 'proving' that you are wrong. If this is the case, you need to decide whether you still want to try and engage assertively, or whether there is something else that would be more helpful to do. For instance, if someone seems only interested in blaming, and this is consistently upsetting, it may be more helpful to avoid in-depth communication altogether.

This latter point is particularly important, and for therapists to bear in mind as well as clients. For instance, if clients are being subjected to domestic violence, encouraging them to engage assertively with their partner may be an extremely inappropriate and dangerous thing to do.

An example of assertiveness work in therapy was with Rima, who was challenged to acknowledge some of her positive qualities (Chapter 2). One of Rima's principal goals for therapy was 'To feel strong and resilient in relation to my mother'. Rima had experienced difficulties with her mother throughout her life. She described her as a self-centred, controlling, and very needy woman, who seemed consistently oblivious to Rima's own needs. Rima also experienced her mother as highly unpredictable: for instance, the last time they had gone shopping together, Rima's mother had started 'ranting' at one of the shop assistants over the price of a dress, much to Rima's embarrassment and horror.

Just before our therapy began, Rima had written to her mother saying that she was thinking of breaking contact with her. Rima had never challenged her mother before in this way, and was waiting anxiously to hear what her mother would say. The response came just before session three – a long, rambling letter – which managed to acknowledged that difficulties did exist in the relationship, but tended to attribute these to Rima's 'mental health problems', such as her fear of being judged in public. Rima felt relieved, but also annoyed and frustrated, and we used the therapy session to talk through how Rima was feeling, and what she might choose to write back.

For Rima, communicating with her mother in this way was a massive step forward from how she had done things in the past, which tended to oscillate between compliance and anger. The basic principles of assertiveness which I introduced into the dialogue, as above, seemed to provide a useful framework for thinking about how to respond constructively. Rima decided that she did want to tell her mother about the frustration that she was feeling, but also to acknowledge that she was pleased her mother had recognised some of the problems between them. Rather than trying to prove to her mother that she *really was* behaving in embarrassing ways, Rima also decided to keep things more simple: reiterating how difficult *she* found her mother's behaviour, and that *she* wanted her mother to acknowledge this. Later on in the work, when Rima's mother had again responded in a quite defensive way, Rima decided that the most assertive things she could do would simply be to ask her mother if she was willing, at this point, to hear how Rima was feeling. If not, and if the mother was simply concerned with defending herself, then Rima felt that the best option would be to have a break from contact for some time.

Exploring, and testing out, our own perceptions and metaperceptions as therapists

We can also apply this analysis of perceptions and metaperceptions to our own development as therapists. Ask yourself, for instance, this question: *What do you think your clients see when they see you?* Imagine, for instance, a client coming in to your consulting room for the first time. How do you imagine they experience you? Do you think, for instance, they perceive you as friendly, distant, powerful or engaged?

Whatever your answer to this question, there is a very good chance that you are wrong – at least to some extent. Indeed, research suggests that therapists are even less accurate than clients in judging how they are seen by others (Michels, 2000)! Furthermore, as with other people (see above), the evidence suggests that therapists tend to underestimate the esteem with which they are held in: assuming, for instance, that clients see them as more neurotic, and as less conscientious, agreeable and supportive, than they actually do (Michels, 2000).

Hence, it would seem important that therapists also develop an awareness of any potential discrepancies between how they assume others perceive them and how those others actually do. This would help to minimise the likelihood that such misperceptions cause miscommunications and ruptures in the therapeutic relationship (see Metaperceptions exercise on the companion website for a structured means of doing this). Take the example of a therapist who feels very inexperienced, and therefore puts up a confident front to his clients to try and compensate for this. If a client then responds to this front by making fun of the therapist, the therapist should be ok with it if he knows that the client is responding to his perceived confidence. But if the therapist makes the metaperceptual error of assuming that the client, also, perceives him as inexperienced and inadequate, then the teasing may be experienced in a much more hostile way, potentially leading to a more defensive response by the therapist.

METAPERCEPTIONS: A GROUP TRAINING EXERCISE

Given that the therapeutic relationship is there for the client and not the therapist, it would rarely be appropriate for therapists to use this encounter to test out the accuracy of their metaperceptions. However, one important implication of this analysis is that therapists can try to hold their metaperceptions 'lightly': with a flexibility and fluidity that means they are open to their clients' *actual* perceptions of them. For example, some years ago, I worked with a young artist, Zed. After our first session together, I had a deep sense of warmth and empathy towards her; and implicitly assumed that she had experienced something of that from me. At the beginning of the second session, then, I was shocked when Zed presented me with a picture she had drawn of me earlier that week. In it, I was portrayed as a cold, aloof and unwelcoming figure, dressed entirely in black. Here, I tried my hardest to let go of my metaperceptual assumptions, and acknowledge – and respond to – how Zed actually seemed to be experiencing me. So we explored her perception of me more fully, and we also compared it against what I felt I had been experiencing, to see what Zed might learn about her interpersonal perceptions. The next session, Zed said that she felt much better about the relationship – something that may not have happened if I had steadfastly held on to my metaperceptual assumption that she experienced me as empathic from the start.

An openness to feedback from clients – whether verbal or through the use of written post-session evaluation forms, such as the Helpful Aspects of Therapy Form (see www.experientialresearcher.com) – can also help us learn how clients, more generally, might experience us. These are things we may be totally unaware of. For instance, Zed indicated that she had been very conscious of the fact that I was wearing all black in our session, and this had added to her sense that I might be quite serious and imposing. In fact, in those days, pretty much everything I ever wore was black – partly a consequence of being anxious about my weight as a teenager, and partly as a hangover from my post-punk youth – and it had never occurred to me that this might convey an altogether different message to what was intended. The feedback from Zed helped me to re-think this: not to radically change my wardrobe (as I sit here 15 years on, I still have a black t-shirt on, though at least my jeans now are dark blue); but to be more aware of how I might be experienced by clients.

USING
FEEDBACK
MEASURES

Critical reflections

Do we need to go beyond a linear worldview?

A phenomenological, experience-centred approach (Chapter 3) produces a relatively linear and unidimensional worldview: Person A experiences X, Y and Z. But when we combine this with a relational perspective (Chapter 2) – if, for instance, X is actually 'Person B' – then things become a lot more complicated. Now, Person A experiences Person B, but Person B also experiences Person A; and, Person A will have a metaperception of how Person B perceives them, and likewise for Person B. Moreover, Person A's perceptions and metaperceptions of Person B will affect how they behave towards Person B, which will affect Person B's perceptions and behaviours towards A, *ad infinitum*. Now, we can no longer think in terms of simple linear processes, but of a complex, interweaving gestalt (Chamberlain & Bütz, 1998). In this respect, the kind of social phenomenological analysis developed in this chapter may be essential in trying to make deeper sense of human experiencing, relating and behaviour.

Is this analysis consistent with existential ideas?

As we have seen, such an analysis does lead to a break down in assumptions about the intelligibility of primary human experiencing (Chapter 3). Indeed, from an existential standpoint, the present analysis could be critiqued for straying too far into CBT territory, with its assumptions about the fundamental irrationality of primary human experiencing. And, indeed, recent research suggests that people may have more insight into how others experience them than has been previously suggested (Carlson et al., 2011). However, when we start to focus on the inter-experiential realm – how one person experiences the experiences of another – then assumptions about the inherent trustworthiness and 'rightness' of our experiences do become more problematic. This is for the following reason. If Person A sees object X in one way, and Person B sees object X in another way, then we can simply accept that they have different perspectives on how things are. But if Person A sees Person B's experiences in one way, and Person B sees their own experiences in a different way, then we cannot simply accept both their perceptions. Here, if we trust Person B to know their own experiencing, then Person A's experiencing *must* be wrong. Likewise, if we trust Person A's perceptions of Person B's experiencing, then Person B *must* be wrong.

Can interpersonal problems be resolved so easily?

From some existential positions, the present analysis could also be critiqued for being too naïve and optimistic about the possibilities for human relating and accord. In the present chapter, there is an assumption that, with assertive and effective communication, people can exist in relative harmony with each other. By contrast, existential philosophers like Sartre (1958) have argued that the very essence of human being is to be in conflict with others. For Sartre, the 'look' of the other constantly threatens to turn us into an object: to 'it-ify' us. Hence, in attempting to defend ourselves against such objectification, we may strive to objectify the other instead, entering a battle of objectify-or-be-objectified. Alternatively, we may submit to the other's objectification, and in doing so lose touch with our own humanity. Sartre (1989: 45) famously wrote: 'Hell is – other people!'; and, from this standpoint, we cannot escape from the struggles of interpersonal existence. Here, then, it might be suggested that we should help clients come to terms with interpersonal conflict as an existential given (see Chapter 5), rather than fostering an illusion that such difficulties can ultimately be overcome.

How does an understanding of metaperceptions compare across orientations?

From a pluralistic standpoint, one of the particular strengths of the present analysis is that it forms a meeting point for a range of therapeutic orientations. Not only is it consistent with an existential emphasis on being-in-relationship and phenomenology, but it fits closely with a cognitive understanding of distress in terms of 'errors of thinking' (albeit at an interpersonal level), and a behavioural emphasis on testing out assumptions in the real world. There is also a meeting with the interpersonal psychotherapy tradition (Stuart & Robertson, 2003; Sullivan, 1953), which holds that 'a large part of mental disorder results from and is perpetuated by inadequate communication' (Cohen, 1953: xii); and with systemic and family therapy, which often focuses on nonlinear, interlocking feedback mechanisms between persons (e.g. Kaslow, Dausch & Celano, 2003). Many commonalities also exist with the psychodynamic concepts of transference and countertransference, in terms of misperceiving the intentions, experiences and characteristics of others. However, while psychodynamic thinking attributes such misperceptions to experiences in early relationships, the present analysis suggests that they may also arise through basic cognitive biases.

Personalising practice

The methods described in this chapter may be most helpful for clients who:

- Want to work on interpersonal and relational issues in therapy, or have interpersonal difficulties.
- Seem to have inaccurate assumptions about how others experience their worlds – as may be manifest in misperceptions of what their therapist is experiencing.
- Seem to have inaccurate assumptions about how others experience them – as may be manifest in inaccurate metaperceptions about how their therapist perceives them.

Summary

Research and theory suggests that we often have inaccurate perceptions of others' experiences, and this can lead to interpersonal discord and distress. Equally, we may often misjudge how others perceive us – our *metaperceptions* – and this can also be a source of interpersonal conflict and difficulties. To help clients address this, we can support them to explore, and test out, their perceptions and metaperceptions; and encourage them to communicate more assertively with others. We can also examine our own perceptions and metaperceptions and test out their accuracy, such that they do not interfere with the development of an effective therapeutic alliance.

Questions for reflection and discussion

- How accurately do you think you know how other people perceive you? Has reading this chapter changed your view on that at all?
- Think of a client you are struggling with: How accurately do you think she or he perceives how others experience her or him? How might you work with this in therapy?

Recommended reading

Laing, R.D., Phillipson, H. & Lee, A.R. (1966) *Interpersonal Perception: A Theory and a Method of Research*. London: Tavistock. The original text that stimulated work in this area. Relatively dry and technical, but a useful read for those with a special interest.

Kenny, D.A. & Depaulo, B.M. (1993) Do people know how others view them – an empirical and theoretical account. *Psychological Bulletin, 114*(1), 145–161. A little dated, but the most comprehensive review of the evidence in this area.

Cooper, M. (2009) Interpersonal perceptions and metaperceptions: Psychotherapeutic practice in the inter-experiential realm. *Journal of Humanistic Psychology, 49*(1), 85–99. Practitioner-friendly review, covering similar content to the present chapter. Available on the companion website.

EXPLORING THE
INTER-PERCEPTUAL
WORLD

8

Discussion

This chapter draws together two themes of this book that, for me, are of particular importance:

- The tragic optimism at the heart of an existential worldview.
- The radical potential of existential thought and practice.

It then goes on to summarise:

- The similarities and differences between existential therapy and other therapeutic orientations.
- The principal contributions that an existential approach can make to the therapeutic field.
- The key critiques of existential therapy.
- A pluralistic perspective on existential therapy.
- The particular clients for whom an existential approach might be appropriate.

A tragic optimism

Life as suffering

In the introduction to my 2003 book *Existential Therapies* (2003b: 1), I half-jokingly described existential therapy as 'similar to person-centred therapy ... only more miserable!' I say 'half-jokingly' because, although existentialism is ultimately a philosophy of passion, intensity and care in living, it does have a decidedly melancholic side (Manafi, 2010; Tengan, 1999). From an existential standpoint, life is not the fun-filled adventure many of us would like it to be. Rather, beneath the Technicolor gloss lies a much bleaker reality. As we have seen, from this existential perspective, to be human means having to choose and to be responsible (Chapter 4). It means facing the limitations of human existence, such as death, uncertainty and the paradoxes of life (Chapter 5). It means striving to find meanings and purposes in a world that may be devoid of them, but in which we are unable to step off the treadmill of wanting and desiring (Chapter 6). And to be human means to be caught up in interpersonal misperceptions, entanglements and conflicts that arise from the very grounds of our being (Chapter 7). 'Life', writes van Deurzen (1998: 132), 'is an endless struggle, where moments of ease and happiness are the exception rather than the rule'. Like Sisyphus rolling his boulder up the hill (Camus, 1955), we must battle to move forward in our lives. There are some successes, but most often they are followed by further failures. And after all that there is decrepitude and death.

Throughout all this, from an existential standpoint, there is the inevitability and pervasiveness of anxiety (Kierkegaard, 1980; May, 1977; Spinelli, 2015). We feel anxious because we have to make choices within a world that is unpredictable and unforgiving, and where the choice of one thing means a choice against something else. And, from an existential perspective, we also feel anxious because we are aware of the fundamental nothingness of our being: that we have no absolute certainty, groundedness or meaning. As human beings, we are compelled towards creating stability, definiteness and purposes. But, like building a house on sand, we cannot escape an awareness of how shaky our foundations truly are; or that one day it will all be swept away. Becker writes (1973: 87):

> Anxiety is the result of the perception of the truth of one's condition. What does it mean to be a *self-conscious animal*? The idea is ludicrous, if it is not monstrous. It means to know that one is food for worms. This is the terror: to have emerged from nothing, to have a name, consciousness of self, deep inner feelings, an excruciating yearning for life and self-expression – and with all this yet to die.

In the same vein, to be human is to experience regret for the possibilities that we have failed to actualise (Heidegger, 1962; Kierkegaard, 1980), guilt for failing others (Buber, 1988), and the pain of endlessly wanting (Schopenhauer, 1969). Indeed, the existentially oriented philosopher

Schopenhauer (1969: 310) argues that *all life is suffering*. 'The shortness of life, so often lamented', he writes (1969: 325), 'may perhaps be the very best thing about it'; and he goes on to state that, 'no man, if he be sincere and at the same time in possession of his faculties, will ever wish to go through it again' (1969: 324).

This emphasis on the tragic dimensions of existence makes the existential approach relatively unique in the therapeutic field. As we saw earlier, in the person-centred approach, there is a tendency to believe in a 'good life' (Rogers, 1961): that there are a series of stages that we can go through to achieve a more fully functioning state. Similarly, from a CBT perspective (e.g., Moorey, 2014), psychological difficulties tend to be seen as a product of distorted and primitive thinking, which have the capacity to be corrected. What an existential perspective adds here, then, is the possibility that our psychological distress is not a sign of pathology or failure to actualise, but an intelligible and meaningful response to the reality of human existence. We suffer – feel guilt, anxiety and pain – not because we are maladjusted, but because it is the very essence of human existence to do so. Indeed, for existential philosophers such as Kierkegaard (1980) and Schopenhauer (1969), the more that we experience such distressing feelings as anxiety, the more self-aware, intelligent and actualised we may be.

Standing naked in the storm of life

Yet the message of existentialism is not that we should feel sorry for ourselves or bemoan the human fate. Rather, as with a contemporary 'recovery' agenda (National Institute for Mental Health in England, 2005), it is that we should live and thrive *despite*. That is, the challenge is to 'stand naked in the storm of life' (Becker, 1973: 86) and to engage with existence in all its downs as well as ups. 'Life means challenge, trouble and difficulties', writes van Deurzen (2009b: 167). 'Sorrows and problems about everywhere: to become real in therapy means to be prepared to meet these head on and to have an attitude of willingness and eagerness to be in tune with life and to find good in the bad, moving forward courageously and confidently, no matter what may come'. Here, the 'secret' to life is not about always getting it right, but about learning to *bear* failures, difficulties and challenges. It is to be *resilient* (Children and Young People's Mental Health Coalition, 2012) and *hardy* (Maddi, 2004): meeting our problems squarely in the face, rather than running away from them (van Deurzen & Adams, 2011). In addition, the existential message is that we should make the most of our lives *now*, rather than waiting for some fantasised perfection 'just around the corner'. Here, we can see parallels with behavioural and psychodynamic approaches which also emphasise the importance of learning to tolerate anxiety, and learning to live and thrive despite.

Taking life seriously

In this respect, an existential approach is a commitment to 'taking life seriously' (May, 1983: 169). It rejects an apathetic, cynical and indifferent stance; and instead calls on us to actualise our genuine *care* for life (May, 1969a). Life matters; and rather than seeing this concern as a sign of dysfunction or irrationality, it argues that we should nurture our care for life and draw on it to actualise our being. In this existential perspective, we have just one life – so, incredibly precious – and we can choose to either fritter it away or make the most of our very limited moments on earth. Here the point of being alive is to do the things that we cannot do when we are un-alive: when we are dead. We can be indifferent when we are dead, we can be quiet and immobile. But while we are alive, we have the opportunity to be passionate, zestful and fiery. We can love, we can care, we can live every moment of our lives to the fullest degree, all the time under the shadow of finitude and death.

Living life to the full

Honest confrontation with our existential situation may evoke 'fear and trembling' but, from an existential perspective, it has the potential to be deeply 'healing and enriching' (Yalom, 1999: 125). This is the 'tragic optimism' that Frankl (1984) describes: a hope and a belief that we can find meaning and fulfilment on the far side of our suffering. Through an immersion in the 'churning broth that is the human condition' (Bugental, 1981: 54), we can discover a vibrancy and intensity of living, an openness to the world that allows us to live existence to the full (Spira, 2000). This is about allowing sorrow to carve into our being, so that we can contain that much more joy (Gibran, 1923: 35). Far from being a philosophy, then, of hopelessness and despair, 'existentialism celebrates life and epitomises an attitude of passion, commitment, brevity and perseverance' (Manafi, 2010: 173).

Implications for practice

What are the implications of this tragic-optimistic worldview for therapeutic practice? One potential application is psycho-education: we can help our clients to understand that life is a challenge to be faced (van Deurzen, 2009b, 2012a). From a pluralistic standpoint, however, we may need to be very cautious in adopting this path. These ideas may make sense to us, but for some clients, such a perspective on life may make no sense at all. It may just seem unnecessarily intense and morbid. 'What kind of miserable freak', they might ask, 'would want to see the world in this way?' It is a bit like listening to Bob Dylan (the greatest existential musician of all time, see Appendix, and a lifelong personal favourite). Some people experience a deep, soulful beauty in the bleakness, intensity and passion. Others just hear a nasal, whiny dirge. Who is right? From a pluralistic standpoint, however much we might love listening to Bob Dylan, we also have to acknowledge that some people might prefer listening to Miley Cyrus, and that neither is ultimately 'right'. It hurts, it really does; but that is what Levinas' openness to otherness is all about!

From a pluralistic standpoint, then, the key value of this tragic optimism may be in helping us deeply empathise with those clients who *do* see the world in this way. For those clients who want to ask these existential questions, and do not want to be 'jollied out' of their pain, it allows us to sit deeply with them and genuinely, deeply respect what they are asking and feeling. And not in the sense of 'I know how bad things are for you, now let me help you out of it'. Rather, it is in the sense of 'I know how bad things are for you, and it *really* makes sense to me that things feel so difficult'. It is a deep valuing and staying with the client in the tragic (Bugental, 1981) – not reassuring or trying to make things better – and with the genuine belief that this can be an intelligible, legitimate part of a fully lived life. From a pluralistic existential stance, no-one should be forced to listen to Bob Dylan. But for the person whose soul is touched deeply by his songs – and who may be otherwise surrounded by superficial pap – it may be the most exquisite pleasure and relief to listen to it.

What an existential therapeutic approach offers, moreover, is the chance to listen to this music *in the presence of another.* Remember being a teenager and listening to some music with a friend, and being mesmerised by the power of that shared experience? In existential therapy, clients can not only go into their darkest places, but they can go there with someone alongside. More than that, they can go there with someone who shows that they also, deeply, know what that place might be like: that they, the therapist, have also touched that sadness, suffering and despair. And through connecting, at one and the same time, with both their own pain and that of the therapist, they may come to feel that they are less alone in their suffering: that they are part of a common humanity that is struggling and striving to make sense of their lives. Here, there is no real distinction between the 'afflicted' and the 'healed' (Yalom, 2001), we are all in this together. And even though this may not resolve the client's primary pain, there may be a world of difference between struggling alone, and struggling alongside others. Perhaps this is one way of reading Beckett's *Waiting for Godot* (see Box 6.2). Things are not easy for Vladimir and Estragon, but at least they have each other: to argue with, to play with, to feel that they are not totally alone. In some way, relationality assuages the meaninglessness of existence: we find hope and possibilities through connections with others.

Of course, as therapists, this means that we 'must learn how to name and accept our own despair' (Farber, 1967: 601). Through connecting with our own *existential touchstones* (Mearns & Cooper, 2005) – the difficulties, challenges and struggles we have faced in our own lives – we can develop the capacity to relate to clients in their own darkest depths. As Yalom (2008: 274) writes, 'We have to abandon those vestiges of a medical model that posit that ... patients are suffering from a strange affliction and are in need of a dispassionate, immaculate, perma-sealed healer. We all face the same terror, the wound of mortality, the worm at the core of existence'.

A radical therapeutic perspective

Closely related to this tragic optimism is another theme that has permeated this text. This is the radical, socially critical potential of an existential worldview (Spinelli, 2001). Most of the principal psychological therapies, such as CBT, focus on helping clients return to a state of 'normal' social functioning. Here, the emphasis is on facilitating change within the individual. From a pluralistic perspective, such work can be very important. However, an existential perspective – as with the more radical humanistic (e.g., Proctor, Cooper, Sanders & Malcolm, 2006) and psychodynamic approaches (Fromm, 1965) – suggests that something more may be needed for optimal psychological health: social, political and cultural change. This is consistent with the broader thrust of existential philosophy which, at least in its French version (de Beauvior, Sartre, Camus) 'is a deeply politically engaged philosophy whose adherents manifest a real concern with helping to eliminate the oppressive structures that keep human beings enslaved' (Wartenberg, 2008: 147).

This perspective can be traced right back to the discussion of primary and secondary experiencing in Chapter 3. Here, it was argued, it is not the primary experiencing of human beings that leads to psychological difficulties. Rather, it is the distortion, denial or subjugation of those experiences, at the secondary level, through social forces. 'We are born into a world where alienation awaits us,' argues Laing (1967: 12), and become a 'shrivelled, desiccated fragment of what a person can be' (Laing, 1967: 22). More than that, he says, we are then duped into thinking that this crippled, self-estranged state is 'normality' (Laing, 1965): the way that we should, and are expected to, be. Hence, not only are we alienated from ourselves, but blind to our own alienation. Normality just *is*, and to question this 'collusive madness' (Laing, 1967: 62) risks stigmatisation and ridicule.

In this respect, there are many elements of existential therapy that can be seen as radical political acts. Through the process of bracketing (Chapter 3), for instance, clients are encouraged to stand back from, and question, assumed norms (Langdridge & Barker, 2013). Indeed, as we saw in Chapter 6, even the most fundamental meanings for why we exist may be challenged. And clients are also encouraged to acknowledge and actualise their freedom. That is, to take responsibility for their acts; and to make their own choices rather than relying on what others say or do.

In these respects, existential therapists might be seen as the *anarchists* of the counselling and psychotherapy world: inviting clients to question the world around them, and to live their lives as *they* see fit. More critically, however, they could also be seen as the *difficult adolescents:* unwilling to fit into social structures and to do what everyone else does. And, indeed, while facilitating existential workshops, I have had more than one participant say to me: 'Yes, you know I was also really into existential ideas ... when I was *15!*'

For most clients, having an anarchist or a stroppy adolescent as their therapist is unlikely to be what they need. However, where these radical, counter-normative ideas may really come into their own is when working with groups who are, themselves, marginalised or stigmatised by social norms (Barker & Langdridge, 2013): for instance, clients who are transgendered, immigrants or disabled. Here, as with a social model of disability (Crow, 1996), the focus is not on what is 'wrong' with clients. Rather, it is on clients' experiences of confronting a world that may oppress, objectify and discriminate against them. And, as the research suggest (e.g., Liddle, 1996), engaging with clients in such a de-pathologising way may be experienced as profoundly helpful, validating and empowering.

More than this, an existential standpoint also invites therapists to consider social activism as a means towards improved psychological wellbeing: for their clients, themselves, and for society as a whole. Counsellors and psychotherapists generally consider this outside their remit. But in a world, for instance, where transgendered clients are stigmatised, discriminated against and repressed, there may be only so much that individual therapeutic work can do to help such clients feel better. Instead, laws may need to be changed; stereotypes may need to be campaigned against. In the United States, an engagement with social justice issues is increasingly being seen as part of a counselling psychologist's role (e.g., Vera & Speight, 2003). In the UK, too, there are groups such as Psychotherapists and Counsellors for Social Responsibility (pcsr-uk.ning.com), which strive to provide a forum in which therapists can develop and actualise a social justice agenda.

Having said all that, it needs to be noted that this is very much a *potentiality* of an existential worldview, rather than an *actuality*. Indeed, to date, the involvement of existential therapists with social justice issues has been relatively limited. However, in the United States, existential–humanistic therapists have begun to explore the application of existential therapy to minority and marginalised groups, with the development of feminist perspectives (Brown, 2008), gay and lesbian perspectives (Monheit, 2008), and the application of existential therapies across cultures (Alsup, 2008; Comas-Diaz, 2008; Galvin, 1995; Rice, 2008). In the UK, too, recent years have seen some important applications of existential therapy to counter-normative ideas and practices, particularly around sexuality and gender identity (e.g., Milton, 2014).

Comparing across orientations: a summary

In drawing together an understanding of existential thought and practice, it may be useful to now review the similarities and differences with other therapeutic orientations. As indicated earlier, such an exercise needs to be conducted with considerable caution, as each of the orientations are, in reality, spectra of ideas and practices. Hence, similarities and differences between orientations depend very much on which aspects of each orientation are being referred to. In comparing existential therapy and CBT, for instance, there are many similarities between logotherapy and a cognitive therapeutic approach; but daseinsanalysis and behavioural therapy would be very far apart. Nevertheless, an indicative set of comparisons is presented in Table 8.1, which considers each of these therapies in a prototypical form.

As this table suggests, the existential approach probably has the strongest similarities with the humanistic orientation. Indeed, they are often considered a single school of therapy (e.g., Rowan, 1999). In both, practice tends to orientate around an exploration of lived-experiences within the context of a deepened therapeutic relationship. However, both approaches make somewhat different assumptions about the nature of that experiencing, and consequently take the therapeutic exploration off in somewhat different directions.

Table 8.1 Similarities and differences between existential therapies and other orientations

	Similarities	Differences (how existential approach differs)	Suggested reading
Humanistic	• I–Thou relationship as healing • Intelligibility of primary experiencing • Phenomenological/experiential focus • Exploration of here-and-now encounter • Authenticity as therapeutic goal	• Greater emphasis on givens, limits and tragic elements of existence • Less emphasis on actualising tendency/ innate goodness • More philosophical exploration/less emotion-centred	(Burston, 2003; Cooper, 2003a; Rowan, 1999; Spinelli, 1994, 1999)
Psycho-dynamic	• Orientation around therapeutic relationship • Exploration of here-and-now encounter • Unstructured • Inevitability of disappointment and conflict in life • Encouragement to bear anxiety	• Emphasis on conscious vs. unconscious • Real relationship vs. transferential relationship • Emphasis on present and future vs. past • Descriptive exploration vs. interpretative • More use of self-disclosure • Less emphasis on therapeutic boundaries and frame • Warmer therapeutic stance	(Boss, 1963; Cannon, 1991; Cohn, 1997: 13; Spinelli, 1994)
CBT	• Encouragement to face fears • Challenge to question sedimented beliefs	• Less structured and directive • Emphasis on relationship as agent of change	(Hickes & Mirea, 2012; Mirea, 2012; Spinelli, 1994; Wolfe, 2008)

(Continued)

Table 8.1 (Continued)

	Similarities	Differences (how existential approach differs)	Suggested reading
	• Exploration of meaning-making processes • Warm and collaborative therapeutic relationship	• Intelligibility of primary experiencing vs. irrationality • Less pathologising and disorder-focused • Less psycho-educational • Being as in-the-world and in-relation-to-others • Explicit emphasis on freedom and choice	
'Third wave' CBTs/mindfulness	• Focus on awareness and mindfulness of experiencing • Being as flow • Focus on acceptance of experiencing • Encouragement to be open and allow being to be	• Less structured, directive and technique based • Less psycho-educational	(Bunting & Hayes, 2008; Claessens, 2009a, 2009b; Harris, 2013; Nanda, 2010, 2012)
Narrative/ constructionist/ solution-focused	• Focus on meaning-making • Focus on future • Phenomenological exploration • Embeddedness in social relations • Warm and collaborative therapeutic relationship	• Greater emphasis on givens, limits and tragic elements of existence • Less technique based	(Langdridge, 2006; Medina, 2010)

Existential therapy also shares a relational focus with the psychodynamic approach, and particularly an exploration of the here and now therapeutic encounter. However, within the existential field, people tend to be seen as more able to access their primary experiencing, such that there is less emphasis on interpretation. The existential therapeutic relationship also tends to be warmer and more flexible.

Differences between existential therapy and CBT can be quite marked. This is primarily because the latter tends to adopt a more structured, directive, technique-based and psycho-educational approach. As we have seen, this is rooted in different assumptions about the nature of primary experiences. If they are intelligible (as in existential therapy), they need acceptance and empathy; if they are prone to biases (as in CBT), they need questioning and challenge. However, at the core of both approaches is the belief that clients need to learn to face their fears and anxieties; and that they do this best in the context of a warm and collaborative therapeutic relationship.

'Third wave' CBTs, such as acceptance and commitment therapy (Hayes, Strosahl & Wilson, 2011), dialectical behaviour therapy (Swales & Heard, 2008), compassion focused therapy (Gilbert, 2010), and mindfulness-based cognitive therapy (Segal, Williams & Teasdale, 2002) also tend to be more structured, directive and technique-based than existential therapy. However, the degree of overlap in the philosophical and psychological assumptions between these two orientations is striking, and this has been an area of considerable attention in recent years (e.g., Bunting & Hayes, 2008; Harris, 2013; Nanda, 2010). In particular, both orientations emphasise an awareness, and acceptance, of the flow of lived-experiencing; and much of this comes from the Eastern philosophies and practices that underpin both orientations (e.g., Boss, 1965; Claessens, 2009b; Heidegger, 2001; Hoffman, Yang & Kaklauskas, 2009).

The existential approach can also be compared against contemporary constructionist approaches, such as narrative therapy (McLeod, 1997) and solution-focused brief therapy (O'Connell, 2012). Here, there is considerable emphasis in both orientations in helping clients look towards their futures, and on the processes by which clients make sense of their lives. However, again, the constructionist approaches tend to incorporate more techniques and active therapeutic strategies, and also tend to be more optimistic in their views on human possibilities.

There are many other therapeutic orientations that an existential approach could be compared against. For instance, as with interpersonal therapy (Stuart & Robertson, 2003), there is an understanding of distress in relational terms; and, as with systemic and families therapies, there is an understanding of the person as being-in-relation to others (see, for instance, Boszormenyi-Nagy & Krasner, 1986). There are also many links between existential therapy and the practice of philosophical counselling (Lahav, 1998; LeBon, 2001), with both inviting clients to reflect on questions of meaning, existence and how to have a good life.

While existential therapy, then, can be understood as a specific set of understandings and practices, it also sits within a broader therapeutic field in which there are considerable commonalities as well as differences. In this respect, the existential approach, as with all therapeutic orientations, should probably not be seen like a picture on a gallery wall, with clearly defined borders against other pictures. Rather, it may be better seen as one part of a collage, with messy and irregular borders that overlap considerably with other parts, but also making a distinctive contribution to the whole. Here, as with a pluralistic perspective, the overlaps are inevitable – indeed, they may be part of the beauty of the overall piece – and we should not get too caught up in trying to disentangle them, or defining which is which. Yet, at the same time, each individual contribution needs to be prized; and through further refinement and embellishment, the overall whole can be enhanced.

Existential therapy: a summary

So how can we summarise the contribution that existential therapy makes? Existentialism takes many forms, but what unites these approaches is a desire to engage with the reality of individual human perspectives in a respectful and humanising way (Chapter 1). This is encapsulated in Buber's concept of the I–Thou stance (Chapter 2): an engagement with the other as an agentic human subjectivity, rather than as an object, mechanism or collection of 'parts'. To deepen an engagement with the concrete realities of human existence, existential philosophers and therapists have drawn extensively from Husserl's phenomenology (Chapter 3): which places human lived-experiencing at the centre of its philosophical and psychological worldview. In contrast to a purely phenomenological perspective, however, existential writers have argued that there are certain givens of the human condition: that we are free (Chapter 4), that that freedom faces certain limitations (Chapter 5), that we are orientated towards our futures (Chapter 6), and that we are caught within webs of interpersonal relationships (Chapter 7).

Although there are a range of different existential approaches to therapy, all hold that psychological wellbeing comes from honestly facing up to the realities of our lives: making the pre-reflected reflected (Chapter 3). This may involve unpacking our lived-experiences and recognising how we really feel and think. It may also involve acknowledging our capacity to choose (Chapter 4), and how it feels to face such limitations of existence as death (Chapter 5). For some existential therapists, there is also a need to rediscover what it is that, at the level of primary experiencing, gives us a sense of meaning and purpose in life (Chapter 6). And, in Chapter 7, we explored the value of honestly acknowledging both our own experiences and those of others towards us.

From an existential standpoint, acknowledging and accepting the reality of our existence has a range of benefits. First, it means that we are likely to feel better about ourselves: a greater sense of self-worth. Second, it means that we are less likely to be worrying about reality coming back to haunt us. Third, it means that we are less likely to develop 'neurotic' defensive strategies, which we have to keep on trying to shore up to keep reality at bay. Fourth, it means we are less likely to fall into vicious circles, in which our negative feelings about our 'negative' feelings makes the original experiencing that much worse. Fifth, it can help us make the most of the life that we do actually have. And finally, it can help us improve our relationships with others.

Existential practices that can help clients achieve this range from the gently exploratory to the firmly challenging. At the former, gentler end, clients may simply be encouraged to describe their experiencing and the choices, limitations, meaning and relationships that exist in their lives. At the latter, firmer end, clients may be directly challenged to acknowledge their freedom and limitations, and to recognise their meanings and interpersonal misperceptions. Between these two poles are a range of strategies, such as personification, that aim to stimulate and structure clients' explorations of their experiencing, but within a supportive and highly affirming context. Most existential practice involves a range of firmer and gentler methods, but existential therapists may tend towards favouring one pole or the other, depending on how much they trust clients to know – and honestly acknowledge – their own experiencing.

From a pluralistic standpoint, existential understandings and methods are not the 'right' way of working with clients, but helpful for some clients some of the time. There is little evidence on who they are best suited to but, based on the material presented in this book, we could summarise that they are most likely to be helpful for clients who:

- Want to be engaged with on an 'equal' level, as a fellow, intelligible human being.
- Want to gain insight and understanding of their experiences rather than cure.
- Want to develop a greater sense of their freedom and possibilities, and make more active choices in life.

- Accept that there are limitations to their lives, and want to work out the best way of thriving despite them.
- Want to develop a greater sense of meaning and purpose in life.
- Want to improve their interpersonal relationships and interpersonal understandings.
- Have a somewhat melancholic worldview, and feel comfortable with seeing the world in that way.
- Are wanting to experience the full spectrum of human emotions: the downs as well as the ups.

Key critiques

In this book, a range of critiques have been levelled at existential understandings and practices. This section summarises some of the most important overarching criticisms – reflecting, again, some of my own personal concerns and interests.

What evidence is there for existential therapies?

First, there is a lack of empirical support for existential therapeutic practices. This was discussed in Chapter 1, and is a major Achilles heel for the orientation as a whole. This is not just in terms of having the capacity to influence commissioners and policy-makers, but in terms of existential therapists genuinely knowing whether what they do helps or does not. And it is not just research on the outcomes of existential therapy that is needed, but also more research on what actually happens in existential therapy (e.g., Olivereira et al., 2012), as well as what clients find helpful (e.g., Edwards & Milton, 2014). The existential approach might also benefit greatly from forming closer links with – and drawing on – the psychological evidence in such fields as Terror Management Theory (Greenberg et al., 2004), Self-determination Theory (Deci & Ryan, 2002) and personal projects (Little, 1983).

Do existential therapists really do anything different?

Without further research in this field, it may also be difficult to dispel a cloud that is beginning to loom over the existential therapies. To date, what research there is suggests that the actual practices of most existential therapists may be much less distinctive than the existential literature would suggest (e.g., Correia et al., in preparation-b; Norcross, 1987; Olivereira et al., 2012; Sousa & Alegria, in preparation; Wilkes & Milton, 2006). As we have seen, research suggests that the two forms of practice that overwhelmingly seem to dominate in actual existential practice are relational and phenomenological ways of working; and these are not only characteristics of most humanistic ways of working (e.g., Rogers, 1957), but are also amongst the most common therapeutic practices across all orientations (Cook et al., 2010). Concomitantly, the more distinctive existential methods – such as helping clients to confront death – are only minimally reported or witnessed in actual existential practice. For all its discussion of philosophy and existential givens, then, it is really not clear whether the actual practice of existential therapists is that different from a more general phenomenological-relational practice, as seen, for instance, in person-centred or gestalt therapies.

How elitist is the existential view?

This links in to a third criticism of the existential approach. Despite its emphasis on mutuality and a respectful valuing of the other, it can have a decidedly elitist and judgemental side. In its critique of 'normality' (see above), for instance, there is a disparaging of the 'idle talk' of the masses (Heidegger, 1962) and their 'monologue disguised as dialogue' (Buber, 1947). 'Just see the superfluous crowd!' writes (Nietzsche, 1967: 105), 'Sick are they always; they vomit their bile and call it a newspaper'. Of course, it is very unlikely that existential therapists would bring such attitudes into therapy (or, indeed, hold them). But what might be brought in is some degree of tension between a radical acceptance of clients, and a more normative view of how they should live their lives. When existential therapists, for instance, call on clients to 'confront anxiety and move ahead despite it' (May, 1977: 40), they are doing something very different from bracketing their assumptions and supporting clients to find their own way of being in the world. Therapeutically, there is nothing wrong with providing such guidance. Indeed, it may be very helpful to clients. But if it is presented as a neutral standpoint, and simply a facilitation of the client's own way of experiencing the world, then existential therapists might be guilty of the same covering up of their agenda that they may level at society.

Conclusion

The aim of this book has been to take readers on a journey through the landscape of the existential therapies: exploring core understandings and therapeutic practices. It is a rich, complex and varied field, with much that therapists may be able to take away to enhance their own work. This journey is supported by a pluralistic worldview, which reminds us that this is not the only culture we can inhabit. There are wonderful sights, and we may choose to spend the remainder of our working lives here; but there are also many other fabulous lands we may want to explore, such as CBT, psychodynamic and humanistic approaches. When we see these different cultures as *truisms*, we may come to see them as warring perspectives: if we believe one, we cannot believe the other. But if we see them as different *narratives* about the way the world is and how people can be helped, then they can all be suitable for different people at different times. Pluralism, then, can be likened to a spirit of internationalism: we do not need to have travelled everywhere in the world, but we can still respect, value and honour diversity. This provides an ideal framework for the development of existential understandings and practices and, more than that, it is an articulation of existential values in itself, extending a deep appreciation of otherness and difference to the therapeutic field as a whole.

Questions for reflection and discussion

- Which of the existential understandings and methods do you consider most helpful? Which do you consider least helpful?
- In what ways do you think an existential perspective is consistent with a pluralistic one, and in what ways do you think it is different?

Recommended reading

Van Deurzen, E. (2009) *Psychotherapy and the Quest for Happiness*. London: Sage. Existential challenge to 'get real' and not expect endless happiness in our life.

Vos, J., Craig, M. & Cooper, M. (2014) Existential therapies: a meta-analysis of their effects on psychological outcomes. *Journal of Consulting and Clinical Psychology*. Systematic summary of results of existential therapy interventions, indicating good effects for meaning therapies.

Appendices

One of the great strengths of existential philosophy is that it stretches far beyond psychotherapy and counselling; into art, literature and many other forms of popular culture. This means that there are many – including films, novels and songs that convey the key messages of existentialism. These may be useful for trainees of existential therapy, and also as recommendations for clients to deepen an understanding of this way of seeing the world.

In order to identify the most helpful resources, an online survey was conducted in the summer of 2014 to identify the key existential films, books and novels. Invites were sent out via email to existential training institutes and societies, and through social media. Participants were invited to nominate up to three of each art media that 'most strongly communicate the core messages of existentialism'.

In total, 119 people took part in the survey (i.e., gave one or more response; see the companion website for full details of participants and results). Approximately half were female (n = 57) and half were male (n = 56), with one of other gender. The average age was 47 years old (range 26–89). The participants were primarily distributed across the UK (n = 37), continental Europe (n = 34), North America (n = 24), Australia (n = 15) and Asia (n = 6). Around 90% of the respondents were either qualified therapists (n = 78) or in training (n = 26). Of these, around two-thirds (n = 69) considered themselves existential therapists, and one third (n = 32) did not.

Existential Films: Ten to Watch

There were 304 nominations for the key existential film. The most popular responses, in descending order, were as follows (with director, date of release, and illustrative explanation(s) for the nominations).

1 = *The Matrix* (Andy Wachowski, 1999) 'Invites us to be observers of our paradigms and in so doing be in a state of consciousness that transcends paradigm'.

1 = *Groundhog Day* (Harold Ramis, 1993) 'The story of a man who needs a lot of repetition before he learns the lessons he needs to learn – he begins to care about people and as a result he is very cared about; it gives hope that anyone can change'.

3 = *Harold and Maude* (Hal Ashby, 1971) 'Love transcending boundaries and the willingness to open up to life without allowing anything to become an anchor'.

3 = *I Heart Huckabees* (David Russell, 2004) 'Existential detectives trying to help people figure out their meaning', 'Great existential comedy – fun, relevant, smart. Makes existentialism topical for today'.

3 = *Into the Wild* (Sean Penn, 2007) 'A story about existential loneliness and the dilemma between being an individual and belongingness to a community'.

6 = *Being There* (Hal Ashby, 1979) 'Chance (the Gardener) appears and then exists. [He] Lives, largely misconstrued by others, and then ceases to exist'.

6 = *Three Colours: Blue* (Krzysztof Kieslowski, 1997) 'Negotiates both literally and symbolically existential issues of freedom, equality and brotherhood/sisterhood but also other big issues of love, death and meaning'.

8 =   *Fight Club* (David Fincher, 1999) 'Excruciatingly existential .... captures the polarities of human existence with our aiming for values but descending into the dark side too'.

8 =   *Melancholia* (Lars von Trier, 2011) '[A film] about key challenges of the human condition, not merely local or idiosyncratic problems'.

8 =   *Wild Strawberries* (Ingmar Bergman, 1957) 'Dealing with the meaninglessness of life, trying to be open even if it is meaningless, choosing in the face of despair, and faith'.

This Top 10 film list can be accessed on IMDB at: www.imdb.com/ rg/s/1/list/ls071374530/. The full list of nominated films is available on the companion website.

EXISTENTIAL
FILMS

Existential Novels: Ten to Read

There were 288 nominations for the key existential novel. The top ten, in descending order, were:

1   *The Stranger* (aka *The Outsider*, Albert Camus, 1942) 'The greatest existential novel written', 'Provides a model of living authentically, without attempting to fit a mould or behave according to norms, and ultimately dying authentically, by accepting, not religion, but that the universe is indifferent'.

2   *Nausea* (Jean-Paul Sartre, 1938) 'A journey into the mundane and dealing with nothingness on an everyday basis'.

3   *Crime and Punishment* (Fyodor Dostoyevsky, 1866) 'A man's inescapable relationship with existential guilt and agency'.

4   *The Death of Ivan Ilyich* (Leo Tolstoy, 1886) 'How death reminds us to live a full life'.

5=   *The Trial* (Franz Kafka, 1925) 'A parable about dealing with the ultimate meaninglessness, arbitrariness, and unfairness of life'.

5=   *The Plague* (Albert Camus, 1947) 'Explores how there are adversarial and threatening conditions of life (death) that cannot be avoided, and yet the relatedness we have that is our salvation'.

5=   *Steppenwolf* (Hermann Hesse, 1927) 'Presents a story about loneliness and the need to connect to another person'.

5=   *Man's Search for Meaning* (Viktor Frankl, 1946) 'A great depiction of living with meaning despite the suffering that life brings', 'Frankl's book is a "must be read" for everyone'.

9   *Metamorphosis* (Franz Kafka, 1915) 'Presents issues that deal with identity, family relation, loneliness and ultimately rejection'.

10   *The Unbearable Lightness of Being* (Milan Kundera, 1984) 'Deals
     with the struggle to make life meaningful'.

This Top 10 book list can be accessed on Amazon at: www.amazon.
co.uk/registry/wishlist/MHVLFKNY9QIO. The full list of nominated
books is available on the companion website.

EXISTENTIAL
NOVELS

Existential Songs: Ten to Singalong to

There were 235 nominations for the key existential song, with enormous variation across the different respondents. In terms of artists, the most commonly nominated were (in descending order): Bob Dylan, Pink Floyd, The Beatles, Leonard Cohen, Talking Heads, David Bowie, Bruce Springsteen, John Lennon, Radiohead, and Simon and Garfunkel. The top ten nominated songs, in descending order, were:

1   *Once in a Lifetime* (Talking Heads, 1981) 'The words say something familiar to me'.

2 =   *Imagine* (John Lennon, 1971) 'A generation's mass conscious, hope and vision of a world of unity and peace'.

2 =   *Time* (Pink Floyd, 1973) 'A powerful statement about the fleetingness of life'.

2 =   *Somewhere Over the Rainbow* (Eva Cassidy, 2001/Izzy, 2010/Jeff Beck, 2007) 'So full of angst it's deadly'.

5 =   *Like a Rolling Stone* (Bob Dylan, 1965)

5 =   *Blowin' in the Wind* (Bob Dylan, 1962) 'The sense of the cosmic, the enigmatic, and the call for a vital response – beyond the canned and the programmatic, to great human predicaments'.

5 =   *Darkness on the Edge of Town* (Bruce Springsteen, 1978) 'About trying to create meaning and survive in the face of despair'.

5 =   *My Way* (Frank Sinatra, 1969)

5 =   *Hope There's Someone* (Antony and the Johnsons, 2005)

5 =   *Hallelujah* (Leonard Cohen, 1984)

EXISTENTIAL
SONGS

This Top 10 songlist can be accessed as a YouTube playlist, search 'Existential Songs: The Top 10'. The full list of nominated songs is also available as a YouTube playlist, search 'Existential songlist'. The full list can also be found on the companion website.

References

Adams, M. (2001) Practicing phenomenology: some reflections and considerations. *Journal of the Society for Existential Analysis*, *12*(1), 65–84.

Adams, M. (2013) *A Concise Introduction to Existential Counselling*. London: Sage.

Aked, J., Marks, N., Cordon, C. & Thompson, S. (2008) *Five Ways to Wellbeing: The Evidence*. London: New Economics Foundation.

Alsup, R. (2008) Existentialism of personalism: A native American perspective. In K.J. Schneider (ed.), *Existential-Integrative Psychotherapy: Guideposts to the Core of Practice* (pp. 121–127). New York: Routledge.

Armor, D.E. & Taylor, S.E. (1998) Situated optimism: specific outcome expectancies and self-regulation. In M.P. Zanna (ed.), *Advances in Experimental Social Psychology* (Vol. 30). San Diego: Academic Press.

Arndt, J., Cook, A. & Routledge, C. (2004) The blueprint of terror management. In J. Greenberg, S.L. Koole & T. Pyszczynski (eds), *Handbook of Experimental Existential Psychology* (pp. 35–53). New York: Guilford.

Aron, A. & Aron, E.N. (2013) The meaning of love. In P.T.P. Wong (ed.), *The Human Quest for Meaning: Theories, Research and Applications* (2nd edn, pp. 185–208). New York: Routledge.

Aylindar, S. (2014) What do clients want? An investigation of clients' preferences using the Therapy Personalisation Form–Assessment. (Unpublished doctoral dissertation). University of Strathclyde/Glasgow Caledonian University, Glasgow.

Bannink, F.P. (2007) Solution-focused brief therapy. *Journal of Contemporary Psychotherapy*, *37*(2), 87–94.

Barak, A., Hen, L., Boniel-Nissim, M., & Shapira, N.A. (2008) A comprehensive review and a meta-analysis of the effectiveness of internet-based psychotherapeutic interventions. *Journal of Technology in Human Services*, *26*(2-4), 109–160.

Barker, M. & Langdridge, D. (2013) The challenge of sexuality and embodiment in human relationships. In E. van Deurzen & S. Iacovou (eds), *Existential Perspectives on Relationship Therapy* (pp. 54–67). London: Palgrave.

Barren, J.R. (2005) Use of existential-phenomenological counseling for police officers. *Policing – an International Journal of Police Strategies & Management*, *28*(2), 255–268.

Bateson, G., Jackson, D.D., Haley, J. & Weakland, J. (1956) Towards a theory of schizophrenia. *Behavioral Science, 1*, 251–264.

Baumeister, R.F. (1991) *Meanings of Life*. New York: Guilford Press.

Baumeister, R.F. & Leary, M.R. (1995) The need to belong – desire for interpersonal attachments as a fundamental human-motivation. *Psychological Bulletin, 117*(3), 497–529.

Beck, A.T., John, R.A., Shaw, B.F. & Emery, G. (1979) *Cognitive Therapy of Depression*. New York: Guilford Press.

Becker, E. (1973) *The Denial of Death*. New York: Free Press Paperbacks.

Bedi, R.P., Davis, M.D. & Williams, M. (2005) Critical incidents in the formation of the therapeutic alliance from the client's perspective. *Psychotherapy: Theory, Research, Practice, Training, 42*(3), 311–323.

Bennett-Levy, J., Butler, G., Fennell, M., Hackmann, A., Mueller, M. & Westbrook, D. (2005) *Oxford Guide to Behavioural Experiments in Cognitive Therapy*. Oxford: Oxford University Press.

Bergman, S.H. (1991) *Dialogical Philosophy from Kierkegaard to Buber*. New York: State University of New York.

Binswanger, L. (1958) The case of Ellen West: An anthropological-clinical study. In R. May, E. Angel & H.F. Ellenberger (eds), *Existence: A New Dimension in Psychiatry and Psychology* (pp. 237–364). New York: Basic Books.

Binswanger, L. (1963) *Being-in-the-World: Selected Papers of Ludwig Binswanger* (J. Needleman, Trans.). London: Condor Books.

Bohart, A.C. (2001) Emphasising the future in empathy responses. In S. Haugh & T. Merry (eds), *Empathy* (pp. 99–111). Ross-on-Wye: PCCS Books.

Bohart, A.C. & Tallman, K. (1999) *How Clients Make Therapy Work: The Process of Active Self-Healing*. Washington: American Psychological Association.

Borrell-Carrio, F., Suchman, A.L. & Epstein, R.M. (2004) The biopsychosocial model 25 years later: principles, practice, and scientific inquiry. *Annals of Family Medicine, 2*(6), 576–582.

Boss, M. (1963) *Psychoanalysis and Daseinsanalysis*. New York: Basic Books.

Boss, M. (1965) *A Psychiatrist Discovers India* (H.A. Frey, Trans.). London: Oswald Wolff.

Boss, M. (1977) *'I Dreamt Last Night...'* (S. Conway, Trans.). New York: John Wiley and Sons, Inc.

Boss, M. (1979) *Existential Foundations of Medicine and Psychology* (S. Conway & A. Cleaves, Trans.). Northvale, NJ: Jason Aronson Inc.

Boszormenyi-Nagy, I. & Krasner, B.R. (1986) *Between Give and Take: A Clinical Guide to Contextual Therapy*. Hove: Brunner-Routledge.

Boucher, T. (2010) Cognitive-behavioural contributions to pluralistic practice: reflections on an issue of some contention. In M. Milton (ed.), *Therapy and Beyond: Counselling Psychology Contributions to Therapeutic and Social Issues* (pp. 155–169). London: Wiley-Blackwell.

Bowlby, J. (1969) *Attachment*. New York: Basic Books.

Bozarth, J.D. & Wilkins, P. (eds) (2001) *Unconditional Positive Regard*. Ross-on-Wye: PCCS Books.

Breitbart, W., Rosenfeld, B., Gibson, C., Pessin, H., Poppito, S., Nelson, C., Tomarken, A., Timm, A.K., Berg, A., Jacobson, C., Sorger, B., Abbey, J. and Olden, M. (2010) Meaning-centered group psychotherapy for patients with advanced cancer: a pilot randomized controlled trial. *Psycho Oncology*, *19*(1), 21–28.

Brown, L.S. (2008) Feminist therapy as a meaning-making practice: where there is now power, where is the meaning? In K.J. Schneider (ed.), *Existential-Integrative Psychotherapy: Guideposts to the Core of Practice* (pp. 130–140). New York: Routledge.

Brunstein, J.C. (1993) Personal goals and subjective well-being: A longitudinal study. *Journal of Personality and Social Psychology*, *65*(5), 1061–1070.

Buber, M. (1947) *Between Man and Man* (R.G. Smith, Trans.). London: Fontana.

Buber, M. (1958) *I and Thou* (R.G. Smith, Trans. 2nd edn). Edinburgh: T & T Clark Ltd.

Buber, M. (1964) *Daniel: Dialogues on Realisation* (M. Friedman, Trans.). New York: Holt, Reinhart and Winston.

Buber, M. (1970) *I and Thou* (W. Kaufman, Trans.). New York: Charles Scribner's Sons.

Buber, M. (1988) *The Knowledge of Man: Selected Essays* (M. Friedman & R.G. Smith, Trans.). Atlantic Highlands, NJ: Humanities Press International Inc.

Bugental, J.F.T. (1976). *The Search for Existential Identity: Patient-Therapist Dialogues in Humanistic Psychotherapy*. San Francisco: Jossey-Bass Publishers.

Bugental, J.F.T. (1978) *Psychotherapy and Process: The Fundamentals of an Existential-Humanistic Approach*. Boston, MA: McGraw-Hill.

Bugental, J.F.T. (1981) *The Search for Authenticity: An Existential-Analytic Approach to Psychotherapy* (exp. edn). New York: Irvington.

Bugental, J.F.T. (1987) *The Art of the Psychotherapist: How to Develop the Skills that Take Psychotherapy Beyond Science*. New York: W.W. Norton and Co.

Bunting, K. & Hayes, S.C. (2008) Language and meaning: acceptance and commitment therapy and the EI model. In K.J. Schneider (ed.), *Existential-Integrative Psychotherapy: Guideposts to the Core of Practice* (pp. 217–234). New York: Routledge.

Burns, D.D. & Spangler, D.L. (2000) Does psychotherapy homework lead to improvements in depression in cognitive-behavioral therapy or does improvement lead to increased homework compliance? *Journal of Consulting and Clinical Psychology*, *68*(1), 46–56.

Burston, D. (2003) Existentialism, humanism and psychotherapy. *Existential Analysis*, *14*(2), 309–319.

Camus, A. (1955) *The Myth of Sisyphus* (J. O'Brien, Trans.). London: Penguin.

Cannon, B. (1991) *Sartre and Psychoanalysis: An Existentialist Challenge to Clinical Metatheory.* Lawrence, KN: University Press of Kansas.

Carlson, E.N., Vazire, S. & Furr, R.M. (2011) Meta-insight: Do people really know how others see them? *Journal of Personality and Social Psychology, 101*(4), 831.

Cayne, J. & Loewenthal, D. (2011) Post-phenomenology and the between as unknown. In D. Loewenthal (ed.), *Post-existentialism and the Psychological Therapies: Towards a Therapy without Foundations.* London: Karnac.

Chamberlain, L.L. & Bütz, M.R. (eds) (1998) *Clinical Chaos: A Therapist's Guide to Nonlinear Dynamics and Therapeutic Change.* Philadelphia: Brunner/Mazel.

Children and Young People's Mental Health Coalition (2012) *Resilience and Results: How to Improve the Emotional and Mental Wellbeing of Children and Young People in your School.* London: Children and Young People's Mental Health Coalition.

Claessens, M. (2009a) Mindfulness-based third wave CBT therapies and existential-phenomenology. Friend or foes? *Existential Analysis, 21*(2), 295–308.

Claessens, M. (2009b) Mindfulness and existential therapy. *Existential Analysis, 20*(1), 109–119.

Claiborn, C.D., Goodyear, R.K. & Horner, P.A. (2002) Feedback. In J.C. Norcross (ed.), *Psychotherapy Relationships that Work: Therapist Contributions and Responsiveness to Patients* (pp. 217–233). New York: Oxford University Press.

Clarkson, P. (2003) *The Therapeutic Relationship* (2nd edn). London: Wiley-Blackwell.

Cohen, M.B. (1953) Introduction. In H.S. Sullivan (ed.), *The Interpersonal Theory of Psychiatry* (pp. xi–xviii). New York: W.W. Norton and Co.

Cohn, H.W. (1997) *Existential Thought and Therapeutic Practice: An Introduction to Existential Psychotherapy.* London: Sage.

Cohn, H.W. (2002) *Heidegger and the Roots of Existential Therapy.* London: Continuum.

Comas-Diaz, L. (2008) Latino spirituality. In K.J. Schneider (ed.), *Existential-Integrative Psychotherapy: Guideposts to the Core of Practice* (pp. 100–109). New York: Routledge.

Cook, J.M., Biyanova, T., Elhai, J., Schnurr, P.P. & Coyne, J.C. (2010) What do psychotherapists really do in practice? An Internet study of over 2,000 practitioners. *Psychotherapy: Theory, Research, Practice, Training, 47*(2), 260.

Cooper, M. (1996) Modes of existence: towards a phenomenological poly-psychism. *Journal of the Society for Existential Analysis, 7*(2), 50–56.

Cooper, M. (1999a) The discourse of existence: existential-phenomenological psychotherapy in a postmodern world. *Journal of the Society for Existential Analysis, 10*(2), 93–101.

Cooper, M. (1999b) If you can't be Jekyll be Hyde: An existential-phenomenological exploration on lived-plurality. In J. Rowan & M. Cooper (eds), *The Plural Self: Multiplicity in Everyday Life* (pp. 51–70). London: Sage.

Cooper, M. (2001a) Embodied empathy. In S. Haugh & T. Merry (eds), *Empathy* (pp. 218–229). Ross-on-Wye: PCCS Books.

Cooper, M. (2001b) The genetic given: towards an existential understanding of inherited 'personality traits'. *Journal of the Society for Existential Analysis, 12*(1), 2–12.

Cooper, M. (2001c) The tools of being: an existential perspective on the past. *Counsellor and Psychotherapist Dialogue, 1*(3), 12–15.

Cooper, M. (2003a) Between freedom and despair: Existential challenges and contributions to person-centred and experiential therapy. *Person-Centered and Experiential Psychotherapies, 2*(1), 43–56.

Cooper, M. (2003b) *Existential Therapies*. London: Sage.

Cooper, M. (2003c) 'I–I' and 'I–Me': Transposing Buber's interpersonal attitudes to the intrapersonal plane. *Journal of Constructivist Psychology, 16*(2), 131–153.

Cooper, M. (2004a) Encountering self-otherness: 'I–I' and 'I–Me' modes of self-relating. In H.J.M. Hermans & G. Dimaggio (eds), *Dialogical Self in Psychotherapy* (pp. 60–73). Hove: Brunner-Routledge.

Cooper, M. (2004b) Existential approaches to therapy. In P. Sanders (ed.), *The Tribes of the Person-Centred Nation: An Introduction to the Schools of Therapy Related to the Person-Centred Approach* (pp. 95–124). Ross-on-Wye: PCCS Books.

Cooper, M. (2004c) Viagra for the brain: psychotherapy research and the challenge of existential therapeutic practice. *Existential Analysis, 15*(1), 2–14.

Cooper, M. (2005a) From self-objectification to self-affirmation: The 'I–Me' and 'I–I' self-relational stances. In S. Joseph & R. Worsley (eds), *Person-Centred Psychopathology: A Positive Psychology of Mental Health* (pp. 60–74). PCCS Books: Ross-on-Wye.

Cooper, M. (2005b) The inter-experiential field: perceptions and metaperceptions in person-centered and experiential psychotherapy and counseling. *Person-Centered and Experiential Psychotherapies, 4*(1), 54–68.

Cooper, M. (2006) Socialist humanism: a progressive politics for the twenty-first century. In G. Proctor, M. Cooper, P. Sanders & B. Malcolm (eds), *Politicising the Person-Centred Approach: An Agenda for Social Change* (pp. 80–94). Ross-on-Wye: PCCS Books.

Cooper, M. (2007) Humanizing psychotherapy. *Journal of Contemporary Psychotherapy, 37*(1), 11–16.

Cooper, M. (2008a) *Essential Research Findings in Counselling and Psychotherapy: The Facts are Friendly*. London: Sage.

Cooper, M. (2008b) Existential psychotherapy. In J. LeBow (ed.), *Twenty-First Century Psychotherapies: Contemporary Approaches to Theory and Practice* (pp. 237–276). London: Wiley.

Cooper, M. (2009a) Interpersonal perceptions and metaperceptions: psychotherapeutic practice in the inter-experiential realm. *Journal of Humanistic Psychology, 49*(1), 85–99.

Cooper, M. (2009b) Welcoming the other: actualising the humanistic ethic at the core of counselling psychology practice. *Counselling Psychology Review, 24*(3&4), 119–129.

Cooper, M. (2010) The challenge of counselling and psychotherapy research. *Counselling and Psychotherapy Research, 10*(3), 183–191.

Cooper, M. (2012a) Clients' and therapists' perceptions of intrasessional connection: an analogue study of change over time, predictor variables, and level of consensus. *Psychotherapy Research, 22*(3), 274–287.

Cooper, M. (2012b) *Existential Counselling Primer*. Ross-on-Wye: PCCS Books.

Cooper, M. (2012c) Existentially informed person-centred therapy. In P. Sanders (ed.), *The Tribes of the Person-centred Nation: An Introduction to the Schools of Therapy Related to the Person-centred Approach* (2nd edn, pp. 131–160). Ross-on-Wye: PCCS Books.

Cooper, M. (2012d) *A Hierarchy of Wants: Towards an Integrative Framework for Counselling, Psychotherapy and Social Change*. University of Strathclyde, Glasgow. Retrieved from download from pure.strath.ac.uk/portal.

Cooper, M. (2013a) Experiencing relational depth in therapy: what we know so far. In R. Knox, D. Murphy, S. Wiggins & M. Cooper (eds), *Relational Depth: New Perspectives and Developments* (pp. 62–76). Basingstoke: Palgrave.

Cooper, M. (2013b) Experiencing relational depth: self-development exercises and reflections. In R. Knox, D. Murphy, S. Wiggins & M. Cooper (eds), *Relational Depth: New Perspectives and Developments* (pp. 137–152). Basingstoke: Palgrave.

Cooper, M. (2014) *Strathclyde Pluralistic Protocol*. London: University of Roehampton.

Cooper, M. & Adams, M. (2005) Death. In E. van Deurzen & C. Baker (eds), *Existential Perspectives on Human Issues: A Handbook for Therapeutic Practice* (pp. 78–85). London: Palgrave.

Cooper, M. & Bohart, A.C. (2013) Experiential and phenomenological foundations. In M. Cooper, P.F. Schmid, M. O'Hara & G. Wyatt (eds), *The Handbook of Person-centred Psychotherapy and Counselling* (2nd edn). Basingstoke: Palgrave.

Cooper, M., Chak, A., Cornish, F. & Gillespie, A. (2012) Dialogue: bridging personal, community and social transformation. *Journal of Humanistic Psychology, 53*(1), 70–93.

Cooper, M. & Cruthers, H. (1999) Facilitating the expression of subpersonalities: a review and analysis of techniques. In J. Rowan & M. Cooper (eds), *The Plural Self: Multiplicity in Everyday Life* (pp. 198–212). London: Sage.

Cooper, M. & Hermans, H. (2007) Honouring self-otherness: alterity and the intrapersonal. In L.M. Simão & J. Valsiner (eds), *Otherness in Question: Labyrinths of the Self* (pp. 305–315). Charlotte, NC: Information Age.

Cooper, M. & Ikemi, A. (2012) Dialogue: a dialogue between focusing and relational perspectives. *Person-Centered & Experiential Psychotherapies, 11*(2), 124–136.

Cooper, M. & Joseph, S. (in press) Psychological foundations for humanistic psychotherapeutic practice. In D. Cain, K. Keenan & S. Rubin (eds), *Humanistic Psychotherapies*. Washington: APA.

Cooper, M. & McLeod, J. (2007) A pluralistic framework for counselling and psychotherapy: implications for research. *Counselling and Psychotherapy Research, 7*(3), 135–143.

Cooper, M. & McLeod, J. (2011a) Person-centered therapy: a pluralistic perspective. *Person-Centered and Experiential Psychotherapies, 10*(3), 210–223.

Cooper, M. & McLeod, J. (2011b) *Pluralistic Counselling and Psychotherapy*. London: Sage.

Cooper, M., Schmid, P.F., O'Hara, M. & Bohart, A.C. (eds) (2013) *The Handbook of Person-Centred Psychotherapy and Counselling* (2nd edn). Basingstoke: Palgrave.

Cooper, M. & Spinelli, E. (2012) A dialogue on dialogue. In L. Barnett & G. Madison (eds), *Existential Psychotherapy: Vibrancy, Legacy and Dialogue* (pp. 141–157). London: Routledge.

Cooper, M. & Stumm, G. (2015) Existential approaches and pluralism. In M. Cooper & W. Dryden (Eds.), *Handbook of Pluralistic Counselling and Psychotherapy*. London: Sage.

Cooper, M., Vos, J. & Craig, M. (2011) *Protocol for EXIST Review*. Glasgow: University of Strathclyde.

Cooper, M., Watson, J.C. & Hölldampf, D. (eds) (2010) *Person-centred and Experiential Therapies Work: A Review of the Research on Counseling, Psychotherapy and Related Practices*. Ross-on-Wye: PCCS Books.

Cooper, M., Wild, C., van Rijn, B., Ward, T., McLeod, J., Cassar, S., ... Sreenath, S. (submitted) Pluralistic therapy for depression: acceptability, outcomes and helpful aspects in a multisite open-label trial. *Counselling Psychology Review*.

Correia, E., Cooper, M. & Berdondini, L. (2014a) Existential psychotherapy: an international survey of the key authors and texts influencing practice. *Journal of Contemporary Psychotherapy*, 1–8. doi: 10.1007/s10879-014-9275-y.

Correia, E., Cooper, M. & Berdondini, L. (2014b) The worldwide distribution and characteristics of existential psychotherapists and counsellors. *Existential Analysis, 25*(2), 321–337.

Correia, E., Cooper, M., Berdondini, L. & Correia, K. (in preparation-a) Existential psychotherapies: similarities and differences among the main branches. *Journal of Humanistic Psychology*.

Correia, E., Cooper, M., Berdondini, L. & Correia, K. (in preparation-b) Characteristic practices of existential psychotherapy: a worldwide survey of practitioners' perspectives.

Cox, G. (2012) *The Existentialist's Guide to Death, the Universe and Nothingnesss*. London: Continuum.

Craig, M., Vos, J., Cooper, M. & Correia, E. (in press) Existential psychotherapies. In D. Cain, K. Keenan & S. Rubin (eds), *Humanistic Psychotherapies*. Washington: APA.

Crits-Christoph, P., Connolly Gibbons, M.B. & Mukherjee, D. (2013) Psychotherapy process-outcome research. In M.J. Lambert (ed.), *Bergin and Garfield's Handbook of Psychotherapy and Behavior Change* (pp. 298–340). New Jersey: John Wiley.

Crossley, N. (1996) *Intersubjectivity: The Fabric of Social Becoming*. London: Sage.

Crow, L. (1996) Including all of our lives: renewing the social model of disability. In C. Barnes & G. Mercer (eds), *Exploring the Divide*. Leeds: Disability Press.

Crumbaugh, J.C. & Carr, G.L. (1979) Treatment of alcoholics with logotherapy. *International Journal of the Addictions, 14*(6), 847–853.

Crumbaugh, J.C. & Maholick, L.T. (1964) An experimental study in existentialism: the psychometric approach to Frankl's concept of noogenic neurosis. *Journal of Clinical Psychology, 20*(2), 200–207.

D'Zurilla, T.J. & Nezu, A.M. (1999) *Problem-Solving Therapy: A Social Competence Approach to Clinical Interventions*. New York: Academic Press.

De Beauvoir, S. (1948a) *The Ethics of Ambiguity*. New York: Citadel.

De Beauvoir, S. (1948b) *The Second Sex*. London: Vintage.

De Unamuno, M. (1954) *Tragic Sense of Life* (J.E.C. Flitch, Trans.). New York: Dover.

Deci, E.L. & Ryan, R.M. (eds) (2002) *Handbook of Self-determination Research*. Rochester, NY: University of Rochester Press.

Department of Health (2009) *New Horizons: Towards a Shared Vision for Mental Health* (consultation document). London: Department of Health.

Depaulo, B.M., Hoover, C.W., Webb, W., Kenny, D.A. & Oliver, P.V. (1987) Accuracy of person perception – do people know what kinds of impressions they convey. *Journal of Personality and Social Psychology, 52*(2), 303–315.

Derrida, J. (1974) *Of Grammatology* (G.C. Spivak, Trans.). Baltimore, MY: The John Hopkins University Press.

Dewey, J. (1958) *Experience and Nature*. New York: Dover.

Diener, E. & Seligman, M.E. (2002) Very happy people. *Psychological Science, 13*(1), 81–84.

Dreyfus, H.L. (1997) *Being-in-the-World: A Commentary on Heidegger's Being and Time, Division 1*. Cambridge, MA: The MIT Press.

Dryden, W. (1999) *Rational Emotive Behavioural Counselling in Action* (2nd edn). London: Sage.

DuPlock, S. (ed.) (1997) *Case Studies in Existential Psychotherapy and Counselling*. Chichester: John Wiley.

Edwards, A. & Elwyn, G. (eds) (2009) *Shared Decision-making in Health Care: Achieving Evidence-based Patient Choice* (2nd edn). Oxford: Oxford University.

Edwards, W. & Milton, M. (2014) Retirement therapy? Older people's experiences of existential therapy relating to their transition to retirement. *Counselling Psychology Review, 29*(2), 43–53.

Ellenberger, H.F. (1958) A clinical introduction to psychiatric phenomenology and existential analysis. In R. May, E. Angel & H.F. Ellenberger (eds), *Existence: A New Dimension in Psychiatry and Psychology*. New York: Basic Books.

Elliott, R., Bohart, A.C., Watson, J.C. & Greenberg, L.S. (2011) Empathy. In J.C. Norcross (ed.), *Psychotherapy Relationships that Work: Evidence-based Responsiveness* (2nd edn, pp. 132–152). New York: Oxford University Press.

Elliott, R., Watson, J.C., Goldman, R. & Greenberg, L.S. (2004) *Learning Emotion-focused Therapy: The Process-experiential Approach to Change*. Washington, DC: American Psychological Association.

Emmelkemp, P.M.G. (2013) Behavior therapy with adults. In M.J. Lambert (ed.), *Bergin and Garfield's Handbook of Psychotherapy and Behavior Change* (6th edn, pp. 343–392). Chicago: John Wiley and Sons.

Emmons, R.A. & Diener, E. (1986) A goal-affect analysis of everyday situational choices. *Journal of Research in Personality, 20*(3), 309–326.

Erikson, E.H. (1998) *The Life Cycle Completed*. New York: W.W. Norton and Co.

Fabry, J. (1980) *The Pursuit of Meaning: Viktor Frankl, Logotherapy and Life* (rev. edn). San Francisco: Harper and Row.

Farber, B.A. & Doolin, E.M. (2011) Positive regard. In J.C. Norcross (ed.), *Psychotherapy Relationships that Work: Therapist Contributions and Responsiveness to Patients* (2nd edn, pp. 168–186). New York: Oxford University Press.

Farber, E.W. (2010) Humanistic–existential psychotherapy competencies and the supervisory process. *Psychotherapy: Theory, Research, Practice, Training, 47*(1), 28–34.

Farber, L.H. (1967) Martin Buber and psychotherapy. In P.A. Schlipp & M. Friedman (eds), *The Philosophy of Martin Buber* (pp. 577–601). London: Cambridge University Press.

Farber, L.H. (2000a) *O Death, Where is thy Sting-A-Ling-Ling? The Ways of the Will* (exp. edn). New York: Basic Books.

Farber, L.H. (2000b) *The Ways of the Will* (exp. edn). New York: Basic Books.

Festinger, L. (1954) A theory of social comparison processes. *Human Relations, 7*, 117–140.

Fillion, L., Duval, S., Dumont, S., Gagnon, P., Tremblay, I., Bairati, I. & Breitbart, W.S. (2009) Impact of a meaning-centered intervention on job satisfaction and on quality of life among palliative care nurses. *Psycho-Oncology, 18*(12), 1300–1310.

Finlay, L. (2012) Research: an existential predicament for our profession? In L. Barnett & G. Madison (eds), *Existential Psychotherapy: Vibrancy, Legacy and Dialogue* (pp. 183–191). London: Routledge.

Frankl, V.E. (1984) *Man's Search for Meaning* (revised and updated edn). New York: Washington Square Press.

Frankl, V.E. (1986) *The Doctor and the Soul: From Psychotherapy to Logotherapy* (R. Winston & C. Winston, Trans., 3rd edn). New York: Vintage Books.

Frankl, V.E. (1988) *The Will to Meaning: Foundations and Applications of Logotherapy* (exp. edn). London: Meridian.

Freud, S. (1923) The ego and the id (J. Strachey, Trans.). *The Standard Edition of the Complete Psychological Works of Sigmund Freud* (Vol. 19, pp. 12–59). London: Hogarth Press.

Friedman, M. (1985) *The Healing Dialogue in Psychotherapy*. New York: Jason Aronson, Inc.

Friedman, M. (1999) Dialogical psychotherapy. In *Understanding the Counselling Relationship* (pp. 76–89). Thousand Oaks, CA: Sage Publications Ltd.

Friedman, M., Carel, H., Hassan, J. & Orange, D. (2012) On reading Irvin Yalom's *Staring at the Sun*: overcoming the dread of death. In L. Barnett & G. Madison (eds), *Existential Psychotherapy: Vibrancy, Legacy and Dialogue* (pp. 209–232). London: Routledge.

Fromm, E. (1942) *The Fear of Freedom*. London: Routledge.

Fromm, E. (1965) The application of humanist psycho-analysis and Marx's thought (A. Ross, Trans.). In E. Fromm (ed.), *Socialist Humanism* (pp. 207–222). London: Penguin.

Fromm, E. (2005) *To Have or to Be?* London: Continuum.

Galvin, J. (1995) Brief encounters with Chinese clients: the case of Peter. In K.J. Schneider & R. May (eds), *The Psychology of Existence: An Integrative, Clinical Perspective*. New York: McGraw-Hill, Inc.

Gavin, V.J. (2013) Creative existential therapy for children, adolescents and adults (with special reference to training). *Existential Analysis, 24*(2), 318–341.

Geller, S.M. (2013) Therapeutic presence. In M. Cooper, P.F. Schmid, M. O'Hara & G. Wyatt (eds), *The Handbook of Person-Centred Psychotherapy and Counselling* (2nd edn, pp. 209–236). Basingstoke: Palgrave.

Gendlin, E.T. (1962) *Experiencing and the Creation of Meaning: A Philosophical and Psychological Approach to the Subjective*. Evanston, IL: Northwestern University.

Gendlin, E.T. (1981) *Focusing*. New York: Bantam Books.

Gendlin, E.T. (1996) *Focusing-Oriented Psychotherapy: A Manual of the Experiential Method*. New York: The Guilford Press.

Gibran, K. (1923) *The Prophet*. London: Penguin.

Gilbert, P. (2010) *Compassion Focused Therapy*. Hove: Routledge.

Goffman, E. (1971) *The Presentation of Self in Everyday Life*. Harmondsworth, Middlesex: Penguin.

Goldenberg, H. & Isaacson, Z. (1996) Between persons: the narrow bridge where I and Thou meet. *Existential Analysis*, 7(2), 118–130.

Gordon, L.R. (1997) Black existential philosophy. In L.R. Gordon (ed.), *Existence in Black: An Anthology of Black Existential Philosophy* (pp. 1–9). London: Routledge.

Greenberg, J., Koole, S.L. & Pyszczynski, T. (2004) *Handbook of Experimental Existential Psychology*. New York: Guilford Publications.

Greenberg, L.S. & Dompierre, L.M. (1981) Specific effects of gestalt 2-chair dialog on intrapsychic conflict in counseling. *Journal of Counseling Psychology*, 28(4), 288–294.

Greenberg, L.S. & Rice, L.N. (1981) The specific effects of a gestalt intervention. *Psychotherapy – Theory, Research and Practice*, 18(1), 31–37.

Greenberg, L.S., Rice, L.N. & Elliott, R. (1993) *Facilitating Emotional Change: The Moment-by-Moment Process*. New York: Guilford Press.

Guignon, C. (ed.) (1993) *The Cambridge Companion to Heidegger*. Cambridge: Cambridge University.

Guttman, D. (1996) Research in the service of logotherapy. *Journal des Viktor-Frankl-Instituts*, 4(1), 15–36.

Gyani, A., Shafran, R., Layard, R. & Clark, D.M. (2013) Enhancing recovery rates: lessons from year one of IAPT. *Behaviour Research and Therapy*, 51(9), 597–606.

Harris, W. (2013) Mindfulness-based existential therapy: connecting mindfulness and existential therapy. *Journal of Creativity in Mental Health*, 8(4), 349–362.

Hayes, S.C., Strosahl, K.D. & Wilson, K.G. (2011) *Acceptance and Commitment Therapy: The Process and Practice of Mindful Change* (2nd edn). New York: Guilford Press.

Hegel, G.W.F. (1949) *The Phenomenology of Mind* (J.B. Baillie, Trans., 2nd edn). London: Allen and Unwin.

Heidegger, M. (1962) *Being and Time* (J. Macquarrie & E. Robinson, Trans.). Oxford: Blackwell.

Heidegger, M. (1996) *Being and Time* (J. Stambaugh, Trans.). Albany, NY: State University of New York Press.

Heidegger, M. (2001) *Zollikon Seminars: Protocols–Conversations–Letters* (F. Mayr & R. Askay, Trans.). Evanston, IL: Northwestern University Press.

Helliwell, J.F. & Wang, S. (2010) *Trust and Well-being*, NBER Working Paper 15911. Cambridge: National Bureau of Economic Research.

Hendricks, M.N. (2002) Focusing-oriented/experiential psychotherapy. In D.J. Cain & J. Seeman (eds), *Humanistic Psychotherapies: Handbook of Research and Practice* (pp. 221–252). Washington, DC: American Psychological Association.

Henry, P. (1997) African and Afro-Caribbean existential philosophies. In L.R. Gordon (ed.), *Existence in Black: An Anthology of Black Existential Philosophy* (pp. 13–36). London: Routledge.

Hickes, M. & Mirea, D. (2012) Cognitive behavioural therapy and existential-phenomenological psychotherapy: rival paradigms or fertile ground for therapeutic synthesis? *Existential Analysis*, 23(1), 15–31.

Hill, C.E., Helms, J.E., Tichenor, V., Spiegel, S.B., O'Grady, K.E. & Perry, E.S. (1988) Effects of therapist response modes in brief psychotherapy. *Journal of Counseling Psychology*, 35(3), 222–233.

Hill, C.E. & Knox, S. (2002) Self-disclosure. In J.C. Norcross (ed.), *Psychotherapy Relationships that Work: Therapist Contributions and Responsiveness to Patients* (pp. 255–265). New York: Oxford University Press.

Hoffman, L., Yang, M. & Kaklauskas, F.J. (2009) *Existential Psychology East-West*. Colorado Springs, CO: University of the Rockies.

Hollanders, H. (2014) Integrative therapy. In W. Dryden & A. Reeves (eds), *The Handbook of Individual Therapy* (6th edn, pp. 519–545). London: Sage.

Holt-Lunstad, J., Smith, T.B. & Layton, J.B. (2010) Social relationships and morality risk: a meta-analytic review. *ploS Medicine*, 7(7). Available from: www. plosmedicine.org.

Horvath, A.O., Del Re, A.C., Fluckinger, C. & Symonds, D. (2011) Alliance in individual psychotherapy. In J.C. Norcross (ed.), *Psychotherapy Relationships that Work: Evidence-based Responsiveness* (2nd edn, pp. 25–69). New York: Oxford University Press.

Husserl, E. (1960) *Cartesian Meditations: An Introduction to Phenomenology*. The Hague: Martinus Nijhoff.

Hycner, R. (1991) *Between Person and Person: Towards a Dialogical Psychotherapy*. Highland, NY: Gestalt Journal Press.

Hycner, R. & Jacobs, L. (1995) *The Healing Relationship in Gestalt Therapy*. Highland, NY: Gestalt Journal Publications.

Ihde, D. (1986) *Experimental Phenomenology: An Introduction*. Albany, NY: State University of New York Press.

Jacobsen, B. (2007) *Invitation to Existential Psychology*. Chichester: John Wiley.

Jaspers, K. (1932a) Boundary situations (E.B. Ashton, Trans.) *Philosophy* (Vol. 2). Chicago: The University of Chicago Press.

Jaspers, K. (1932b) *Philosophy* (E.B. Ashton, Trans., Vol. 2). Chicago: The University of Chicago Press.

Jaspers, K. (1963) *General Psychopathology* (J. Hoenig & M.W. Hamilton, Trans., Vol. 1). Baltimore: The John Hopkins University Press.

Jaspers, K. (1986) *Karl Jaspers: Basic Philosophical Writings* (E. Ehrlich, L.H. Ehrlich & G.B. Pepper, Trans.). New Jersey: Humanities Press.

Jordan, J.V., Kaplan, A.G., Miller, J.B., Stiver, I.P. & Surrey, J.L. (eds) (1991) *Women's Growth in Connection: Writings from the Stone Centre*. New York: Guilford Press.

Kahneman, D. (2011) *Thinking, Fast and Slow*. London: Penguin.

Kaslow, N.J., Dausch, B.M. & Celano, M. (2003) Family therapies. In A.S. Gurman & S.B. Messer (eds), *Essential Psychotherapies* (pp. 400–462). New York: Guilford Press.

Kaufmann, W. (1978) *Existentialism, Religion and Death: Thirteen Essays*. New York: New American Library.

Kazantzis, N., Deane, F.P. & Ronan, K.R. (2000) Homework assignments in cognitive and behavioral therapy: a meta-analysis. *Clinical Psychology: Science and Practice, 7*(2), 189–202.

Kenny, D.A. & Depaulo, B.M. (1993) Do people know how others view them – an empirical and theoretical account. *Psychological Bulletin, 114*(1), 145–161.

Keshen, A. (2006) A new look at existential psychotherapy. *American Journal of Psychotherapy, 60*(3), 285–298.

Kierkegaard, S. (1980) *The Concept of Anxiety: A Simple Psychologically Orienting Deliberation on the Dogmatic Issue of Hereditary Sin* (R. Thomte, Trans., Vol. 8). Princeton, NJ: Princeton University Press.

Kierkegaard, S. (1985) *Fear and Trembling* (A. Hannay, Trans.). London: Penguin.

Kierkegaard, S. (1992) *Concluding Unscientific Postscript to Philosophical Fragments* (H.V. Hong & E.H. Hong, Trans., Vol. 12:1). Princeton, NJ: Princeton University Press.

King, L.A. & Hicks, J.A. (2013) Positive affect and meaning in life. In P.T.P. Wong (ed.), *The Human Quest for Meaning: Theories, Research, and Applications* (2nd edn, pp. 125–141). New York: Routledge.

Kissane, D.W., Bloch, S., Smith, G.C., Miach, P., Clarke, D.M., Ikin, J., ... McKenzie, D. (2003) Cognitive-existential group psychotherapy for women with primary breast cancer: a randomised controlled trial. *Psycho-Oncology, 12*(6), 532–546.

Klein, M.J., Mathieu-Coughlan, P. & Kiesler, D.B. (1986) The experiencing scales. In L.S. Greenberg & W.M. Pinsof (eds), *The Psychotherapeutic Process: A Research Handbook* (pp. 21–71). New York: Guilford Press.

Klinger, E. (2013) The search for meaning in evolutionary goal-theory perspective and its clinical implications. In P.T.P. Wong (ed.), *The Human Quest for Meaning: Theories, Research, and Applications* (2nd edn, pp. 23–56). New York: Routledge.

Knox, R. (2013) Relational depth from the client's perspective. In R. Knox, S. Wiggins, D. Murphy & M. Cooper (eds), *Relational Depth: New Perspectives and Developments* (pp. 21–35). Basingstoke: Palgrave.

Knox, R. & Cooper, M. (2010) Relationship qualities that are associated with moments of relational depth: the client's perspective. *Person-Centered and Experiential Psychotherapies, 9*(3), 236–256.

Knox, R., Murphy, D., Wiggins, S. & Cooper, M. (eds) (2013) *Relational Depth: New Perspectives and Developments*. Basingstoke: Palgrave.

Koestenbaum, P. (1971) *The Vitality of Death: Essays in Existential Psychology and Philosophy*. New York: Greenwood Publishing Company.

Kolden, G.G., Klein, M.H., Wang, C.-C. & Austin, S.B. (2011) Congruence. In J.C. Norcross (ed.), *Psychotherapy Relationships that Work: Evidence-based Responsiveness* (2nd edn, pp. 187–203). New York: Oxford University Press.

Kroenke, K., Spitzer, R.L. & Williams, J.B. (2001) The Phq-9. *Journal of General Internal Medicine, 16*(9), 606–613.

Lahav, R. (1998) On the possibility of a dialogue between philosophical counselling and existential psychotherapy. *Existential Analysis, 9*(1), 129–144.

Laing, R.D. (1965) *The Divided Self: An Existential Study in Sanity and Madness*. Harmondsworth: Penguin.

Laing, R.D. (1967) *The Politics of Experience and the Bird of Paradise*. Harmondsworth: Penguin.

Laing, R.D. (1969) *Self and Others* (2nd edn). London: Penguin Books.

Laing, R.D. (1970) *Knots*. London: Penguin.

Laing, R.D. (1985) *Wisdom, Madness and Folly: The Making of a Psychiatrist 1927–1957*. London: Macmillan.

Laing, R.D. & Esterson, A. (1964) *Sanity, Madness and the Family*. London: Penguin Books.

Laing, R.D., Phillipson, H. & Lee, A.R. (1966) *Interpersonal Perception: A Theory and a Method of Research*. London: Tavistock.

Lander, N.R. & Nahon, D. (2005) *The Integrity Model of Existential Psychotherapy in Working with the 'Difficult Patient'*. Hove: Routledge.

Langdridge, D. (2006) Solution focused therapy: a way forward for brief existential therapy? *Existential Analysis, 17*(2), 359–370.

Langdridge, D. (2012) *Existential Counselling and Psychotherapy*. London: Sage.

Langdridge, D. & Barker, M. (2013) Relationship therapy with lesbian, gay, bisexual and trans clients. In E. van Deurzen & S. Iacovou (eds), *Existential Perspectives on Relationship Therapy* (pp. 148–160). London: Palgrave.

Langer, S.L. & Wurf, E. (1999) The effects of channel-consistent and channel-inconsistent interpersonal feedback on the formation of metaperceptions. *Journal of Nonverbal Behavior, 23*(1), 43–65.

Längle, A., Gortz, A., Probst, C., Probst, M., Lopatka, C., Kubin, M. & Steinert, K. (2005) How effective is existential analytical psychotherapy: a study about the efficiency of existential analysis. *Psychotherapie Forum, 13*(2).

Layard, R. (2006) *Happiness: Lessons from a New Science*. London: Penguin.

Lazarus, A.A. (1993) Tailoring the therapeutic relationship: on being an authentic chameleon. *Psychotherapy, 30*(3), 404–407.

LeBon, T. (2001) *Wise Therapy: Philosophy for Counsellors*. London: Continuum.

LeMay, K. & Wilson, K.G. (2008) Treatment of existential distress in life threatening illness: A review of manualized interventions. *Clinical Psychology Review, 28*(3), 472–493.

Leontiev, D. (2013) The challenge of otherness: relationships, meaning and dialogue. In E. van Deurzen & S. Iacovou (eds), *Existential Perspectives on Relationship Therapy* (pp. 15–31). London: Palgrave.

Lester, D. (1992) The disunity of self. *Personality and Individual Differences, 13*(8), 947–948.

Leung, J. (2008) *A Quantitative Online Study Exploring the Factors Associated with the Experience and Perception of Relational Depth*. (Unpublished doctoral dissertation). University of Strathclyde/Glasgow Caledonian University, Glasgow.

Levinas, E. (1969) *Totality and Infinity: An Essay on Exteriority* (A. Lingis, Trans.). Pittsburgh, PA: Duquesne University Press.

Levinas, E. (1982) *Ethics and Infinity: Conversations with Philip Nemo* (R.A. Cohen, Trans.). Pittsburgh, PA: Duquesne University Press.

Libet, B., Gleason, C.A., Wright, E.W. & Pearl, D.K. (1983) Time of conscious intention to act in relation to onset of cerebral activity (readiness-potential): the unconscious initiation of a freely voluntary act. *Brain, 106*(3), 623–642.

Liddle, B.J. (1996) Therapist sexual orientation, gender, and counseling practices as they relate to ratings on helpfulness by gay and lesbian clients. *Journal of Counseling Psychology, 43*, 394–401.

Little, B.R. (1983) Personal projects: a rationale and method for investigation. *Environment and Behavior, 15*(3), 273–309.

Macquarrie, J. (1972) *Existentialism*. Harmondsworth: Penguin Books.

Maddi, S.R. (2004) Hardiness: An operationalization of existential courage. *Journal of Humanistic Psychology, 44*(3), 279–298.

Madison, G. (ed.) (2014) *Theory and Practice of Focusing-oriented Psychotherapy: Beyond the Talking Cure*. London: Jessica Kingsley.

Manafi, E. (2010) Amor Fati*: existential contributions to pluralistic practice. In M. Milton (ed.), *Therapy and Beyond: Counselling Psychology Contributions to Therapeutic and Social Issues* (pp. 171–187). London: Wiley-Blackwell.

Marien, H., Custers, R., Hassin, R.R. & Aarts, H. (2012) Unconscious goal activation and the hijacking of the executive function. *Journal of Personality and Social Psychology, 103*(3), 399.

Marks, I.M. (1978) *Living with Fear: Understanding and Coping with Anxiety*. New York: McGraw-Hill.

Markus, H. & Sentis, K. (1982) The self in social information processing. In J. Suls (ed.), *Psychological Perspectives on the Self* (Vol. 1, pp. 41–70). Hillsdale, NJ: Lawrence Erlbaum.

Martin, L., Campbell, W.K. & Henry, C.D. (2004) The roar of awakening: mortality acknowledgement as a call to authentic living. In J. Greenberg, S.L. Koole & T. Pyszczynski (eds), *Handbook of Experimental Existential Psychology* (pp. 431–448). New York: Guilford.

Maslow, A.H. (1971) *The Farther Reaches of Human Nature*. London: Penguin.

May, R. (1953) *Man's Search for Himself*. New York: W.W. Norton and Co.

May, R. (1958) Contributions of existential psychotherapy. In R. May, E. Angel & H.F. Ellenberger (eds), *Existence: A New Dimension in Psychiatry and Psychology* (pp. 37–91). New York: Basic Books.

May, R. (1969a) *Love and Will*. New York: W.W. Norton and Co.

May, R. (ed.) (1969b) *Existential Psychology*. New York: Random House.

May, R. (1975) *The Courage to Create*. New York: W.W. Norton and Co.

May, R. (1977) *The Meaning of Anxiety* (rev. edn). New York: W.W. Norton and Co.

May, R. (1981) *Freedom and Destiny*. London: W.W. Norton and Co.

May, R. (1983) *The Discovery of Being*. New York: W.W. Norton and Co.

May, R. (1999) Existential psychology and the problem of death. *Review of Existential Psychology and Psychiatry*, 24, 40–48.

May, R., Angel, E. & Ellenberger, H.F (eds) (1958) *Existence: A New Dimension in Psychiatry and Psychology*. New York: Basic Books.

McLeod, J. (1997) *Narrative and Psychotherapy*. London: Sage.

McLeod, J. & Cooper, M. (2012) Pluralistic counselling and psychotherapy. In C. Feltham & I. Horton (eds), *The Sage Handbook of Counselling and Psychotherapy* (pp. 368–371). London: Sage.

McLeod, J., McLeod, J., Cooper, M. & Dryden, W. (2014) Pluralistic therapy. In W. Dryden & A. Reeves (eds), *Handbook of Individual Therapy* (6th edn, pp. 547–573). London: Sage.

McMillan, M. & McLeod, J. (2006) Letting go: the client's experience of relational depth. *Person-Centered and Experiential Psychotherapies*, 5(4), 277–292.

Mead, G.H. (1934) *Mind, Self and Society*. Chicago: University of Chicago Press.

Mearns, D. (1997) *Person-centred Counselling Training*. London: Sage.

Mearns, D. (2003) *Developing Person-centred Counselling* (2nd edn). London: Sage.

Mearns, D. & Cooper, M. (2005) *Working at Relational Depth in Counselling and Psychotherapy*. London: Sage.

Medina, M. (2010) All for one and one for all? *Existential Analysis*, 21(2), 263–270.

Merleau-Ponty, M. (1962) *The Phenomenology of Perception* (C. Smith, Trans.). London: Routledge.

Merry, T. (2004) Classical client-centred therapy. In P. Sanders (ed.), *The Tribes of the Person-Centred Nation: An Introduction to the Schools of Therapy Related to the Person-Centred Approach* (2nd edn, pp. 21–46). Ross-on-Wye: PCCS Books.

Michalak, J., Heidenreich, T. & Hoyer, J. (2004) Goal conflicts: concepts, findings, and consequences for psychotherapy. In W.M. Cox & E. Klinger (eds), *Handbook of Motivational Counseling* (pp. 83–97). New York: John Wiley.

Michels, J.L. (2000) *Perceptions and Metaperceptions among Clinicians and Clients in First Therapy Sessions*. Carbondale, IL: Southern Illinois University.

Milton, M. (2010a) Coming home to roost: counselling psychology and the natural world. In M. Milton (ed.), *Therapy and Beyond: Counselling Psychology Contributions to Therapeutic and Social Issues* (pp. 293–308). London: Wiley-Blackwell.

Milton, M. (2010b) *Therapy and Beyond: Counselling Psychology Contributions to Therapeutic and Social Issues*. London: Wiley-Blackwell.

Milton, M. (ed.) (2014) *Sexuality: Existential Perspectives*. Ross: PCCS Books.

Milton, M. & Gillies, F. (2007) From biology to being: evolutionary theory and existential practice. *Existential Analysis, 18*(2), 247–260.

Milton, M., Charles, L., Judd, D., O'Brien, M., Tipney, A. & Turner, A. (2003) The existential-phenomenological paradigm: the importance for psychotherapy integration. *Existential Analysis, 14*(1), 112–136.

Minkowski, E. (1958) Findings in the case of schizophrenic depression. In R. May, E. Angel & H.F. Ellenberger (eds), *Existence: A New Dimension in Psychiatry and Psychology* (pp. 127–138). New York: Basic Books.

Mirea, D. (2012) Cognitive behavioural coaching – friend or foe for the existential coach. In E. van Deurzen & M. Hanaway (eds), *Existential Perspectives on Coaching* (pp. 166–174). London: Palgrave.

Moja-Strasser, L. (1996) The phenomenology of listening and the importance of silence. *Journal of the Society for Existential Analysis, 7*(1), 90–102.

Monheit, J. (2008) A lesbian and gay perspective: the case of Marcia. In K.J. Schneider (ed.), *Existential-Integrative Psychotherapy: Guideposts to the Core of Practice* (pp. 140–146). New York: Routledge.

Moorey, S. (2014) Cognitive therapy. In W. Dryden & A. Reeves (eds), *Handbook of Individual Therapy* (6th edn, pp. 243–269). London: Sage.

Moran, D. (2000) *Introduction to Phenomenology*. London: Routledge.

Morrow-Bradley, C. & Elliott, R. (1986) Utilization of psychotherapy research by practicing psychotherapists. *American Psychologist, 41*(2), 188–197.

Morse, S. & Gergen, K. (1970) Social comparison, self-consistency, and the concept of the self. *Journal of Personality and Social Psychology, 16*(1), 148–156.

Mosher, L.R. & Hendrix, V. (2004) *Soteria: Through Madness to Deliverance*. Bloomington, IN: Xlibris.

Mullan, B. (1995) *Mad to be Normal: Conversations with R.D. Laing*. London: Free Association Books.

Mullan, B. (1999) *R.D. Laing: A Personal View*. London: Duckworth.

Murphy, D. (2013) Mutuality and relational depth in counselling and psychotherapy. In R. Knox, S. Wiggins, D. Murphy & M. Cooper (eds), *Relational Depth: New Perspectives and Developments* (pp. 185–195). Basingstoke: Palgrave.

Murphy, D. & Cramer, D. (2014) Mutuality of Rogers's therapeutic conditions and treatment progress in the first three psychotherapy sessions. *Psychotherapy Research*, 1–11.

Nanda, J. (2010) Embodied integration: Reflections on mindfulness based cognitive therapy (MBCT) and a case for mindfulness based existential therapy (MBET). A single case illustration. *Existential Analysis, 21*(2), 331–350.

Nanda, J. (2012) Why mindfulness-based existential coaching. In E. van Deurzen & M. Hanaway (eds), *Existential Perspectives on Coaching* (pp. 175–187). London: Palgrave.

National Institute for Mental Health in England (2005) *NIMHE Guiding Statement on Recovery*. London: Department of Health.

Neimeyer, R.A. (1997–98) Special article: Death anxiety research – the state of the art. *Omega, 36*(2), 97–120.

Nietzsche, F. (1967) *Thus Spake Zarathustra* (T. Common, Trans.). London: George Allen and Unwin Ltd.

Norcross, J.C. (1987) A rational and empirical analysis of existential psychotherapy. *Journal of Humanistic Psychology, 27*(1), 41–68.

Norcross, J.C. (ed.) (2011) *Psychotherapy Relationships that Work: Evidence-based responsiveness* (2nd edn). New York: Oxford University Press.

Norcross, J.C. & Lambert, M.J. (2011) Evidence-based therapy relationships. In J.C. Norcross (ed.), *Psychotherapy Relationships that Work: Evidence-based Responsiveness* (2nd edn, pp. 3–21). New York: Oxford University.

Norcross, J.C. & Wampold, B.E. (2011) Evidence-based therapy relationships: research conclusions and clinical practices. *Psychotherapy, 48*(1), 98–102.

O'Connell, B. (2012) *Solution-focused Therapy* (3rd edn). London: Sage.

Olivereira, A., Sousa, D. & Pires, A.P. (2012) Significant events in existential psychotherapy: the client's perspective. *Existential Analysis, 23*(2), 288–304.

Orlinsky, D.E., Rønnestad, M.H. & Willutzki, U. (2004) Fifty years of psychotherapy process-outcome research: continuity and change. In M.J. Lambert (ed.), *Bergin and Garfield's Handbook of Psychotherapy and Behavior Change* (5th edn, pp. 307–389). Chicago: John Wiley and Sons.

Park, C.L. (2013) Meaning and meaning making in cancer survivorship. In P.T.P. Wong (ed.), *The Human Quest for Meaning: Theories, Research, and Applications* (2nd edn, pp. 521–538). New York: Routledge.

Park, N., Park, M. & Peterson, C. (2010) When is the search for meaning related to life satisfaction? *Applied Psychology: Health and Well Being, 2*(1), 1–13.

Paulson, B.L. & Worth, M. (2002) Counselling for suicide: client perspectives. *Journal of Counseling and Development, 80*(1), 86–93.

Plomin, R., DeFries, J.C., McClearn, G.E. & McGuffin, P. (2001) *Behavioral Genetics* (4th edn). New York: Worth Publishers.

Proctor, G., Cooper, M., Sanders, P. & Malcolm, B. (eds) (2006) *Politicising the Person-Centred Approach: An Agenda for Social Change*. Ross-on-Wye: PCCS Books.

Pyszczynski, T., Greenberg, J. & Koole, S.L. (2004) Experimental existential psychology: exploring the human confrontation with reality. In J. Greenberg, S.L. Koole & T. Pyszczynski (eds), *Handbook of Experimental Existential Psychology* (pp. 3–9). New York: Guilford Press.

Quinn, F. (2010) The right to choose: existential-phenomenological psychotherapy with primary school-aged children. *Counselling Psychology Review, 25*(1), 41–48.

Rayner, M. & Vitali, D. (in press) Short-term existential psychotherapy in primary care: a quantitative report. *Journal of Humanistic Psychology*.

Reinecke, M.A. & Freeman, A. (2003) Cognitive therapy. In A.S. Gurman & S.B. Messer (eds.), *Essential Psychotherapies* (pp. 224–271). New York: Guilford Press.

Rennie, D.L. (1994) Clients' deference in psychotherapy. *Journal of Counseling Psychology, 41*(4), 427–437.

Rescher, N. (1993) *Pluralism: Against the Demand for Consensus.* Oxford: Oxford University.

Rice, D.L. (2008) An African-American perspective: the case of Darrin. In K.J. Schneider (ed.), *Existential-Integrative Psychotherapy: Guideposts to the Core of Practice* (pp. 110–121). New York: Routledge.

Rogers, C.R. (1951) *Client-centered Therapy.* Boston: Houghton and Mifflin.

Rogers, C.R. (1957) The necessary and sufficient conditions of therapeutic personality change. *Journal of Consulting Psychology, 21*(2), 95–103.

Rogers, C.R. (1959) A theory of therapy, personality and interpersonal relationships as developed in the client-centered framework. In S. Koch (ed.), *Psychology: A Study of Science* (Vol. 3, pp. 184–256). New York: McGraw-Hill.

Rogers, C.R. (1961) *On Becoming a Person: A Therapist's View of Therapy.* London: Constable and Co.

Rogers, C.R. (1980) *A Way of Being.* Boston: Houghton and Mifflin.

Rosenberg, S.S. & Gara, M.A. (1985) The multiplicity of personal identity. In P. Shaver (ed.), *Self, Situations and Social Behaviour: Review of Personality and Social Psychology* (Vol. 6, pp. 87–113). Beverly Hills, CA: Sage.

Rowan, J. (1999) Existential analysis and humanistic psychotherapy. *Journal of the Society for Existential Analysis, 10*(1), 44–64.

Rowan, J. (2009) *Personification: Using the Dialogical Self in Psychotherapy and Counselling.* London: Routledge.

Rowan, J. (2010) *Personification: Using the Dialogical Self in Psychotherapy and Counselling*: New York, NY: Routledge/Taylor & Francis Group.

Ryan, R.M. & Deci, E.L. (2000) Self-determination theory and the facilitation of intrinsic motivation, social development, and well-being. *American Psychologist, 55*(1), 68–78.

Ryle, A. (1990) *Cognitive Analytic Therapy: Active Participation in Change.* Chichester: Wiley.

Sachse, R. & Elliott, R. (2002) Process-outcome research on humanistic therapy variables. In D.J. Cain & J. Seeman (eds), *Humanistic Psychotherapies: Handbook of Research and Practice* (pp. 83–115). Washington, DC: American Psychological Association.

Safran, J.D. & Muran, J.C. (2000) *Negotiating the Therapeutic Alliance: A Relational Treatment Guide.* New York: Guilford Press.

Salmela-Aro, K. & Little, B.R. (2007) Relational aspects of project pursuit. In B.R. Little, K. Salmela-Aro & S.D. Phillips (eds), *Personal Project Pursuit: Goals, Action, and Human Flourishing* (pp. 199–219). Mahwah, NJ: Lawrence Erlbaum Associates Publishers.

Sanchez, V.C., Lewinsohn, P.M. & Larson, D.W. (1980) Assertion training: effectiveness in the treatment of depression. *Journal of Clinical Psychology, 36*(2), 526–529.

Sartre, J.-P. (1958) *Being and Nothingness: An Essay on Phenomenological Ontology* (H. Barnes, Trans.). London: Routledge.

Sartre, J.-P. (1989) *No Exit and Three Other Plays*. New York: Vintage.

Sartre, J.-P. (1996) Existentialism. In L. Cahoone (ed.), *From Modernism to Postmodernism: An Anthology* (pp. 259–265). Cambridge, MA: Blackwells Publishers Ltd.

Scalzo, C. (2010) *Therapy with Children: An Existentialist Perspective*. London: Karnac.

Scheler, M. (1967) In N. Lawrence & D. O'Connor (eds), *Readings in Existential Phenomenology* (pp. 19–30). Englewood Cliffs, NJ: Prentice-Hall.

Schmid, P.F. (2006) The challenge of the other: towards dialogical person-centered psychotherapy and counseling. *Person-Centered and Experiential Psychotherapies, 5*(4), 240–254.

Schneider, K.J. (2000) R.D. Laing's existential-humanistic practice: what was he actually doing? *Psychoanalytic Review, 87*(4), 591–600.

Schneider, K.J. (2003) Existential-humanistic psychotherapies. In A.S. Gurman & S.B. Messer (eds.), *Essential Psychotherapies* (pp. 149–181). New York: Guilford Press.

Schneider, K.J. (ed.) (2008) *Existential-Integrative Psychotherapy: Guideposts to the Core of Practice*. New York: Routledge.

Schneider, K.J. & Krug, O.T. (2010) *Existential-humanistic Therapy*. Washington, DC: APA.

Schneider, K.J. & May, R. (eds) (1995) *The Psychology of Existence*. New York: McGraw-Hill.

Schopenhauer, A. (1969) *The World as Will and Representation* (E.F.J. Payne, Trans.). New York: Dover.

Schulenberg, S.E., Hutzell, R.R., Nassif, C. & Rogina, J.M. (2008) Logotherapy for clinical practice. *Psychotherapy: Theory, Research, Practice, Training, 45*(4), 447–463.

Schwartz, B. (2005) *The Paradox of Choice*. London: Harper.

Segal, Z.V., Williams, J.M.G. & Teasdale, J.D. (2002) *Mindfulness-based Cognitive Therapy for Depression: A New Approach to Preventing Relapse*. New York: Guilford Press.

Segrin, C. (2001) *Interpersonal Processes in Psychological Problems*. New York: Guilford Press.

Segrin, C.G. (2011) Depressive disorders and interpersonal processes. In L.M. Horowitz & S. Strack (eds), *Handbook of Interpersonal Psychology: Theory, Research, Assessment, and Therapeutic Interventions* (pp. 425–448). Hoboken, NJ: John Wiley & Sons Inc.

Serlin, I. (1999) An interview with Irvin Yalom. *Review of Existential Psychology and Psychiatry, 24*, 142–151.

Shandy, T. [pseudonym] (2012) On pluralistic counselling and psychotherapy by Mick Cooper and John McLeod. *Hermeneutic Circular*, 7–9.

Shrauger, J.S. & Schoeneman, T.J. (1979) Symbolic interactionist view of self-concept: Through the looking glass darkly. *Psychological Bulletin, 86*(3), 549–573.

Sheldon, K.M. & Elliot, A.J. (1999) Goal striving, need satisfaction, and longitudinal well-being: The self-concordance model. *Journal of Personality and Social Psychology, 76*(3), 482–497.

Smith, B. & Woodruff Smith, D. (eds) (1995) *The Cambridge Companion to Husserl.* Cambridge: Cambridge University.

Smith-Pickard, P. (2014) Merleau-Ponty and existential sexuality. In M. Milton (ed.), *Sexuality: Existential Perspectives* (pp. 79–91). Ross: PCCS Books.

Snyder, C.R., Michael, S.T. & Cheavens, J.S. (1999) Hope as a foundation of common factors, placebos, and expectancies. In M. Hubble, B.L. Duncan & S.D. Miller (eds), *The Heart and Soul of Change: What Works in Therapy* (pp. 179–200). Washington, DC: American Psychological Association.

Soon, C.S., Brass, M., Heinze, H.J. & Haynes, J.D. (2008) Unconscious determinants of free decisions in the human brain. *Nature Neuroscience, 11*(5), 543–545.

Sousa, D. & Alegria, S. (in preparation) An analysis of the practices of existential psychotherapists using the Psychotherapy Process Q-Sort Manual.

Spector, P.E., Cooper, C.L., Sanchez, J.I., O'Driscoll, M., Sparks, K. et al. (2002) Locus of control and well-being at work: how generalizable are western findings? *Academy of Management Journal, 45*(2), 453–466.

Spiegel, D., Bloom, J.R. & Yalom, I. (1981) Group support for patients with metastatic cancer. *Archive of General Psychiatry, 38*, 527–533.

Spinelli, E. (1989) *The Interpreted World: An Introduction to Phenomenological Psychology.* London: Sage.

Spinelli, E. (1994) *Demystifying Therapy.* London: Constable.

Spinelli, E. (1997) *Tales of Un-Knowing: Therapeutic Encounters from an Existential Perspective.* London: Duckworth.

Spinelli, E. (1999) An open letter to John Rowan in reply to his article 'Existential analysis and humanistic psychotherapy'. *Existential Analysis, 10*(1), 65–71.

Spinelli, E. (2001) *The Mirror and the Hammer: Challenges to Therapeutic Orthodoxy.* London: Continuum.

Spinelli, E. (2005) *The Interpreted World: An Introduction to Phenomenological Psychology* (2nd edn). London: Sage.

Spinelli, E. (2007) *Practising Existential Psychotherapy: The Relational World.* London: Sage.

Spinelli, E. (2014a) An existential challenge to some dominant perspectives in the practice of contemporary counselling psychology. *Counselling Psychology Review, 29*(2), 7–24.

Spinelli, E. (2015) *Practising Existential Therapy: The Relational World* (2nd edn). London: Sage.

Spira, J. (2000) Existential psychotherapy in palliative care. In H. Chochinov & W. Breitbart (eds), *Handbook of Psychiatry in Palliative Medicine* (pp. 197–214). Oxford: Oxford University.

Stålsett, G., Gude, T., Rønnestad, M.H. & Monsen, J.T. (2012) Existential dynamic therapy ("VITA") for treatment-resistant depression with Cluster C disorder: matched comparison to treatment as usual. *Psychotherapy Research, 22*(5), 579–591.

Steger, M.F. (2013) Experiencing meaning in life. In P.T.P. Wong (ed.), *The Human Quest for Meaning: Theories, Research, and Applications* (2nd edn, pp. 165–184). New York: Routledge.

Steger, M.F., Frazier, P., Oishi, S. & Kaler, M. (2006) The meaning in life questionnaire: assessing the presence of and search for meaning in life. *Journal of Counseling Psychology, 53*(1), 80–93.

Stern, D.N. (2004) *The Present Moment in Psychotherapy and Everyday Life*. New York: W.W. Norton and Co.

Stiles, W.B., Elliott, R., Firthcozens, J.A., Llewelyn, S.P., Margison, F.R., Shapiro, D.A. & Hardy, G. (1990) Assimilation of problematic experiences by clients in psychotherapy. *Psychotherapy, 27*(3), 411–420.

Storms, M. (1973) Videotape and the attribution process: Reversing actors' and observers' points of view. *Journal of Personality and Social Psychology, 27*, 165–175.

Strasser, F. & Strasser, A. (1997) Existential time-limited therapy: the wheel of existence. In E. van Deurzen (ed.), *Wiley Series in Existential Counselling and Psychotherapy*. Chichester: John Wiley.

Stuart, S. & Robertson, M. (2003) *Interpersonal Psychotherapy: A Clinician's Guide*. London: Arnold.

Sullivan, H.S. (1953) *The Interpersonal Theory of Psychiatry*. New York: W.W. Norton and Co.

Swales, M.A. & Heard, H.L. (2008) *Dialectical Behaviour Therapy*. Hove: Routledge.

Tengan, A. (1999) *Search for Meaning as the Basic Human Motivation: A Critical Examination of Viktor Emil Frankl's Logotherapeutic Concept of Man* (Vol. 556). Frankfurt am Main: Peter Lang.

Tillich, P. (2000) *The Courage to Be* (2nd edn). New Haven: Yale University Press.

Timulak, L. (2007) Identifying core categories of client-identified impact of helpful events in psychotherapy: a qualitative meta-analysis. *Psychotherapy Research, 17*(3), 310–320.

Travelbee, J.E. (1979) Nursing. In J.B. Fabry, R.P. Bulka & W.S. Sahakian (eds), *Logotherapy in Action*. New York: Jason Aronson.

Trüb, H. (1964) Selected readings. In M. Friedman (ed.), *The Worlds of Existentialism: A Critical Reader* (pp. 497–505). Chicago: University of Chicago Press.

Van Deurzen, E. (1998) *Paradox and Passion in Psychotherapy: An Existential Approach to Therapy and Counselling*. Chichester: John Wiley and Sons.

Van Deurzen, E. (2009a) *Everyday Mysteries* (2nd edn). London: Routledge.

Van Deurzen, E. (2009b) *Psychotherapy and the Quest for Happiness*. London: Sage.

Van Deurzen, E. (2012a) *Existential Counselling and Psychotherapy in Practice* (3rd edn). London: Sage.

Van Deurzen, E. (2012b) The existential ideology and framework for coaching. In E. van Deurzen & M. Hanaway (eds), *Existential Perspectives on Coaching* (pp. 3–20). London: Palgrave.

Van Deurzen, E. (2012c) Reasons for living: existential therapy and spirituality. In L. Barnett & G. Madison (eds), *Existential Psychotherapy: Vibrancy, Legacy and Dialogue* (pp. 171–182). London: Routledge.

Van Deurzen, E. & Adams, M. (2011) *Skills in Existential Counselling and Psychotherapy*. London: Sage.

Van Deurzen, E. & Hanaway, M. (eds) (2012) *Existential Perspectives on Coaching*. London: Palgrave.

Van Deurzen, E. & Iacovou, S. (eds) (2013) *Existential Perspectives on Relationship Therapy*. London: Palgrave.

Vargiu, J.G. (1974) Psychosynthesis workbook: subpersonalities. *Synthesis, 1*, 52–90.

Ventegodt, S. & Merrick, J. (2013) The human heart or recovering the meaning of life. In P.T.P. Wong (ed.), *The Human Quest for Meaning: Theories, Research, and Applications* (2nd edn, pp. 573–584). New York: Routledge.

Vera, E.M. & Speight, S.L. (2003) Multicultural competence, social justice, and counseling psychology: expanding our roles. *The Counseling Psychologist, 31*(3), 253–272.

Vohs, K.D. & Baumeister, R.F. (2004) Ego depletion, self-control, and choice. In J. Greenberg, S.L. Koole & T. Pyszczynski (eds), *Handbook of Experimental Existential Psychology* (pp. 398–410). New York: Guilford Press.

Von Hildenbrand, D. (2009) *The Nature of Love* (J.F. Crosby, Trans.). South Bend, IN: St Augustine.

Vos, J., Craig, M. & Cooper, M. (2014) Existential therapies: a meta-analysis of their effects on psychological outcomes. *Journal of Consulting and Clinical Psychology*.

Vygotsky, L.S. (1962) *Thought and Language*. Cambridge, MA: MIT Press.

Wahl, B. (2003) Working with 'existence tensions' as a basis for therapeutic practice. *Existential Analysis, 14*(2), 265–278.

Walsh, R.A. & McElwain, B. (2002) Existential psychotherapies. In D.J. Cain & J. Seeman (eds), *Humanistic Psychotherapies: Handbook of Research and Practice* (pp. 253–278). Washington, DC: American Psychological Association.

Warnock, M. (1970) *Existentialism* (rev. edn). Oxford: Oxford University Press.

Wartenberg, T.E. (2008) *Existentialism: A Beginner's Guide*. London: Oneworld.

Watson, V., Cooper, M., McArthur, K. & McLeod, J. (2012) Helpful therapeutic processes: a pluralistic analysis of client activities, therapist activities and helpful effects. *European Journal of Psychotherapy and Counselling, 14*(1), 77–90.

Wellman, H.M. & Lagattuta, K.H. (2000). Developing understanding of mind. In S. Baron-Cohen, H. Tager-Flusberg & D.J. Cohen (eds.),

Understanding Other Minds: Perspectives from Developmental Cognitive Neuroscience (pp. 21–49). Oxford: Oxford University Press.

Whiddon, M.F. (1983). Logotherapy in prison. *International Forum for Logotherapy*, 6(1), 34–39.

Wiggins, S. (2011) *Relational Depth and Therapeutic Outcome*. Paper presented at the 17th Annual BACP Research Conference, Portsmouth.

Wilkes, R.S. & Milton, M. (2006) Being an existential therapist: an IPA study of existential therapists' experiences. *Existential Analysis*, 17(1), 71–83.

Williams, C. & Garland, A. (2002) A cognitive–behavioural therapy assessment model for use in everyday clinical practice. *Advances in Psychiatric Treatment*, 8(3), 172–179.

Wolfe, B.E. (2008) Existential issues in anxiety disorders and their treatment. In K.J. Schneider (ed.), *Existential-Integrative Psychotherapy: Guideposts to the Core of Practice* (pp. 204–216). New York: Routledge.

Wolitzky, D. (2003) The theory and practice of traditional psychoanalytic treatment. In A.S. Gurman & S.B. Messer (eds), *Essential Psychotherapies: Theory and Practice* (2nd edn, pp. 69–106). New York: Guilford Press.

Wong, P.T. (2013) Introduction. In P.T.P. Wong (ed.), *The Human Quest for Meaning: Theories, Research, and Applications* (2nd edn, pp. xxix-xlvi). New York: Routledge.

Wong, P.T.P. (1998) Meaning-centred counseling. In P.T. Wong & P. Fry (eds), *The Quest for Human Meaning: A Handbook of Theory, Research and Application* (pp. 395–435). Mahway, NJ: Lawrence Erlbaum Inc.

Wood, R.E. (1969) *Martin Buber's Ontology: An Analysis of I and Thou*. Evanston, IL: Northwestern University Press.

Yakeley, J. (2012) Psychoanalytic therapy. In C. Feltham & I. Horton (eds), *The Sage Handbook of Counselling and Psychotherapy* (pp. 268–272). London: Sage.

Yalom, I.D. (1980) *Existential Psychotherapy*. New York: Basic Books.

Yalom, I.D. (1989) *Love's Executioner and Other Tales of Psychotherapy*. London: Penguin Books.

Yalom, I.D. (1999) *Momma and the Meaning of Life: Tales of Psychotherapy*. London: Piatkus.

Yalom, I.D. (2001) *The Gift of Therapy: Reflections on Being a Therapist*. London: Piatkus.

Yalom, I.D. (2008) *Staring at the Sun*. London: Piatkus.

Yalom, I.D. & Elkin, G. (1974) *Every Day Gets a Little Closer: A Twice-told Therapy*. New York: Basic Books.

Yalom, I.D. & Lieberman, M.A. (1991) Bereavement and heightened existential awareness. *Psychiatry: Interpersonal and Biological Processes*, 54(4), 334–345.

You, S., Van Orden, K.A. & Conner, K.R. (2011) Social connections and suicidal thoughts and behavior. *Psychology of Addictive Behaviors*, 25(1), 180–184.

Index